C000056288

Studies in Scottish Church History

Studies in Scottish Church History

A. C. CHEYNE

T&T CLARK
EDINBURGH

T&T CLARK LTD
59 GEORGE STREET
EDINBURGH EH2 2LQ
SCOTLAND

First published 1999

ISBN 0 567 08644 5

British Library Cataloguing-in-Publication Data
A catalogue record for this book is available from the British Library

Typeset by Waverley Typesetters, Galashiels
Printed and bound in Great Britain by MPG Books, Bodmin

For Mona

Contents

Acknowledgements

Most of the papers collected in this volume were first published elsewhere, though in some instances considerable changes have subsequently been made in them. 'Diversity and Development in Scottish Presbyterianism' and 'Piety and Learning: Three Edinburgh Exemplars', both appeared in *New College Bulletin*, the former (my inaugural lecture as Professor of Ecclesiastical History in the University of Edinburgh) in 1965, the latter (as part of New College's contribution to the University's Quatercentenary celebrations) in 1983; 'The Ten Years' Conflict and the Disruption: An Overview' was published by the Scottish Academic Press in 1993; 'The Bible and Change in the Nineteenth Century' was included by the Saint Andrew Press in *The Bible in Scottish Life and Literature* (ed. D. F. Wright, 1988); 'Church Reform and Church Defence: the Contribution of John Tulloch' (my presidential address to the Scottish Church History Society) appeared in the Society's *Records*, vol. xxiii, pt. 3, in 1989; 'John Caird: Preacher, Professor, Principal' (a Stevenson Lecture delivered in the University of Glasgow in its Quincentenary year), was published by the Scottish Academic Press in *Traditions of Theology in Glasgow 1450–1990* (ed. W. I. P. Hazlett, 1993); 'The Religious World of Henry Drummond' appeared in *Theology in Scotland*, vol. V, no. 1, in the Spring of this year; the two articles on the Baillie brothers appeared in *Christ, Church and Society: Essays on John Baillie and Donald Baillie* (ed. D. Fergusson), which was published by T&T Clark in 1993; and 'Church History in Edinburgh, c. 1840–1990' was included in *Disruption to Diversity: Edinburgh Divinity 1846–1996* (eds, D. F. Wright and G. D. Badcock), published by T&T Clark in 1996. I offer my thanks to those who have allowed me to republish them.

Chapter 1

Diversity and Development in Scottish Presbyterianism

In the nineteenth century, it has been observed, human thought in every field seemed to run to history. At that time, certainly, the discipline of history, along with the attitudes which it tends to foster, enjoyed a remarkable prestige in the theological faculties and seminaries of the world. All is now changed. A gulf of more than years divides us from men like Philip Schaff in the United States, Adolf Harnack and Ernst Troeltsch in Germany, and T. M. Lindsay, A. R. MacEwen and James Mackinnon in Scotland; and history no longer dominates the Divinity curriculum. Yet if its methods and spirit have ceased to be regarded as the open sesame to all truth one cannot help noticing how frequently, and how hopefully, churchmen and theologians still turn to it for inspiration and support. In ecumenical conversation and theological controversy alike it remains indispensable, providing olive branches for the one and powder and shot for the other with even-handed liberality; and its usefulness has been demonstrated by the number of historical references included, over recent years, in reports made to the Church of Scotland's General Assembly by its Commission on Baptism, its Committee on Inter-Church Relations and its Panel on Doctrine.

Naturally enough, the ecclesiastical historian is gratified to see that contemporaries still consider his discipline relevant or even valuable; but in his satisfaction there is an element of unease. The reason for this should be fairly obvious. One can very easily become so obsessed with the practical uses of history – its serviceability, for example, in the life of the Church – as to overlook the dangers implicit in too exclusively utilitarian an approach. There is, of course, the crude temptation to regard the records of the past simply as a kind of immense haystack whose chief interest lies in the somewhat widely dispersed needles which it may be supposed to contain. But there are others more sophisticated and more deadly, of which two in particular spring to mind. The first is the temptation to let our historical conclusions be shaped by theological or ecclesiastical preconceptions – to brainwash our ancestors, as it were, into corroborating our opinions and sentiments. The second is the temptation to simplify (it may be for the most eirenic of reasons) the story of past time, to suppress its discordant voices and silence its minorities, to iron out its complexities and transpose its hesitancies into a bolder key. Each, if succumbed to, would be fatal to the historian's integrity and to truth itself. What I mean may be explicated by reference to the Scottish situation.

In the 'Articles Declaratory of the Constitution of the Church of Scotland in Matters Spiritual' which are appended to the 'Basis and Plan of Union, 1929' we read as follows:

> The principal subordinate standard of the Church of Scotland is the Westminster Confession of Faith.... Its government is Presbyterian ... Its system and principles of worship, orders, and discipline are in accordance with 'The Directory for the Public Worship of God', 'The Form of Presbyterian Church Government', and 'The Form of Process', as these have been or may hereafter be interpreted or modified by Acts of the General Assembly or by consuetude.[1]

There is a comforting clarity and definiteness about these words (particularly if we overlook the important qualifying phrase with which they end) that would seem to admit of no gainsaying. Here, apparently, is the answer to interested enquirers from other traditions who question us about the doctrine, the government or the worship of Presbyterianism in Scotland! Perhaps so, but we should not allow ourselves to be beguiled into receiving a constitutional document as an entirely adequate description of a spiritual body and – still less – of its historical development. The churchmanship and the piety of four centuries cannot be comprehensively represented in a phrase or two from the Declaratory Articles, nor even in the masterly conciseness of the Kirk's

---

[1] 'Articles Declaratory of the Constitution of the Church of Scotland in Matters Spiritual' (Appendix to Uniting Act, 1929), in J. T. Cox and J. B. Longmuir (eds), *Practice and Procedure in the Church of Scotland* (5th edn, 1964), pp. 366–7.

subordinate standards, for the simple reason that the Scottish Church is not and never has been a tidy, smooth-surfaced and immutable monolith. It is, rather, a highly diversified, multifarious structure – indeed, not a structure at all, but a living organism in a constant process of growth and change. As any scrutiny of the religious scene in Scotland since the Reformation clearly indicates, on numerous matters of importance there has been, and continues to be, marked diversity even within the national Church; and in those very areas where the greatest measure of agreement can be found there has nonetheless been considerable adaptation and development over the past four centuries.

Consider first the sphere of *church government* – its practical exercise as well as the principles underlying it. No reader of Gordon Donaldson's classic study, *The Scottish Reformation*, can ever again maintain that the new order introduced by John Knox and his associates was unequivocally Presbyterian in either fact or intention. Yet within a generation of the 'uproar for religion' the Melvillian blue-print for a fully organised Presbyterian church, set out in the Second Book of Discipline, had been approved by the General Assembly and was being put into effect in various parts of the country: a major administrative change, on any interpretation. How would Knox have viewed it? Would he, as Professor Donaldson argued so persuasively in the work just referred to, have recognised that it was contrary to the whole character of the 1560 polity?[2] There cannot be absolute certainty, though I am inclined to doubt whether he would have discerned an unbridgeable gulf between his own achievement and his successor's. And in any case the situations confronting the two men were vastly different, and Scotland's leading reformer was hardly the man to veto all adjustment to changing circumstances. Despite his inflexibility on what he regarded as essentials, he was not without an opportunist streak; and it would be fair to say that it was he who, in the formative years of the reformed Church of Scotland, wrote into some of its classic documents the positive obligation to adapt. His History contains a solemn reference to the possibility of 'a more perfect' polity being established in days to come; and the Scots Confession, as is well known, disclaims the notion that 'any policie, and an ordour in ceremonies can be

---

[2] G. Donaldson, *The Scottish Reformation* (1960), chs 8 and 9, passim.

appoynted for al ages, times and places', and affirms that 'ceremonies, sik as men have devised, ar but temporall' and ought to be changed if fostering 'superstition'.[3] I do not think it is stretching the evidence, therefore, to say that in these early years the Church presented future generations with both the example of drastic organisational change and – through Knox if not through Melville – some idea of the principles which might well inspire it. Development has always been at least a possibility in this whole realm of church government.

With equal truth it may be said that diversity of opinion has always been in evidence. Not on the great essentials, admittedly, concerning which virtual unanimity has almost invariably existed. No Scottish Presbyterian would dissent from the authors of the Confession of 1560 when they declare that

> As we beleeve in ane God, Father, Sonne and haly Ghaist; sa do we maist constantly beleeve that from the beginning there has been, and now is, and to the end of the warld sall be, ane Kirk, that is to say, ane company and multitude of men chosen of God ... quha have communion and societie with God the Father, and with His Son Christ Jesus, through the sanctificatioun of his haly Spirit.[4]

Every Scottish Presbyterian would also agree with that same Confession when it describes the identification marks of the Church as 'trew preaching', 'the right administration of the Sacraments' and 'discipline uprightlie ministred'; and with the *Form of Presbyterial Church Government*'s assertion that 'Jesus Christ ... gave officers necessary for the edification of His Church and perfecting of His saints ... some extraordinary ... others ordinary and perpetual'.[5] But here agreement ends. Who are the divinely authorised 'officers' just mentioned, and what is the Church's part in their appointment? Perfect identity does not exist between the answers of Melville's *Second Book of Discipline* and Westminster's *Form of Church Government*, though each had been accepted at one time or another by the General Assembly. How are the clergy of the Reformed Church related to the clergy of medieval times? (That is to say, is there an uninterrupted

[3] Scots Confession, art. xx, in P. Schaff (ed.), *The Creeds of Christendom*, vol. 3 (4th edn, 1919), p. 466.

[4] Ibid., art. xvi, in Schaff, *Creeds*, p. 458.

[5] Ibid., art. xviii, in Schaff, *Creeds*, p. 461.

successio presbyterorum – and is it important?) Two respected teachers, Principal R. H. Story and Professor G. D. Henderson, have reacted quite differently from each other to that question.[6] Can one distinguish, in anything like the Roman or the Anglo-Catholic fashion, between clergy and laity? And is the ministry of Word and Sacraments the only real ministry, or should that of 'other church officers' be included? Here a divergence is to be noted between the Auld Kirk and the United Presbyterian traditions of the nineteenth century. To not a single one of these questions would Knox and Melville, Alexander Henderson and George Gillespie, the Seceders of the 1730s and the founders of the Scottish Church Society in the 1890s feel able to give an agreed reply. That is a measure of the diversity within Scottish Presbyterianism concerning the whole area of Church government.

Within the same general field two topics in particular – ministerial orders (and succession) and the place of the elder – have provoked fierce controversy. On the ministry, one view emerges very clearly from a letter written in 1879 by James Cooper, then a minister in Broughty Ferry and later Professor of Ecclesiastical History in the University of Glasgow, to his friend Dr G. W. Sprott of North Berwick.

'I venture to ask assistance from you', began the younger man, 'in what I feel to be a great crisis in my spiritual life. . . . I have torturing doubts as to the validity of my Presbyterian Orders. . . . If I cannot be satisfied that I am really a Presbyter in Christ's Catholic Church – however imperfect our branch may be – I feel that I cannot (without sin that would be fatal to my hope of Heaven) continue to minister where I do. . . . The thorn has long been in my flesh, and the whole neighbourhood of it is inflamed and sore. A year ago it was aggravated by a statement that ordination was omitted in the Church of Scotland for some thirty years at the time of the Reformation, and that our succession hangs on nothing. . . . I implore you as a scholar, a priest, and a Christian, to give me what help you can.[7]

(It was the year of Newman's elevation to the cardinalate: had young Cooper been re-reading the *Apologia*?) The doubts thus expressed yielded to Dr Sprott's treatment, and Cooper remained a minister of the Church of Scotland to his death: significantly

⁶ R. H. Story, *The Apostolic Ministry in the Scottish Church* (1897); G. D. Henderson, *Church and Ministry* (1951).
⁷ H. J. Wotherspoon, *James Cooper . . . A Memoir* (1926), pp. 105–6.

enough, the subtitle of H. J. Wotherspoon's biography of him is *Presbyter in the Church of God*. It would seem that the distinctive outlook which prompted Cooper's early questionings and shaped his entire ministry has been common to quite a few ministers of the National Church (though never, one suspects, more than an influential minority) during the last hundred years or so – years in which the heirs of the Oxford Movement have transformed much more than their own communion. As far back as 1897, Principal Story's Baird Lectures on *The Apostolic Ministry in the Scottish Church* included the following phrases:

> Those who take a natural interest in tracing the regular sequence of office and order in the Church, and who attribute a proper value to the element of a true apostolic succession, find with satisfaction that the great transformation which passed upon the Kirk in the sixteenth century . . . involved no break in that sequence and succession. The old order changed, giving place to the new; but between the two there was no disruption.[8]

Only six years later, Donald MacLeod (brother of the more famous Norman) was maintaining that 'the continuity of the National Church through the presbyterate . . . is as unbroken as that of the Episcopacy through the Episcopate'.[9] In his study of *The Presbyterian Tradition* (1933), Charles Warr asserted: 'The Church of Scotland insists on the Order of Presbyters as the one essential ministry within the Catholic Church, through which, and from the time of the apostles, the full ministry of the Word and Sacraments has been transmitted throughout the Catholic Church in a regular and valid succession.' And in its emphasis on succession, as in much else, Wotherspoon and Kirkpatrick's *Manual of Church Doctrine* (1st edition, 1920, 2nd revised edition, 1960) is clearly of the same school, though it is careful to point out that 'the Church of Scotland has always sought to find its justification not in its own orders and succession . . . but solely in Him who in Word and Sacrament freely extends to us His Covenant of Grace'.[10]

[8] Story, *Apostolic Ministry*, pp. 243–4.
[9] D. MacLeod, *The Ministry and Sacraments of the Church of Scotland* (1903), p. 3.
[10] C. L. Warr, *The Presbyterian Tradition* (1933), p. 369; H. J. Wotherspoon and J. M. Kirkpatrick, *A Manual of Church Doctrine According to the Church of Scotland* (2nd rev. edn, 1960), pp. 97–8.

6

It is noteworthy that all the most impressive statements of this point of view come either from the fairly recent past (the Scoto-Catholics of the late nineteenth and early twentieth centuries) or from the mid-seventeenth century (muted, in the Westminster *Form of Church Government*, strident in the *Jus Divinum Ministerii Evangelici* of 1654). In both periods the representatives of Presbyterianism were involved in what our contemporary jargon describes as 'ecumenical dialogue'. In the 1640s and 1650s that dialogue was with the Independents, who set little store by ministerial orders or continuity; during the past hundred years or so it has been with the Anglicans, who certainly cannot be accused of doing the same. May we not attribute the somewhat anxious and occasionally even shrill assertions concerning Catholicity and continuity which have been made by Scotland's spokesmen to their desire not to lose out in what Professor Gordon Rupp once called the negotiating churches' game of 'Beggar-my-neighbour'? However that may be, we should not overlook another, very different, strain within the Church of Scotland's thinking on the ministry. It goes back to the eve of the Reformation, appearing for example in Henry Balnaves's *Treatise on Justification* (which Knox edited):

> Ye which have entered in the Church of Christ, by the Bishoppe of Romes law and aucthoritie, with his faire bulles, your shaven crounes, smearing you with oyle or chreame, and cloathing you with all ceremonies commanded in your law. If ye think you there-through the successours of the Apostles and fathers of the Church, ye are greatly deceaved, for that is but a politike succession or ceremonial.[11]

It crops up in the Scots Confession's rejection of 'Antiquity, Title usurpit, lineal Descence, Place appointed' as the 'notes' of the true Church, and receives more extended expression in the *First Book of Discipline*'s bellicose statement that

> It is neither the clipping of their crownes, the greasing [crossing] of their fingers, nor the blowing of the dumb dogges called the Bishops, neither the laying on of their hands, that maketh thame true ministers of Christ Jesus. But the Spirit of God inwardly first moving the hearts to seek Christs glorie, and the profit of his Kirk, and thereafter the nomination of the people, the examination of the learned, and publick

---

[11] D. Laing (ed.), *The Works of John Knox*, vol. III (1854), p. 460.

admission ... make men lawfull ministers of the Word and Sacraments.[12]

The same way of looking at things is evident in certain sixteenth-century pronouncements on the historic (indeed, apostolic) rite of imposition of hands at the ordination of a minister. 'Other ceremonie', so runs the famous phrase in the *First Book of Discipline*, 'than the publick approbation of the people, and declaration of the chiefe minister, that the person there presented is appointed to serve the [that] kirk, we cannot approve, for albeit the Apostles used imposition of hands, yet seeing the miracle is ceased, the using of the ceremonie we judge not necessary.'[13] Calderwood the historian tells us that a similar view was very much alive as late as 1597, when 'the brethren of the Synod of Fife', on being asked the question, 'Is he a lawful minister who wanteth *impositio manuum?*', answered the King: 'Imposition, or laying on of hands, is not essential and necessary, but ceremonial and indifferent, in admission of a pastor.'[14]

The attitude of which these remarks were the expression did not entirely disappear even in the Westminster period, although other and perhaps contradictory emphases undoubtedly existed alongside it. It survived, for example, in Samuel Rutherford's stress upon the necessary part played by popular consent in the lawful admission of a minister – an emphasis which (if we are to believe such an authority as Professor Wilhelm Pauck) goes right back to Luther himself: 'in principle the congregational call of the minister was henceforth more important than ordination. Indeed, in early Protestantism ordination was nothing else than the confirmation of the calling and election of the minister.'[15] And in summing up his general impression of the great seventeenth-century divines one of our ablest historical theologians, James Walker, contended in his Cunningham Lectures (published in 1872) that 'Whatever

---

[12] Scots Confession, art. xvii, in Schaff, *Creeds*, p. 461; *First Book of Discipline*, 9th Head, in J. K. Cameron (ed.), *The First Book of Discipline* (1972), p. 207.

[13] *First Book of Discipline*, 4th Head, in Cameron, *Book of Discipline*, p. 102.

[14] T. Thomson (ed.), *David Calderwood's History of the Kirk of Scotland*, vol. v (1844), p. 586.

[15] W. Pauck, *The Heritage of the Reformation* (rev. edn, 1961), p. 134.

high and stringent views of church authority and church order were held by Gillespie, Rutherford, Dickson, Wood, Durham and others, we think they cannot be charged with any sympathy with a doctrine of orders such as developed in our time out of apostolic succession.'[16] Whether or not Walker was right, few would care to deny that within the Scottish Church today there continues to exist, over against the spiritual descendants of Cooper, MacLeod and Wotherspoon, a very considerable body of opinion which in no way shares their attitude to questions of ministry and order and – every bit as firmly as they – believes itself to be rooted not only in the Reformation but also in the best thought of the Westminster period as well.

The eldership too has known change and controversy: indeed it is remarkable that Knox had scarcely passed from the scene when Melville introduced changes in the office which Principal Story, long afterwards, was to stigmatise as 'error' and 'innovation'. Over the centuries, conflict seems to have gathered round three interrelated questions. First, is the eldership a divinely ordained, scripturally appointed institution, like the ministry of Word and Sacraments, or is it a mere human expedient? Calvin, we know, believed the former, citing in particular 1 Timothy 5:17 as his proof text.[17] So, presumably, did Knox. So also did Scotland's delegates to the Westminster Assembly, although they failed to get their teaching on the matter accepted. Against all these, however, are ranged the *Form of Presbyterial Church Government*, which (to the distress of men like George Gillespie) speaks pointedly not of 'ruling elders' but of 'such as in the Reformed Churches are commonly called elders' – and also the view, frequently expressed from the middle of this century by the Kirk's Panel on Doctrine and those in sympathy with it, that

> there is no clear evidence in the New Testament for what we call 'elders', let alone the theory that there are two kinds of presbyter.

[16] J. Walker, *The Theology and Theologians of Scotland*, Cunningham Lectures (2nd edn, 1888), p. 195.

[17] J. K. S. Reid (ed.), *Calvin: Theological Treatises*, Library of Christian Classics (1954), vol. XXII, p. 58; G. Baum, E. Cunitz and E. Reuss (eds), *Joannis Calvini Opera*, vol. LI (1895), for sermons on 1 Timothy, esp. p. 506; G. D. Henderson, *Presbyterianism* (1954), p. 56.

The Biblical passages to which appeal is made, when objectively considered, cannot be taken to bear the interpretation Presbyterians put upon them. Moreover, they were never understood in this sense by any of the Church Fathers.[18]

Secondly, is the elder primarily a *representative* of the congregation? The word and the idea seem to be absent from the *Form of Church Government*, as also from the First and Second Books of Discipline; and it may be significant that George Gillespie held the tacit consent of the people to an elder's appointment to be all that was necessary, since to leave matters to the 'most voices' would be 'a mere democracy with many moderators, which is the most monstrous government that ever was heard'.[19] But in the early eighteenth century the notion of the 'representative elder' begins to emerge. We find it in Robert Wodrow, and in an Act of the General Assembly of 1731.[20] It has never died out since. Its vogue at present tends, one suspects, to lower rather than to raise the status of the office, for it minimises the fact that the elder of tradition has exercised discipline over the congregation rather than been representative of it or responsible to it.

Thirdly (and this has a way of becoming the chief point at issue), is the elder properly ranked among the officers or among the members of the Church? Is he a 'layman'? The problem seems to have been first raised in the Westminster period, and although apparently a mere dispute about words it has always caused division at a deep level. On the one side the advocates of the so-called 'Presbyter' theory range themselves: these find in Scripture, above all in 1 Timothy 5:17, support for their belief that there were two types of presbyter, or elder, in the Apostolic Church – preaching presbyters and ruling presbyters, of whom the former are prototypes of the Scottish minister and the latter of the Scottish elder. On the other side stand the exponents of the 'Lay' theory, who contend, as did the *English* majority at the Westminster Assembly, that 'the New Testament hath nowhere distinguished the ruling elder's office'.[21]

---

[18] T. F. Torrance, *The Eldership in the Reformed Church* (1984), p. 7.
[19] Quoted in G. D. Henderson, *The Scottish Ruling Elder* (1935), p. 190.
[20] T. M'Crie (ed.), *The Correspondence of the Revd. Robert Wodrow*, vol. 1 (1842), pp. 179–88; *Acts of the General Assembly, 1638–1842* (1843), p. 614, 'the elders who represent the people'.
[21] Henderson, *Ruling Elder*, p. 194.

For a description of the implications of the 'Lay theory' in its developed form one cannot do better than quote a sentence or two from Professor G. D. Henderson, whose lack of sympathy does not vitiate his customary fairness. He writes:

> There are those in Scotland who . . . hold . . . that Church Government is in the hands of the officers of the Church and not of the members, but with them these Church officers are the fully-ordained clergy, and all others including elders are 'mere' laymen. . . . But the elder as a 'mere' layman is not 'ordained' in any full sense of the word. His function is regulative and administrative. It would according to this view be perhaps admissible even to have women elders, for this would in no way affect the question of women and the ministry. Indeed their admission to the eldership might be useful to emphasise the gulf between the ordained and unordained and ultimately protect the ministry against invasion. . . . [The] elder is simply a layman representing other laymen.[22]

After Professor Henderson had written these words, the view he described found expression in more than one pronouncement of the Panel on Doctrine. The 'Presbyter' theory, on the other hand, has at its heart the Lutheran doctrine of the priesthood of all believers (interpreted in a certain way), sympathises with those among the Covenanters who saw the distinction between clergy and laity as 'popish and unchristian', applauds Samuel Rutherford when he roundly calls it 'a lie' to say that the Church of Scotland has 'lay elders', and at times reciprocates the clericalism of its adversaries with an anti-clerical fervour of equal force.[23] Both now have a history which stretches back over more than three hundred years – the one drawing reinforcement from the predominant ethos of the Auld Kirk in late-Victorian days, from the Moderates of the eighteenth century and from the men who favoured the restoration of Episcopalianism at the Restoration of 1660; the other looking to the example of the Free and United Presbyterian Churches, of the Dissenters who sprang from the Erskines and Thomas Gillespie and of the majority of Covenanting thinkers. It may be, of course, that – as a downright controversialist of the 1960s opined in the correspondence columns of the *Scotsman* newspaper – 'It is high time that we stopped beating

---

[22] Henderson, *Ruling Elder*, pp. 214–15.
[23] Ibid., ch. 6, 'Controversy', passim.

about the ecclesiastical bushes and said precisely what an elder is.' But it is more than questionable whether precision of the kind demanded can be so easily achieved. With the past in mind, the historian may well recommend toleration of the differences still existing and reflect that in a great national Church there should be room for diversity.

*   *   *

Turn now to another facet of the Church's life: its *worship*. Two service books receive mention in the 'Basis and Plan of Union' of 1929. The first, included in a list of 'leading documents, setting forth the constitution, standards, rules and methods of the united church', is the Westminster *Directory for the Public Worship of God* (1645). The second, 'also held in honour as having an important place in the history of Scottish Presbyterianism', is the *Book of Common Order*, or 'Knox's Liturgy' (1564). Each represents the mind of the Church on worship at a turning-point in Scottish history, and together – especially if taken in conjunction with more recent productions such as the 1940, 1979 and 1994 Books of Common Order – they offer invaluable guidance as to the major impulses and emphases of Scottish religion in liturgical matters. We must, however, beware of misinterpreting the evidence which they provide. How convenient it would be if the picture furnished by them could be regarded as complete, requiring no amplification or emendation in the light of other material! How pleasant to interpret them as evidence of the perfect uniformity of worship in Scotland over all periods, or at least within each period! How gratifying to feel able to talk (as has been done) of the 'genuine Scottish tradition of worship' and, by contrast, of certain views as having 'no genuine roots in Scottish tradition'! Yet to do so would be to fly in the face of facts. In worship, as in government, development and diversity confront us at every epoch of the Church's existence; and if there *are* principles whereby its conformity or non-conformity with 'essential Presbyterianism' may be judged they are not deducible from history itself but must rather be brought to that history from elsewhere.

Consider in particular the time between the Reformation and the Westminster Assembly – the years when 'Knox's Liturgy', enjoined upon all ministers by the General Assembly of 1564, shaped the general practice. During that crucial period complete uniformity of worship was neither expected nor achieved. The evidence of the *Book of Common Order* itself strongly suggests that it was designed to be a flexible directory rather than a fixed liturgy. Time and again rubrics of this sort occur: 'it shall not be necessary for the minister daily to repeat all these things before mentioned'; 'this prayer following, or such like'; 'we refer it to the discretion of the godly and prudent minister'; 'he [the minister] either useth the Prayer for all Estates before mentioned, or else prayeth, as the Spirit of God shall move his heart'; and so on. Some of the material looks as if it has been included more for the information of men on the periphery of things, or the illumination of the uninspired, than for the undeviating adherence of all. For example: 'This prayer following is used to be said after the Sermon'; 'A prayer used in the Churches of Scotland, in the time of their persecution by the Frenchmen'; and 'These prayers following are used in the French Church of Geneva'. Even in the Order for Communion a certain freedom is allowed, as when we read: 'Then he taketh bread, and giveth thanks, either in these words following, or like in effect.' It is true that no permissive rubric precedes some of the occasional prayers, but by the time of their inclusion it was probably considered that the generally free approach had been well established. Only in those orders of service – Baptism, Marriage, Excommunication and Public Repentance – which either involved the acceptance of solemn engagements or altered a person's status in society as a whole is there complete inflexibility.

There is, besides, ample evidence from the early seventeenth century that ministers did not consider themselves to be bound in every particular by Knox's book. No doubt Samuel Rutherford, that man of extremes, went too far when he asserted concerning read prayers that 'Our Church never allowed them, but men took them up at their own choice'; but was he exaggerating so very wildly? King James VI could never have complained, as he did, of the libellous prayers of the Scottish clergy had they been adhering to the *ipsissima verba* of the Liturgy; just as there must have been some ground for Archbishop Spottiswoode's lament in 1615 that 'there is lacking in our Church a form of divine service; and whiles every man is left to the framing of public prayer by himself, both the people are neglected and their prayers prove often impertinent'. A little later, in the 1630s and 1640s, various ministers – John Row and David Calderwood among them – put on record their opposition to 'a prescript and stinted form of words' and their conviction that 'none are tied to the prayers of that book'.[24]

Indeed, there exists a little-known description of Scottish worship during those years which deserves fuller quotation for the picture it gives of the very free attitude taken by some ministers towards their so-called liturgy. 'The forms of prayers, admonitions, etc.', it affirms,

> were not precisely enjoined, nor yet the order of them, but might be formed otherwise by the minister and the order enlarged or contracted according to his discretion. In the visitation of the sick, ministers used not the words set down in the book, but comforted the sick as the Lord enabled by his gift. . . . No minister was tied to the form of confession of sins either before sermon or at other times, for the Book itself saith the minister useth this confession or the like in effect. The rehearsing of the Belief hath been disused these many years till now of late that the formalists have revived it, because there is an intention to bring in the English service. At the ministration of Baptism the minister taught summarily the doctrine of Baptism, more amply than is set down in the Book. We call such as accompany the father of the baptised witnesses, not godfathers as at the beginning. At the ministration of the Lord's Supper, after sermon was ended the minister began an exhortation before he came down from the pulpit, not as it is framed in the Book but in a more ample form.[25]

Weightiest of all, because most cautious, is Alexander Henderson's testimony in 1641. Replying to the accusation that (as he put it) Scottish ministers 'had no certain rule or direction for their public worship, but that every man following his corrupt fancy did preach and pray what seemed good in his own eyes', he pointed to the existence of the Book of Common Order as sufficient refutation and commented: 'although they be not tied to set forms and words, yet are they not left at random, but for

---

[24] A. A. Bonar (ed.), *Letters of Samuel Rutherford* (1856), p. 492; W. McMillan, *Worship of the Scottish Reformed Church, 1550–1638* (1931), pp. 69–70; G. Donaldson, *The Making of the Scottish Prayer Book of 1637* (1954), p. 31; D. Laing (ed.), *The History of the Church of Scotland . . . by John Row* (1842), p. 404.

[25] Quoted from Wodrow MSS in Donaldson, *Prayer Book of 1637*, p. 29.

testifying their consent and keeping unity they have their directory and prescribed order. Nowhere hath preaching and the ministry more spiritual and less carnal liberty.'[26] The position might be summed up as follows: 'Knox's Liturgy' was valued as the expression and the safeguard of an actual unity, rather than as the means to be used for the creation of a uniformity not yet in existence. Though men honoured it, they could never regard its authority as ultimate.

This being the case from the first days of the Reformation, it is hardly surprising that the passage of time brought to the fore new attitudes and practices which gradually undermined the status of the *Book of Common Order* as the natural rallying-point of the nation in matters of worship. Of these subversive influences the two which attained most prominence were the Anglicising policy of the monarchists, led by James VI and Charles I themselves, and the increasingly extreme Puritanism which developed in reaction against it. In the party who may (for lack of a better word) be described as Anglicisers or Anglicanisers – they were also, in the main, Royalist and Episcopalian – various considerations were of course at work which cannot be detailed here; but it seems fairly certain that one of their distinguishing marks was a tendency to prefer the English Prayer Book to that which Scotland had received from Geneva at the hand of John Knox. To begin with, this preference was perhaps little more than the expression of a sentimental attachment to their first love. (We remember how in 1557, before the religious revolution took place, the Scottish Protestant Lords in Council resolved that 'the Common Prayers be read weekly on Sunday and other festival days . . . conform to the order of the Book of Common Prayers'.[27]) But from the late 1560s sentiment came to be reinforced by weighty considerations of a political nature. England and Scotland both had Protestant monarchs now. With the way opening up for an ultimate union of the crowns was it not highly desirable that there should be a closer approximation of the religious settlements in the two countries? In Professor Donaldson's words, 'The

[26] A. Henderson, *Government and Order of the Church of Scotland* (1641), Epistle to the Reader.
[27] W. Croft Dickinson (ed.), *John Knox's History of the Reformation in Scotland* (1949), vol. I, p. 137.

tendency so far as church government was concerned was towards at least a superficial imitation of the Anglican system, and contemporaries spoke freely of development in the direction of "conformity with England". . . . Far-seeing Scots could discern many advantages in a "conformity" which would include forms of worship.'[28] By the 1580s, certainly, Archbishop Adamson and men like him were (to use Donaldson's phrase) 'inclining towards the Prayer Book'. Adamson was to be found using 'the English ceremonies' at a marriage service, and earned condemnation from his opponents for 'filthily adulterating the state of public prayer with the simplicity of rites in ministration of the sacraments'.[29] Then came the short-lived Melvillian triumph; but the revival of the Episcopalian cause in the opening years of the seventeenth century brought the English Book into prominence once more. The universities were ordered to use it; on King James's return visit to his native land in 1617 it appeared in the Chapel Royal; it was considered peculiarly suitable for cathedral worship; and – most important of all – the various schemes for liturgical reform which were set in train between 1601 and 1637 and culminated in the fateful 'Laud's Liturgy' clearly betray its powerful influence. 'It may be' (so runs the preface to the 1637 Book)

> that exceptions will be taken against this good and most pious work, and, perhaps, none more pressed than that we have followed the Service-Book of England. But we should desire them that shall take this exception, to consider, that, being as we are by God's mercy of one true profession, and otherwise united by many bonds, it had not been fitting to vary much from theirs, ours especially coming forth after theirs; seeing the disturbers of the Church, both here and there, should by our differences, if they had been great, [have] taken occasion to work more trouble. Therefore did we think meet to adhere to their Form, even in the Festivals, and some other rites not as yet received nor observed in our Church, rather than, by omitting them, to give the adversary to think that we dislike any part of their service.[30]

So much for one of the two attitudes which gradually undermined the ascendancy of the old *Book of Common Order* in late sixteenth- and early seventeenth-century Scotland. The other was

[28] Donaldson, *Prayer Book of 1637*, pp. 22–3.
[29] Ibid., pp. 23–4.
[30] Ibid., p. 102.

what we have called Puritanism. In part this amounted to a violent rejection of the policy of 'Conformity with England' – England being regarded as virtually synonymous with Anglicanism. One of James's servants, Spottiswoode, notes in his history that the King had barely reached his capital in 1617 when the ministers 'began to stir as if the whole rites and ceremonies of England were to be brought upon them without their consents', and that 'Mr. William Struthers, one of the ministers of Edinburgh, did unhappily break out in his sermon upon these matters, condemning the rites received in the Church of England, and praying God to save Scotland from the same';[31] and it is significant that the title of George Gillespie's first publication, given to the world some twenty years later on the eve of the Covenanting revolt, was *A Dispute against the English-Popish Ceremonies obtruded on the Church of Scotland.*

It could nevertheless be argued that the Puritanical viewpoint was in a sense the expression of another and very different 'conformity with England' movement from that already examined: its ideal, the churchmanship not of Hooker and Laud but of Robert Browne and the Independents. Dr Sprott, whose Lee Lecture of 1893 on *The worship of the Church of Scotland during the Covenanting Period 1638–61* still remains (despite some bias) the authoritative modern account of it, tells us elsewhere, quoting contemporaries, that this party

> began with some English Brownists, and some Scotsmen returned from Ireland, where, having been pressed with conformity to the English Liturgy, they had abstained very much from public worship, and had fallen into extreme views. They were hostile to the Minister's kneeling for private devotion when he entered the pulpit, and to the singing of Gloria Patri at the end of the Psalms. They favoured 'private conventicles', 'discountenanced read prayers', and 'scundered at the Lord's Prayer and the Belief'. They were suspected of Independency in church government, and in general were charged with being of a sectarian as opposed to a churchly spirit.[32]

---

[31] *History of the Church of Scotland ... by the Right Revd. John Spottiswoode* (1851), vol. III, pp. 241–2.

[32] G. W. Sprott and T. Leishman (eds), *The Book of Common Order of the Church of Scotland, commonly known as Knox's Liturgy, and The Directory for the Public Worship of God agreed upon by the Assembly of Divines at Westminster* (1868), p. lxiii.

(One cannot help noticing, incidentally, how often Scotland's religious controversialists, both then and later, have played to the gallery of nationalism as a means of commending their case. Episcopacy and liturgical worship are denounced by one party as an English importation – and commended by another as a native growth; and so with presbytery and extempore prayer. In the twentieth century, members of the Church Service Society and the Scottish Church Society have perhaps been specially guilty in this respect, but few ardent churchmen are altogether blameless.)

There is no need to follow the story of Jacobean and Caroline antagonisms into the Civil Wars which they helped to bring about. What is worth noting, however, is the fact that the twin themes of diversity and development were just as evident in the new era signalised by the liturgical work of the Westminster Divines as they had been in the period when Scottish worship conformed more or less closely to the pattern of Knox's Book. Indeed, merely to think of the new *Directory for the Public Worship of God* is to think of change and growth. Its very acceptance by the General Assembly in 1645, hesitant as that was to begin with, meant the supplanting (though by no means the condemnation) of its predecessor; and the *Directory* in its turn was to experience all the vicissitudes of approbation, emendation, neglect and even obloquy. We are told that when the new book, finally adjusted, was sent down to Edinburgh 'the Scots were gratified to find that the arrangement of the ordinary worship was nearly the same as that to which they had been accustomed'.[33] Yet the work as a whole introduced or recognised various alterations, some of them slight but others quite considerable. For example, while the order for administration of Baptism largely followed previous Scottish practice it omitted to prescribe repetition of the Creed or the Lord's Prayer, did not include mention of a godfather in addition to the child's parent, and left the wording of the vows to be taken by sponsors intentionally vague. Again, the order for the celebration of Communion was by no means identical with 'Knox's Liturgy' and the earliest usages associated therewith. It tended to replace extreme simplicity with somewhat fuller forms, put the word of exhortation *before* the words of institution, provided for a distinct

---

[33] T. Leishman, 'The Ritual of the Church of Scotland', in R. H. Story (ed.), *The Church of Scotland, Past and Present* (1890), vol. v, p. 388.

invocation of the Holy Spirit (though whether this should be regarded as equivalent to what the Eastern Church means by the Epiclesis is more than doubtful), probably altered the words of administration from the phraseology hitherto most usual in Scotland and included a crucially important rubric – 'the Table being . . . so conveniently placed, that the Communicants may orderly sit about it, or at it' – which (had it not been for special action by the General Assembly to interpret it) might have been understood as implying permission to abandon the custom of sitting *round* the Table for Communion. The marriage service, unlike its counterpart in the old *Book of Common Order*, indicated the content of a prayer for blessing upon the contracting parties. Above all, the minister's and reader's services, which users of the *Common Order* had regarded as separate parts of a full diet of worship, were now combined, and the controversial practice of 'lecturing' was introduced, though with various safeguards not long respected. The evidence is incontrovertible that the adoption of the *Directory* betokened a material departure from the ways of worship sanctioned by the service book of the first Reformers.

But the *Directory* in its turn was not long adhered to at every point. Despite its ban on private Baptism, which was endorsed by the Revolution Assembly of 1690, we find a minister writing in the following terms as early as 1703: 'I very well remember the practice of prelatical ministers in this matter, and I as well know that of Presbyterians now. And I do assert that where there was one child baptised out of the Church there are six baptised now.'[34] Its stipulation, in the sections dealing with Marriage, that 'the Minister . . . is publicly to solemnise it in the place appointed by authority for Public Worship', was likewise brushed aside, although the advice 'that it be not on the Lord's Day' seems to have been taken very seriously. Its prohibition of funeral services at the graveside became in the event a truly dead letter. Its careful warnings against ministerial abuse of 'lecturing' (that is, detailed commentary on the Scripture reading of the day which could amount to a second sermon) – 'let it not be done until the whole Chapter or Psalm be ended; and regard is always to be had unto the time, that neither Preaching or other Ordinance be straitened

[34] Quoted in Leishman, 'Ritual', p. 408.

or rendered tedious' – were not heeded until the middle of the nineteenth century. Its recommendation of the Lord's Prayer as being 'not only a pattern of prayer but itself a most comprehensive prayer' seems to have been negatived by the General Assembly as early as 1649. And everyone knows that even the bestowal of its blessing upon the old Scottish usage of receiving Communion while seated round the Table did not protect that dearly prized institution from the ravages of nineteenth-century innovators, led by Thomas Chalmers himself. Throughout the generations since Westminster, Scottish worship has been characterised by well-nigh constant growth and change.

Nowhere perhaps is this fact made more obvious than by a comparison of the salient characteristics of 'Knox's Liturgy' and the *Directory* on the one hand with those of the 1940 *Book of Common Order* on the other. The differences are very considerable: the 1564 Book apparently designed for the use of members as well as ministers, the 1940 one exclusively for ministers (the former including private prayers for ordinary folk, the latter vestry prayers and the like for the clergy); 1564 including a *reformed* Confession of Faith, 1940 the Apostles' and Nicene Creeds only; 1564 assigning an inordinately large place to discipline, 1940 giving it practically no room at all; 1564 including rules on fasting, 1940 passing it over in silence; 1564 concentrating its attention on men's internal disposition, 1940 concerning itself also with the externals of the ecclesiastical institution; 1564 'so framed as to make responsive worship impossible', 1940 doing almost the opposite; 1645 going out of its way to affirm that 'Festival days, vulgarly called Holy-days, having no warrant in the Word of God, are not to be continued', 1940 devoting a whole section to 'Prayers for the Seasons of the Christian Year'; 1645 declaring that 'no place is capable of any holiness under pretence of whatsoever dedication or consecration', 1940 including orders 'for laying the foundation stone of a church', 'for the dedication of a church', 'for the dedication of an organ', and 'for the dedication of church furnishings and memorials'; 1645 offering detailed counsel on preaching, 1940 leaving it entirely alone.

The 1940 Book continued for more than half a century to be regarded as the high-water mark of Presbyterian expertise in liturgical matters; but even it eventually succumbed to the influences of change, and movement in a rather different direction can be seen in the freer, less stilted but equally dignified forms of the recently published *Book of Common Order of the Church of Scotland* (1994).

As evident as the changes perceptible in Scottish worship between one generation and another have been the differences and disagreements among worshippers in any one generation. At no period could a discerning observer confidently declare, 'This, without any qualification, is the undivided mind and the universal custom of the Kirk' – not even when there has existed an Act of Assembly to encourage such an assertion. Always there have been parties, antithetical viewpoints, diversities of operations. Even at Westminster, Alexander Henderson and Robert Baillie tended to draw together against George Gillespie and Samuel Rutherford. In the early eighteenth century, controversy raged round the desirability or otherwise of using the Lord's Prayer, with Hugh Campbell of Cawdor and James Anderson of Dumbarton on one side and James Hog of Carnock on the other. In the mid-nineteenth, Pirie of Aberdeen and others clashed with Lee of Edinburgh on various liturgical matters. And at the present time there is almost certainly much less unanimity than the General Assembly's Panel on Worship might desire or certain enthusiasts for its productions might contend.

A great deal more could be said about the strange vicissitudes of Scottish worship in the centuries between the Reformation and our own day: the reaction in 1660, for example, which restored many of the old observances that crusading Puritanism had denounced and proscribed; the Revolution of 1688–90 with its re-establishment of Presbyterianism and its canonisation of such recently acquired practices as disuse of the Creed and the Doxology; the slow revival of concern for a more Catholic style of worship, due largely to the dedicated efforts of the Church Service Society and allied groups since the 1860s; the introduction of hymns and organs; the gradual adoption of the clerical dress generally (but not universally) favoured today; and the controversies that have been stirred up, ever and again, by such 'innovation' or 'revivals'. But a more detailed survey would merely underline the fact that not a single generation since Westminster – or indeed since Knox – has found the Kirk presenting an entirely static or uniform front to the world. Only a very bold or a very bigoted person would claim the unerring ability to detect, in all the welter of divergent views and changing practices, the 'essential' tradition of Scottish Presbyterian worship.

So, finally, to the sphere of *faith and doctrine*. Not until nearly a century after the Reformation did the Church of Scotland acquire what is now officially described, in the language of the 1929 Act of Union, as its 'principal subordinate standard' (i.e. subordinate to the Bible). Until then, the doctrinal rallying-point of Reformed churchmen north of the Border had been the Scots Confession of Knox and his associates, described at its adoption by Parliament in 1560 as 'The Confession of Faith professed and believed by the Protestants within the realm of Scotland . . . and by the Estates thereof ratified and approved as wholesome and sound doctrine, grounded upon the infallible truth of God's Word'. In the late 1640s, however, the tides of Puritan revolution bore a new religious symbol north to Scotland, and the recently completed Westminster Confession displaced its simpler and briefer predecessor. The Church acclaimed it, Parliament ratified it, and every household was ordered to possess a copy. Its long career as a shaping influence in the life of both Church and nation had begun. Even the Cromwellian interregnum and the restoration of monarchy and episcopate in 1660 constituted only a brief interlude in the story, for when the Revolution Settlement of 1690 brought Presbyterianism back to power the Confession immediately regained favour also.

The situation in post-Revolution Scotland, however, was an exceptionally fluid one, and events soon ensured that the Confession's role in the new era would be subtly different from what it had been in the old. The trauma of the Union of the Parliaments in 1707 was quickly followed by a succession of attacks from both north and south of the Border upon Scotland's religious establishment; and in its insecurity the Presbyterian Kirk began to use the Confession not merely as an authoritative statement of faith but as a weapon in the ecclesiastical power-game (against recalcitrant Episcopalians) and as a touchstone of political correctness (against Jacobites). Indeed, Church and State joined forces in imposing it on ministers and other office-bearers with a new rigour and inflexibility. Obligatory compliance reached its extreme in 1711, when licentiates and ordained ministers alike were required to sign a formula which bound them to acknowledge the Confession not merely as a summary of the Church's corporate faith but as their personal confession also, and called for their active support and commendation of every detail contained in it.

Surprisingly enough, confessional obligations imposed at the outset of the century of Enlightenment remained binding at its close – despite the fact that the dominant party in the Church, the so-called Moderates, were, if not hostile, at least indifferent to doctrinal orthodoxy. Perhaps the reason was that the Moderate leader, Principal William Robertson, being very well aware that his party's command of the General Assembly did not really reflect the situation in the country as a whole, was too cautious and diplomatic to allow any obvious loosening of the trammels of Westminster Calvinism. 'Let sleeping dogs lie' seems to have been his motto.

In any case, the Revd Principal had scarcely bowed himself out when the religious scene was utterly transformed. Partly because of the excesses of the French Revolution and the tribulations of the long war which followed it, partly because of the intensified zeal and intransigence resulting from the Evangelical Revival, ardent traditionalism became the order of the day in Scotland as in the rest of Great Britain, and Presbyterian devotion to the 'Westminster Standards' was deepened accordingly.

At the same time, it has to be said that the turn of the eighteenth and nineteenth centuries saw the first signs of a breach in the virtually unbroken facade of recognised Scottish orthodoxy. In 1797, the 'Burgher' Seceders, spiritual descendants of Moderatism's arch-enemy, Ebenezer Erskine, disclaimed any interpretation of their confessional standard which favoured 'compulsory measures in religion'. And in 1806 the 'Anti-Burgher' Seceders went even further, declaring that 'no human composure ... can be supposed to contain a full and comprehensive view of divine truth', and appealing from the Church's subordinate to its ultimate authority, Holy Scripture.[35]

These were the premonitory tremors of a coming earthquake; but it was only in the 1830s and 1840s – decades of rapid and far-reaching change, social, political and intellectual – that the magnitude of the impending upheaval became evident. Only then did the basic doctrines and attitudes of Westminster Calvinism come under serious and sustained attack; only then was the

[35] J. M'Kerrow, *History of the Secession Church* (1841), pp. 443, 591.

relationship of mainstream Presbyterians to their inherited doctrinal standard called in question by persons of quite exceptional vision and forcefulness like Thomas Carlyle, Thomas Erskine of Linlathen and the young John Stuart Blackie. They were also the years of heresy trials – of Edward Irving, John McLeod Campbell, James Morison, Robert Balmer and John Brown – which gave an airing to views that were by no means always reconcilable with time-honoured Calvinist norms.

Campbell, a considerable figure in the Established Church, was condemned for arguing – against traditional Calvinism – that Christ had died, not for the elect only, but for all. In the immediate aftermath of the trial, moreover, he came to realise how incompatible his new emphases were with the overall import of the 'Westminster Standards', and bequeathed to subsequent generations this powerful argument against unrestrained confessionalism:

> When the Church says to both ministers and people, 'This is my Confession of Faith: if anything in it appear to you inconsistent with the Word of God, I am prepared to go with you to the Word of God to settle the matter', then does the Church speak according to her place. But if instead of this she says, 'This I have fixed to be the meaning of the Word of God, and you cannot take any other meaning without being excluded from my communion; and to entitle me so to exclude you I do not need to prove to you that what you hold and teach is contrary to the Scriptures, it is quite enough that it is contrary to my Confession of Faith'; I say, if the Church of Christ uses this language she no longer remembers her place as a Church.[36]

Brown's case is evidence that the questioning spirit was also at work among the Presbyterian Dissenters of Scotland. Indeed, it proved to be a turning-point in their theological history. By persuading the United Secession Synod of 1845 to agree with him that there had always been a kind of duality of emphasis within the Reformed camp concerning the extent of the Atonement (some holding that Christ died only for the elect, others that he died for all), Brown ensured that from then onwards the love of God to all humanity occupied the central place in the preaching and teaching of his denomination and its successor, the United

---

[36] *The Whole Proceedings in the Case of John McLeod Campbell before the Presbytery of Dunbarton, and the Synod of Glasgow and Ayr* (1831), p. 202.

Presbyterian Church.[37] The old emphasis upon election and reprobation slipped further and further into the background, and the tone of Scottish theology became gradually more liberal and charitable.

From the mid- and late forties right on to the end of the next decade there was a perceptible slackening in the pace of theological change. The Disruption forced Church leaders to concentrate their energies on mundane matters like the reconstruction of the sorely battered Auld Kirk or the consolidation and expansion of the emergent Free Kirk; while among the old Dissenters the chief concern was the drawing together of Secession and Relief in the United Presbyterian Church of 1847. Theological criticism and innovation were at a discount. In the Free Church, particularly, such Calvinist heavyweights as William Cunningham and Robert Candlish dominated the scene – the former asserting that the work of the sixteenth- and seventeenth-century reformers (including the Westminster Divines) was 'too firmly rooted in the Word of God and . . . too conclusively established, to be ever again seriously endangered',[38] and the latter that Westminster's doctrinal pronouncements 'will stand the test of time, and ultimately command the assent of universal Christendom'.[39]

Only in the 1860s did a gradually accelerating transformation become apparent. That eventful decade – the decade, be it noted, of England's Clerical Subscription Act – saw the fully-fledged emergence of a very different mood in all the churches, more questioning, less serenely satisfied with its confessional inheritance. In 1862, Robert Lee spoke of 'the inadequacy of the theology of the seventeenth century to be the sole guide or authority for the nineteenth'.[40] In 1865, John Tulloch called for historical and philosophical study of the Church's subordinate Standard, and in 1866 he led a revolt of seventy ministers against the anti-revisionist views of the then Auld Kirk Moderator, Dr Cook.[41] That same year, the Moderator of the Free Church reminded the

[37] J. Cairns, *Memoir of John Brown, D.D.* (1860), ch. vii, passim.
[38] A. Campbell Fraser, *Biographia Philosophica* (2nd edn, 1905), p. 161.
[39] R. S. Candlish, *The Fatherhood of God* (2nd edn, 1865), p. 289.
[40] R. H. Story, *Life and Remains of Robert Lee, D.D.* (1870), vol. II, pp. 34–5.
[41] J. Tulloch, 'Introductory Lecture' (no title) (1865); A. T. Innes, *Studies in Scottish History, chiefly Ecclesiastical* (1892), pp. 257–8.

General Assembly, in terms with which McLeod Campbell would happily have agreed, that 'We claim no infallibility for [the Confession], or for ourselves who declare our belief in the propositions which it contains. . . . It is the Word of God which only abides forever.'[42] Around the same time, a significant if abortive revolt against their confessional obligations took place among Church of Scotland office-bearers, while traditional Sabbatarian views – so deeply embedded in the Confession – took something of a beating at the hands of Norman MacLeod in the Auld Kirk and Walter Chalmers Smith in the Free.[43]

Perhaps most thought-provoking and portentous of all were the contributions of Edinburgh's gifted lay theologian, Alexander Taylor Innes. His great work, *The Law of Creeds in Scotland*, came out in 1867; and readers must have been fascinated by the problems it uncovered and the questions it raised, as well as the mass of informative material it contained. Alongside *The Law of Creeds*, Innes also produced an essay on 'The Theory of the Church and its Creed' which, by the provocative things it had to say about the limited effectiveness of every confessional statement, must have encouraged many of his co-religionists to reconsider their attitude to confession-making and confession-subscribing.

As one approaches the years when Presbyterianism's relationship to the Confession issued at last in definitive action, the influence of European contacts becomes increasingly evident. During the first half of the century Scotland, like the rest of Great Britain, had been almost unprecedentedly isolated and insular; and in the Established Church and its Free Church counterpart things did not change very greatly for some time after the Disruption. But it was rather different among the Seceders and their successors in the United Presbyterian Church. The future leader of the denomination, John Cairns, spent much of 1843 and 1844 in Germany, sitting at the feet of Neander, Schelling, von Ranke and others; and he was only one of many Secession students who passed their long vacations at Halle, Berlin or Bonn. Where they led the way, others like Tulloch of the Establishment and Robertson Smith of the Free Church followed in due course.

---

[42] *Proceedings and Debates of the General Assembly of the Free Church of Scotland, 1866*, pp. 7–8.

[43] J. R. Fleming, *The Church in Scotland, 1843–1874* (1927), pp. 212–20.

Whether they were instrumental (as has been suggested) in rescuing the Christianity of their country from 'the blindness of religious provincialism',[44] they certainly helped to root Continental theology and philosophy in Scottish soil, and paved the way for the time, not so far distant, when Wellhausen, Ritschl, Herrmann and Harnack would be household words in the manses of the land. By the 1860s, indeed, it was not even necessary to travel abroad to encounter strong Continental influences. John Caird, who in his later Croall Lectures (delivered in 1878–9) acknowledged a greater debt to Hegel's *Philosophie der Religion* than to any other book,[45] became Professor of Divinity at Glasgow in 1862, while his brother Edward, an even more pronounced Hegelian, obtained the Chair of Moral Philosophy there in 1866. Between them they fostered a marked lack of enthusiasm for the old Calvinist faith.

The impact upon Scottish theology of *English* thinking was probably even greater, being mediated through an endless torrent of books, periodicals and newspapers. But whatever its origins, a new climate of thought was undeniably developing. Among its manifestations, all of which had their bearing on the views hitherto taken of the Confession and confessional subscription, must be reckoned the following:

1. *A fresh picture of the natural world.* Robert Flint, Professor of Divinity at Edinburgh from 1876, is reported as having declared his 'willingness to review the confessional doctrines of Creation, origin of man, and Fall, in the light of the assured results of science and history'.[46]

2. *A fresh estimate of human nature.* Principal Rainy once told the Free Church Assembly that seventeenth-century thought had been marked by what he called 'a sparingness and timidity' in recognising 'elements in human nature which reminded them of its original greatness'.[47]

3. *A fresh moral sensitivity.* Professor Charteris, an administrative innovator but a theological conservative, nevertheless

[44] A. R. MacEwen, *Life of John Cairns* (1895), p. 150.
[45] J. Caird, *Introduction to the Philosophy of Religion* (1880), Prefatory Note.
[46] W. P. Paterson, 'Outline of the History of Dogmatic Theology' (1916), p. 20.
[47] P. C. Simpson, *Life of Principal Rainy* (1909), vol. II, p. 126.

once confessed that he had 'always held the expression of Calvinism in the Confession of Faith to be ruthless and hard'.[48]

4. *A fresh tentativeness.* As Rainy put it in 1880, contemporary theology tended to ask, 'Did not all those [earlier] theologies overdo the confidence of their interpretations and the sweep of their conclusions?'[49]

5. *A fresh tolerance.* In 1881, the year of Robertson Smith's deposition, Flint commented that 'The Church of Scotland has no right to tolerate sceptical teaching and fundamental heresy, but neither has she a right to repress variety of opinion, or to act in any inquisitorial spirit, or to violate constitutional procedure, or to treat all errors as heresies, or to be over-rigid with any man.'[50]

6. *A fresh preference for the apologetic as opposed to the dogmatic spirit.* Tulloch told his students as early as 1864 that 'men no longer heed utterances which are not weighty in argument as well as in tone, nor bow before a condemnation which is not reasoned as well as authoritative'.[51]

7. *A fresh awareness of the need for a truly comprehensive Gospel.* Imperial expansion and missionary enterprise alike were familiarising Christian people with constantly widening prospects, whereas the Westminster system could be described as 'an exclusive one, concerning itself mainly with the position and prospects of believers, and furnishing only a few loopholes from which furtive glances can be taken at the justice of God's providence and the breadth of His mercy in dealing with all His children'.[52]

8. *A fresh approach to evangelism.* Rainy's biographer, Carnegie Simpson, wrote concerning D. L. Moody's first campaign in 1874 that 'The preaching of a "free Gospel" to all sinners did more to relieve Scotland of the old hyper-

---

[48] A. Gordon, *Life of Archibald Hamilton Charteris* (1912), p. 420.
[49] *Report of the Proceedings of the Second General Council of the Presbyterian Alliance* (1880), p. 83.
[50] D. Macmillan, *Life of Professor Flint* (1914), p. 379.
[51] J. Tulloch, 'Introductory Lecture delivered at St. Mary's College, St. Andrews, November 21, 1864' (1864), p. 10.
[52] MacEwen, *Cairns*, pp. 662–3.

Calvinist doctrine of election, and of what the theologians call limited atonement ... than did even the teaching of McLeod Campbell'.[53]

9. *A fresh hostility to Calvinist theology*. As their Lord Rector, James Anthony Froude the historian, told the students of St Andrews in 1871, 'After being accepted for two centuries in all Protestant countries as a final account of the relations between man and his Maker, it [Calvinism] has come to be regarded by liberal thinkers as a system of belief incredible in itself, dishonouring in its object, and as intolerable as it has been intolerant.'[54]

In the light of an intellectual revolution such as this, we are scarcely surprised to learn from a contemporary that 'in the seventies and early eighties both the United Presbyterian and Free Churches [and conceivably the Church of Scotland as well] lost quite a number of able theological students, who slipped quietly out of the theological halls, finding the traditional *Weltanschauung* too narrow for them'.[55] Nor is it a wonder that calls for the revision or even the abandonment of the Confession were more and more often heard.

Quite suddenly, the trickle of dissatisfaction with the confessional *status quo* swelled into a flood; and in 1879 the United Presbyterian Church's Declaratory Act opened a new era in Scotland's religious history. By this Act the Synod chose not to abandon all use of the Confession as a theological test, but rather to redefine the Church's relationship to it. Henceforth, candidates for the ministry or the eldership were required to signify their adherence to Westminster's formulations in the light of a newly drafted 'Declaratory Statement' which took account of recent changes of attitude. Extreme or erroneous inferences that had sometimes been drawn from Confessional phraseology were disclaimed, and the proclamation of God's love for all humanity counterbalanced the restriction of effectual grace to the elect. Most important of all, the so-called 'conscience clause' allowed liberty

[53] Simpson, *Rainy*, vol. I, p. 408.
[54] J. A. Froude, 'Calvinism', in *Short Studies on Great Subjects* (new edn, 1888), vol. II, p. 3.
[55] D. and A. Cairns (eds), *David Cairns: An Autobiography* (1950), p. 125.

of opinion on matters which fell outside 'the substance of the faith' – a concession whose value to troubled minds both then and ever since can hardly be exaggerated.[56]

The Synod were assured by their leader, John Cairns, that the decision thus made neither contradicted nor cancelled Westminster's teaching, but simply made it more balanced, 'giving counterpoise to what otherwise might be looked upon as too strong and extreme'.[57] Was his judgment sound? Did the new statement really try to reconcile the irreconcilable? What were 'the substance of the faith' and 'the essential articles' to which reference was so confidently made? Such questions are still asked, and no unanimous answer given to them. But the fact remains that from 1879 onwards the Declaratory Act was written into the constitution of the United Presbyterian Church and subtly altered the theological face thereby presented to the world. After much more agonising, the Free Church followed suit in 1892 with a similarly worded enactment. And in 1905 the Church of Scotland produced an altered, and less restrictive, formula of subscription. Reformed theology's traditional exclusiveness – as well, no doubt, as its former precision and consistency – was at an end.

No dramatic change has taken place since then in mainstream Presbyterianism's avowed relationship to its inherited symbol. Ministers at ordination still profess belief in 'the fundamental doctrines of the Christian faith contained in the Confession of Faith of this Church', and that same Confession is still officially described as the Church of Scotland's 'principal subordinate standard' – subordinate, of course, to Holy Scripture. But even the present brief survey has shown that it would be a great mistake to let the underlying continuities in the story of several centuries obscure the equally obvious reconsiderations and reversals. The viewpoint of 1647 differed appreciably from that of 1711; the Moderates of the mid-eighteenth century differed in many important respects from the Evangelicals of one hundred years later; there was a great gulf between the early Victorians and their grandchildren on this confessional issue. Nor was it only individuals – as we have seen – who showed a changing attitude:

[56] J. Cooper, *Confessions of Faith and Formulas of Subscription* (1907), pp. 99–101.
[57] MacEwen, *Cairns*, p. 674.

the Declaratory Acts bear witness to the fact that the whole Church has done so too. *Semper eadem* is most assuredly not the slogan with which to sum up the history of the Kirk in matters of faith.

But we have already seen its inapplicability in the sphere of government and worship also. No matter how we approach it, in fact, the overall story of Scottish Presbyterianism is one of much controversy and fairly steady change. There has never been a 'golden period' in which 'the full Presbyterian position' (to use phrases from Wotherspoon's and Kirkpatrick's *Manual*)[58] is clearly discernible; and to maintain such a view would be to warp our study of the past by theological or ecclesiastical presuppositions of one kind or another – to overcome history by dogma, as a distinguished Roman cardinal once advised should be done. A more excellent way is, however, open to churchmen with a concern for history – a way neatly described by Professor Owen Chadwick in his fascinating account of doctrinal development, *From Bossuet to Newman*. Discussing the special achievements of the great monastic historians of seventeenth-century France, he remarks: 'Historical research was being put forward by Mabillon and St. Maur not as a useful agent of theology, but as a study for the glory of God – which in later and less Christian terminology is to say, a study as an end in itself.'[59]

---

[58] Wotherspoon and Kirkpatrick, p. ix.
[59] O. Chadwick, *From Bossuet to Newman* (1957), p. 62.

Chapter 2

Piety and Learning:
Three Edinburgh Exemplars

We are accustomed these days to think and talk of our
universities as secular institutions in a pluralist society.
So no doubt they are; yet surely it is important to recall how
much the Christian religion has had to do with their origins and
their subsequent history. In the case of Edinburgh, at any rate,
the story of the University cannot be told without acknowledging
the prominent part played in it by ministers of the Reformed
Church. The importance of their contribution is perhaps most
easily brought out by considering the careers of three exceptionally
able men – Robert Rollock, Robert Leighton and William
Carstares – who not only attained great prominence in the life of
the University (each of them figuring as its Principal) but also
served both Church and society at large with great distinction.

*   *   *

For modern academics, who find it difficult to conceive of a
university without hundreds of teachers, squads of secretaries,
banks of telephones and word-processors, lecture theatres and
halls of residence, it may be salutary to remember that the 'Tounis
College' of Edinburgh originally consisted of little more than a
few broken-down houses, a handful of students, and *one*
instructor. When James VI granted a charter for the new institution in the summer of 1582, there were needless to say hopes
that it would eventually become a university in the full sense of
the word. At first, however, the baillies and councillors – together
with the ministers of the Kirk, who may well have been the moving
spirits in the whole exercise – were not so ambitious. Tailoring
their aims to the meagreness of their means, they rejected the
plan favoured by the leading educational reformers of the age

33

(specialist professors, that is, teaching separate subjects), and settled instead for a staff of so-called 'regents', each of whom would take his particular cohort of students through all the departments of the curriculum. By the beginning of the fourth year, four such regents would be required, but in the first year a single one would suffice. For this key figure the patrons turned, on the recommendation of John Knox's successor at the High Kirk, James Lawson, to a young teacher in the University of St Andrews, Robert Rollock by name.

On 14 September 1583 an agreement was signed between Rollock and the Provost, magistrates and Town Council; and on 1 October this round-headed, reddish-haired youngster, still in his twenties but with a reputation for godliness and good learning, opened the first session with a public lecture in the Duke of Chatelherault's lodging near the present Old College. There was a crowded audience of citizens and visitors. Next day he enrolled the first class, which probably numbered something between fifty and seventy students altogether – considerably more than had been expected. It was soon discovered that quite a few of these were not familiar enough with Latin to understand the teaching provided; and before the end of the year Rollock had persuaded the Council to appoint a 'second master', Duncan Nairn, who would drill these inadequates in a preparatory session while Rollock himself took the others through the first Arts or Philosophy class. The following October, Rollock's pupils became 'Semies' or second-year men, while Nairn's were promoted to be 'Bajans'. An outbreak of plague then disrupted things, but in October 1586 another Bajan class was begun and a third regent appointed to instruct it. By this time Rollock had acquired the title of Principal. Finally, in 1587, he withdrew altogether from the drudgery of 'regenting' and became (in addition to his duties as Principal) Professor of Theology – the one-man nucleus, as it were, of the present Faculty of Divinity. Under him there now served a staff of four philosophy regents and one regent of Humanity (i.e. Latin). The new college was fairly launched on its voyage down the centuries.

Consider, therefore, the man who served as first Principal and piloted the little bark to the verge of the seventeenth century. He was not, we must admit, a luminary of the first magnitude. As David Masson observed more than a hundred years ago, looked back upon now through the dense radiance of the subsequent history of the University of Edinburgh, ... Rollock himself ... dwindles into a mere telescopic star. That he is remembered at all now is due mainly to the fact that he was the first president of one of the most important institutions of the Scottish nation, and charged with the affairs of that institution in its struggling commencement, its 'day of small things'.[1]

But that, as Masson went on to say, is still something; and in any case it is by no means all that we have to say about Rollock.

He seems, by all accounts, to have been an exceptionally effective *teacher*, genuinely interested in his students and ever desirous of finding the best way to communicate with them. In 1590, for example, the future historian John Row (son of a leading first-generation reformer) was taken into Rollock's household as a kind of student boarder, 'to wait upon him and to study with him', and here is his account of the relationship:

> Mr. Rollock was very kind to him, and made much of him for his father's sake, he also having been regent to his two elder brethren in the Old College of St Andrews. He used him rather as a friend nor as a servant, and was most communicative with him. He used ordinarily on the Saturday afternoon to walk out to the fields, choosing him to carry a book or two with him, that he might read and meditate in the fields. His ordinary custom was to tell him what was his text that he was to preach upon tomorrow, and what was his reasons and doctrines raised from the text, saying, 'Mr. John, does that doctrine rise clearly from my text?' 'Is this use suitable to the doctrine, and pertinent for our people?' All this, and the like passages, as it argued much humility and condescending self-denial in the learned, pious and prudent man, famous Mr. Rollock, so it shows very much kindness in him and care of his servant, using him rather as a comrade and infinite friend than a servant.'[2]

As Rollock's Victorian editor remarks, 'A fine picture this of the godly man and his youthful attendant, musing at even-tide, in our fields, on the truths that were on the morrow to be addressed to our forefathers.'[3]

---

[1] D. Masson, *Edinburgh Sketches and Memories* (1892), p. 54.
[2] J. Row, *The History of the Kirk of Scotland from the Year 1558 to 1637*, Wodrow Society (1842), p. 469.
[3] W. M. Gunn (ed.), *Select Works of Robert Rollock*, Wodrow Society (1849), vol. I, p. xxvii.

He was an honoured and influential theologian – perhaps the earliest post-Reformation Scottish divine with an international reputation. Admittedly, twentieth-century authorities are hardly enthusiastic where Rollock is concerned. They note uneasily that he may have been the first to print that fateful phrase *foedus operum* ('covenant of works'), as well as the first to enlarge upon the contrast between the 'covenant of works' and the 'covenant of grace', thus foreshadowing later 'federalist' doctrine; indeed, the 1958 Report of the General Assembly's Special Commission on Baptism went so far as to condemn him for his moralising of the Christian life and his intellectualising of faith – that 'new scholasticism' which attained classic expression at the Synod of Dort (1618) and thereafter passed into Scottish theology 'with unhappy consequences, not least for the understanding of baptism'.[4] Yet that percipient Victorian critic, James Walker, could observe of Rollock that he was 'certainly *not* of the scholastic type', and praised him as 'our first commentator of any note . . . no less a theologian than an expositor',[5] while in his own day he won great commendation for his scriptural commentaries (on Ephesians, for example, and Romans) and other theological works, more than twenty volumes in all. Many were printed and reprinted on the Continent, and in 1596 one of the leading scholars of the age, Theodore Beza, paid fulsome tribute to them. Writing to John Johnston of St Andrews, Beza told of how he had 'chanced of late to meet with a great treasure', and continued:

> For why should I not esteem as a treasure, and that most precious, the Commentaries of my honourable brother, Master Rollock . . . ? And, I pray you, take it to be spoken without all flattery or partiality, that I never read or met with anything in this kind of interpretation more pithily, elegantly and judiciously written: so as I could not contain myself, but must needs give thanks, as I ought, unto God, for this so necessary and profitable work, and rejoice that both you and the whole Church enjoy so great a benefit.[6]

As Row's story of him suggests, Rollock was a faithful and effective preacher, who took that part of his duties (he was one

---

[4] 'Interim Report of the Special Commission on Baptism, May 1958' (1958), p. 22.

[5] J. Walker, *Scottish Theology and Theologians*, Cunningham Lectures (2nd rev. edn, 1888), pp. 2–3.

[6] Gunn, *Rollock*, vol. I, p. 10.

of the eight ministers of Edinburgh during the later 1590s) with intense seriousness. 'Believe me', he once remarked, 'it is not a thing of small importance to preach the Word: it is not the same thing as to expound the text of Plato and Aristotle, or to set forth a harangue bedaubed with the colours and allurements of rhetoric. The preaching of the Word depends on holiness, humility, and the efficacious demonstration of the Spirit. God knows how highly I have ever prized it.'[7] And his nineteenth-century translator and editor, W. M. Gunn of Edinburgh's High School, has borne witness – from an almost unrivalled familiarity with Rollock's sermons – to the scholarly yet unpedantic approach of the Principal to his task of preaching. 'There is', we are told,

> no parade of scholastic erudition, and his examination is simple and clear. It is evident that he understood perfectly the difference between a promiscuous audience met to hear the truths of the gospel, and a class of pupils in their course of training. . . . Of this, the reader will be convinced, if he compares the 25th chapter of the 'Treatise on God's Effectual Calling', which treats of original sin, with the 16th sermon, where the same subject is handled. The one is a learned and scholarlike dissertation on the subject, enquiring into opinions and refuting opponents – too often, it must be admitted, degenerating into the varied and useless subtleties peculiar to his time. The latter is a popular, forcible and practical exposition of the truths to which Scripture and reason pointed, and has the fulness without any of the pedantry of scholarship. This is the more to be admired, because the attentive reader will mark an undercurrent of scholarlike thought running through the whole of these discourses. He tacitly gives the results of his study, but the unlearned hearer will never notice the process.[8]

He was also a devoted pastor. When he first came to Edinburgh, Rollock could claim no parish experience – a fact which might occasion some headshaking today though it was fairly common among sixteenth-century teachers of theology. But in any case his students were his parishioners, and most conscientiously did he look after them. (Incidentally, it has been pointed out that in all his writings he never gave himself the title of Principal, or even referred to his connection with the College, but simply styled

[7] Quoted in D. Butler, *Life and Letters of Robert Leighton* (1903), p. 51.
[8] Gunn, *Rollock*, vol. I, p. 27.

himself 'minister of Jesus Christ in the Church of Edinburgh'.[9])
The University of the 1580s and 1590s was in every sense a
religious community, with all the discipline, group pressures and
– occasionally – inquisitorial surveillance which that implies; but
Rollock's regime seems to have been marked by a good deal of
lenity and compassion. As his immediate successor, Henry
Charteris, once testified,

> It was his habit frequently to visit each class, to examine into the
> industry of each individual and his progress in his studies; if any
> disputes or disturbances had arisen, quickly and prudently to settle
> them, to rouse all to a persevering discharge of duty, and daily to
> assemble the whole University in the Hall, and in person to conduct
> the public devotions.... He had this distinguishing characteristic,
> that whether he placed before them the promises of the gospel, or
> sternly threatened them with the judgment of God, he so insinuated
> himself into the minds of even the most profligate youth – and such
> he had sometimes under his care – even although his indignation
> had glowed most fiercely against him, that he aroused warm feelings
> of affection, and led him voluntarily from error to the path of duty,
> not so much from fear as from love.

To this sketch of Rollock, the pastorally minded director of
studies, Charteris appended the following little note on Rollock
the administrator: 'It was also his habit each week, or as occasion
offered, to assemble the regents, that at their meetings they might
consult and consider, whether any reformation or amendment of
the system could be effected. Hence the University acquired a
settled state, increasing in purity of discipline, in attention to
study, and in completeness of system.'[10]

He was not uninvolved in politics, both civil and ecclesiastical.
Until his very last years he shared the mind of the Presbyterian
party led by men like Andrew Melville, John Davidson and Robert
Bruce. On one occasion he delivered a courageous rebuke to the
sovereign for his indulgent treatment of malefactors; on another,
after a particularly disastrous riot in Edinburgh, he helped to
reconcile King James with the Town Council and the ministers.
In the late 1590s, however, his gifts and inclinations as a peace-
maker seem to have drawn him into the King's party, trans-

---

[9] A. Grant, *The Story of the University of Edinburgh* (1884), vol. II, p. 241.

[10] Gunn, *Rollock*, vol. I, pp. lxix–lxx.

forming him (at least according to his critics) into a tool of the Episcopalian counter-attack. Once, he actually received a bitter rebuke from his old ally Robert Bruce; and David Calderwood's obituary notice of him mingled criticism with praise:

> He was a man of good conversation, and a powerful preacher, but simple in matters of church government.... The King and commissioners of the General Assembly abused his simplicity, that by his countenance to their course they might get the more followers. He was not ignorant that the godly were offended with his carriage in these businesses; yea, it was told him plainly ... that he should meddle only with his scholars, for he knew not what the government of the Kirk meant.... Many are of opinion that if he had foreseen the evil effects which have followed since, he would never have been drawn to it.[11]

Yet however much Rollock's alliance with the Crown may have been deplored by his erstwhile comrades-in-arms, they never ceased to admire him as a man; and the general verdict is reflected in Henry Charteris's account of the reaction to his death. 'I should hardly be believed', he wrote,

> if I were to tell the lamentations and the profound grief which the report of his death [on 8 February 1599] occasioned through the whole of this city and the country. The Town Council, the University, the burgesses, the lower orders, mourned as if each had suffered a family bereavement, and his funeral was attended with a greater throng than Edinburgh had been wont to see on similar occasions. For the whole population, of the highest and the lowest ranks, of all ages and sexes, flocked in crowds to pay due honour to his memory.[12]

Had Edinburgh's Town Council turned, for their first University Principal, not to Rollock but to Napier of Merchiston, that mathematician of genius, they might have secured an abler man. They would hardly have got a better – and even in academic appointments it may, just occasionally, be wise to take other things than intellect into consideration.

* * *

[11] D. Calderwood, *The History of the Kirk of Scotland*, Wodrow Society (1844), vol. v, p. 732.
[12] Gunn, *Rollock*, vol. I, p. lxxxvii.

There seems to have been a kind of conspiracy among Victorian biographers and historians to acclaim the union of learning and piety discernible in Robert Leighton, Principal of Edinburgh University from 1653 to 1662 before his translation to be successively Bishop of Dunblane and Archbishop of Glasgow during the unhappy Restoration period. Leighton's younger contemporary, Gilbert Burnet, possibly began the fashion. 'He [Leighton] was accounted as a saint from his youth up,' wrote the future Bishop of Salisbury.

> He had great quickness of parts, a lively apprehension, with a charming vivacity of thought and expression. He had the greatest command of the purest Latin that I ever knew in any man. He was a master both in Greek and Hebrew, and in the whole compass of theological learning, chiefly in the study of the Scriptures. But that which excelled all the rest, he came to be possessed with the highest and noblest sense of divine things that I ever saw in any man. His thoughts were lively, oft out of the way and surprising, yet just and genuine. And he had laid together in his memory the greatest treasure of the best and wisest of all the ancient sayings of the heathens as well as Christians, that I have ever known any man master of: and he used them in the aptest manner possible.[13]

One is almost relieved to learn that this paragon of all the virtues behaved during his student days at Edinburgh like a fairly normal young man. Not being too happy with the condition of the Church under Charles I's Episcopalian regime, he composed a verse in criticism of it which suggested that the High Kirk of Edinburgh had fared much better in the days – not so long past – when Rollock and Bruce had conducted its worship.

> Rise, Rollock, rise, relate, and Bruce, return,
> Deplore the mischiefs of this uncouth change:
> In the prime kirk, which as a lamp did burn,
> Our teachers have set up a worship strange.[14]

Another of his verses, more undergraduate in tone, focussed attention upon the inordinately red nose of no less a dignitary than the Rector of the University (who was also Lord Provost of the burgh) – and for this offence the young man was temporarily

---

[13] G. Burnet, *History of His Own Times* (1815 edn), vol. I, pp. 169–70.
[14] Quoted in Butler, *Leighton*, p. 57.

rusticated.[15] No permanent damage, however, seems to have been done either to the Provost's nose or to the poet's reputation; and Leighton graduated in 1631.

By that time the clouds of religious and political controversy, soon to break in the storm of civil war and half a century of revolution and counter-revolution, were already gathering over these islands. Only a year before Leighton's graduation, his ultra-Puritan father was the object of one of the most appalling sentences ever meted out to a critic of the established order. A portion of the mutilation and disfigurement decreed for Alexander Leighton was not actually inflicted upon him; but the greater part was, and he languished in prison for ten years until the Long Parliament granted his petition for release. It is hardly surprising, therefore, that in the early 1630s young Robert chose to leave Britain for the Continent. No details of his sojourn there have been preserved, and we can only speculate as to where and with whom he stayed. One thing alone seems certain: that during his exile in France he was profoundly impressed by Jansenism, that deviant movement within the Roman Catholic Church which owed a great deal to Augustine and whose greatest figure was Pascal. He came home convinced that *The Imitation of Christ* was the best book outside the canon of Holy Scripture, regretting that the Reformation had entirely rejected monastic life, admiring Bernard and other mystical writers, and strongly in favour of religious toleration.

The Scotland to which he returned had thrown off Episcopacy and restored Melvillian Presbyterianism, but Leighton apparently fitted into the new order without difficulty. Presented to the parish of Newbattle (not far from Edinburgh), he seems to have shared in the Covenanting enthusiasm of the early 1640s, and faithfully attended presbyteries, synods and General Assemblies. But the passage of time found him increasingly uneasy at the bigotry then in the ascendant. After making more than one attempt to demit his charge, he eventually – in January 1653 – persuaded his co-presbyters in Dalkeith to allow him to take up the appointment (over some resistance from the Edinburgh ministers, but with the powerful support of Cromwell's agents in Scotland) of Principal of the University of Edinburgh.

[15] Ibid., pp. 54–5.

Not all observers considered the move a particularly auspicious one for the University, and Robert Baillie – surveying that and other changes – commented gloomily: 'All our colleges are quickly like to be undone.'[16] In actual fact, Leighton proved to be a more than satisfactory choice. If he was thwarted in his schemes for augmenting College revenues and establishing grammar schools to improve the supply of competent Latinists, that was largely due to the unfavourable political circumstances of the day. And as far as his relationship with the students was concerned, reports suggest that he developed into an outstandingly effective communicator. There was a fair amount of communicating to be done. He preached weekly on Sunday mornings in the University Church, and once or twice monthly on Sunday afternoons in the College Hall. He also delivered a number of occasional lectures to the students, particularly at graduations. But of central importance were the lectures which – reviving a custom of his hero, Rollock – he gave each Wednesday in the Common Hall on a variety of theological topics. Scarcely distinguishable from sermons, these 'prelections', of which twenty-four have survived, were cast in elegant Latin and bore the marks of wide reading, both classical and patristic. All were, essentially, exhortations to a devout and holy life, and from first to last they manifested the speaker's deep consciousness of the privileges and responsibilities of his position. As he put it in the introductory lecture:

> Though, in most respects, the ministerial office is evidently superior to that of professors of theology in colleges, in one respect the other seems to have the preference, as it is, at least for the most part, the business of the former to instruct the common sort of men, the ignorant and illiterate; while it is the work of the latter to season with heavenly doctrine the minds of select societies of youth, who have had a learned education and are devoted to a studious life; many of whom, it is to be hoped, will by the Divine blessing become preachers of the same salutary doctrine themselves.[17]

There may have been nothing very exceptional about the content of these lectures, but their form is still arresting, and some at least of those who heard them were profoundly impressed.

---

[16] *The Letters and Journals of Robert Baillie*, Bannatyne Club (1842), vol. III, p. 344.

[17] R. Leighton, *Theological Lectures* (1763), pp. 1–2.

One such was Robert Sibbald, later Sir Robert Sibbald, originator of Edinburgh's Physic Garden, founding member of the Royal College of Physicians of Edinburgh, and first Professor of Medicine in the University. In his autobiography Sibbald bore witness as follows:

> The Principal of the College during the five years I studied was Mr. Robert Leighton, . . . a learned and devout man, who had excellent discourses to us in the Common Hall, sometime in Latin, sometime in English, which, with the blessing of God upon them, then gave me strong inclinations to a serious and good life. I shunned the plays and divertisements the other students followed, and read much in my study, for which my fellows gave me the name of Diogenes in dolio. . . . The impressions I retained from Mr. Leighton his discourses disposed me to affect charity for all good men of any persuasion, and I preferred a quiet life, wherein I might not be engaged in factions of Church and State.[18]

The characteristic features of the religion which Principal Leighton sought to inculcate among the students at Edinburgh are readily distinguishable. First and foremost, assuredly, must come a kind of mystical devotion which he had learned (so it would seem) from the Jansenists at Port Royal. His friend Bishop Burnet tells us that 'these men of extraordinary temper . . . studied to bring things, if possible, to the purity and simplicity of the primitive ages, on which all *his* thoughts were set';[19] and certainly such an attitude informs Leighton's *Rules and Instructions for Spiritual Exercises*. It is a work which, perhaps with the single exception of Henry Scougall's *The Life of God in the Soul of Man* (and Scougall was Leighton's disciple), stands alone among the literary expressions of Scottish religious thought. An almost random selection of the 'rules' to be found in this remarkable manual may serve to convey its overall message. From Section VI:

1. Too much desire to please man mightily prejudgeth the pleasing of God.
2. Too great earnestness and vehemency, and too great delight in bodily work and external doings, scattereth and loseth the tranquillity and calmness of the mind.

---

[18] *The Autobiography of Sir Robert Sibbald* (1833), pp. 14–15.
[19] Burnet, *Own Times*, vol. I, p. 172.

8. Descant not on other men's deeds, but consider thine own.

10. Keep silence and retirement as much as thou canst, and, through God's grace, they will keep thee from many snares and offences.

And from Section VII: 'Draw thy mind, therefore, from all creatures, unto a certain silence and rest from the jangling and company of all things below God: and when thou canst come to this, then is thy heart a place meet and ready for thy Lord to abide in, there to talk with thy soul.'[20] One does not need to be a secularist, or even an exponent of the 'Puritan work ethic', to see the defects as well as the attractiveness of all this, and to sympathise with the critics who have opined that Leighton, while living in the world, was never of the world, and therefore lacked the power to move the world.

Another mark of Leighton's religion was its careful subordination of scholarship – for which he professed the highest regard – to what he would undoubtedly have considered the one thing needful. Speaking once with his nephew about his books, of which he was obviously proud, he remarked that 'one devout thought is worth them all'.[21] Again, when presenting a friend with what he called 'two little pieces of history' (documents relating to Paulinus of Nola and another early churchman), he could not refrain from commenting:

> But when all is done there is one only blessed story, wherein our souls must dwell and take up their rest: for amongst all the rest we shall not read, Venite ad me, omnes lassi et laborantes, et ego vobis requiem prestabo: come unto me, all ye that labour and are heavy-laden, and I shall give you rest; and never any yet that tried him, but found him as good as his word.[22]

This emphasis on essentials (as Leighton saw them) was accompanied by a marked indifference to the details of church government and the quibbles of controversial theology. Where government was concerned, he found it inconceivably absurd that absolute authority should be ascribed to anything merely external and institutional. Contentions about such matters were for him

---

[20] W. West (ed.), *The Whole Works of Robert Leighton* (1870), vol. VI, pp. 328–30.

[21] Quoted in Butler, *Leighton*, p. 522.

[22] *The Works of Robert Leighton*, with Life by J. Aikman (1860), p. xvi.

simply 'a drunken scuffle in the dark', and in the letter which contained that famous phrase he deplored the spectacle of 'a poor Church doing its utmost to destroy both itself and religion in furious zeal and endless debates about the empty name and shadow of a difference in government, and in the meanwhile not leaving of solemn and orderly worship so much as a shadow'.[23] As is well known, Leighton's hopes of 'reconciling the devout on both sides' (to use his own words) dominated the closing period of his life in Scotland, and found expression in the schemes for Episcopal-Presbyterian accommodation which he vainly sought to realise during his troubled – one might almost say tragic – years as Bishop of Dunblane and Archbishop of Glasgow. On the theological front, he was similarly opposed to the prevailing mood of the time, and it is no surprise to find that his lectures to the students in Edinburgh were part of a life-long campaign against dogmatic intolerance. 'As for you, young gentlemen,' he told them in the second of his laureation addresses,

> especially those of you that intend to devote yourselves to theological studies, it is my earnest advice and request to you, that you fly far from that infectious curiosity which would lead you into the depths of that controversial, contentious theology, which, if any doctrine at all deserves the name, may be truly termed 'science falsely so called'. And that you may not, in this respect, be imposed upon by the common reputation of acuteness and learning, I confidently affirm, that, to be master of those trifling disputes that prevail in the schools, is an evidence of a very mean understanding. . . . But, you will say, it is necessary, in order to the defence of truth, to oppose errors, and blunt the weapons of sophists. Be it so; but our disputes ought to be managed with few words, for naked truth is most effectual for its own defence, and when it is once well understood, its natural light dispels all the darkness of error.[24]

Understandably enough, estimates of Leighton differed widely during his lifetime. Eulogised by men like Burnet and Sibbald, he met with hostility from those who deplored his excessive openness – to Canterbury (it might be) or to Rome. 'Certain it was', said John Row, spitefully, 'that he had too great a latitude of charity towards the papists, affirming that there were more holy men in the cloisters of Italy and France, praying against the Covenant,

[23] Quoted in Butler, *Leighton*, p. 480.
[24] West, *Leighton*, vol. VI, p. 266.

than there were in Britain praying for it.'[25] And Robert Wodrow tells us that 'By many he was judged void of any dogmatic principles.'[26] In later centuries, however, his admirers have greatly outnumbered his detractors, though only the naive would offer the accommodation proposals as a blueprint for ecumenical advance in our own day. Philip Doddridge, John Wesley, S. T. Coleridge (who spoke of Leighton's works as occupying a middle space 'between inspired and uninspired writings', and whose *Aids to Reflection* has been felicitously described as 'a volume of *marginalia* on Leighton'), McLeod Campbell, John Tulloch and Robert Flint: all were his debtors or his admirers – or both.[27]

As we take our leave of Leighton, it should be noted that in all the vicissitudes of later life he seems never to have forgotten the institution in which perhaps his happiest years were spent: the University of Edinburgh. Even after demitting the Principalship he retained rooms in College. And in 1677 – by which time he was resident in the south of England – he drew up the following bequest: 'To the College of Edinburgh . . . fifty pounds sterling to be added to one hundred pounds sterling [considerable sums at that time] formerly given by me to the same College, that the rent of the whole together may be for the yearly maintenance of one student in Philosophy there during his four years course.'[28] We may well concede, however, that his richest legacy was the example of his character and the unusual blend of piety and learning which he bequeathed to the academic world. As one of the University's chroniclers, Peter McIntyre, put it only a few years ago:

> In a turbulent century he exerted an important leavening influence – eloquent of eternity in an age which believed in 'preaching to the time', tolerant amid intolerance, accommodating in a time of extremes, breathing the very spirit of fellowship and love, gentle and forbearing in a setting of persecution and brutality. Assuredly Leighton is one of those names, catholic in significance and appeal, honoured by men of every class and outlook, a name much to be prized in the list of Principals of any University.[29]

[25] J. Row, *Life of Robert Blair*, Wodrow Society (1848), p. 404.
[26] Quoted in Butler, *Leighton*, p. 72.
[27] Their tributes, and others, are helpfully quoted in Butler, *Leighton*, ch. xv, passim.
[28] Ibid., p. 593.
[29] D. Talbot Rice (comp.), *The University Portraits* (1957), p. 130.

* * *

Of all the distinguished and influential men who have presided over the fortunes of the University of Edinburgh, the most famous is almost certainly that administrator of genius, that most astute of ecclesiastics, that trail-blazing historian whom his contemporaries did not hesitate to bracket with Edward Gibbon himself: William Robertson, the impresario of the Scottish Enlightenment and doyen of Edinburgh society in the city's Golden Age. Yet William Carstares, the man with whom this little study must conclude, probably deserves to run even Robertson close. For his services to the University, at any rate, he comes little short of Robertson, while the part he played in the history of the Scottish Church and the Scottish Nation – each at a turning-point in its development – may well equal that of his more brilliant and celebrated successor.[30]

Like Leighton, Carstares could be described as a product of the Puritan tradition, for which his Covenanting father suffered almost as much as Leighton's had done. Unlike Leighton, however, he did not abandon his father's cause, but worked and suffered for it until its triumph – modified and liberalised – at the Revolution. After graduating from the University of Edinburgh in 1667 (he had entered it only one year after Leighton left for Dunblane), Carstares turned his back on the Scotland of dragoons and conventicles and betook himself, like many another Presbyterian dissident, to Utrecht, where he studied theology and was probably ordained. Despite his devotion to the work of the ministry, he seems quite early to have decided that the exceptional circumstances of the time called for political involvement; and he had not been long in the Netherlands when he entered the service of the young prince, William of Orange. His association with William, the chief hope of those opposed to Charles II and his successor James, was to be a long and momentous one. It eventually brought Carstares to power and prosperity; but during the 1670s and 1680s it committed him to all the hazards of secret service work – wearisome journeys, danger, acute distress even –

---

[30] Carstares has been fortunate in his biographers: J. McCormick (1784), R. H. Story (1874) and A. I. Dunlop, *William Carstares and the Kirk by Law Established*, Chalmers Lectures (1964).

as he shuttled between Britain and the Continent in the furtherance of William's designs.

Perhaps every high-ranking university politician must undergo a certain apprenticeship in plotting and intrigue. Carstares endured more than most, and became only too familiar with disguises, assumed names ('Mr Red', for example), ciphers and invisible ink, clandestine arrivals and hurried departures, arrests at sea and on land. So far as I know, he is the only one of all Edinburgh University's future Principals who has been a prisoner both in the Tower of London and in the Tolbooth and the Castle at Edinburgh. The climax of his sufferings came in the year 1684, when (after a short period as minister of a Dissenting congregation near London) he fell under suspicion of being implicated in the conspiracies then directed against the government of Charles II. Taken to Scotland so that his interrogation might not be moderated by the somewhat humaner laws of the southern kingdom, he underwent sickeningly awful torture at the hands of the Privy Council in Edinburgh. Eventually, he was tricked into making a lengthy deposition which – he was told – would not be used as evidence against any of his fellow-conspirators. Needless to say, the Council did not keep its word, and while Carstares was released Robert Baillie of Jerviswood went to the scaffold. It seems, however, that even the thumb-screws and the threat of 'the boot' did not induce Carstares to disclose the more important secrets to which he was privy, particularly those which implicated William of Orange himself; and in after years the Prince was very willing to acknowledge his profound indebtedness to the Scottish Presbyterian minister whose courage and constancy had so materially assisted his cause.

Back again in the Netherlands, Carstares became one of William's chaplains, and as a member of the inner circle at the Hague kept the Prince informed about the religious and political situation in Scotland. He was also appointed a minister of the English church in Leyden; but when the time came for William's long-projected invasion of Britain Carstares obtained leave to join the army and sailed in the flagship of the Dutch fleet. On 5 November 1688 he shared in the famous landing at Torbay. At that historic moment, William called upon his Scottish chaplain to lead the troops in a solemn service of thanksgiving. This Carstares did, and none of his fellow-countrymen would have been surprised to learn that a metrical psalm (the 118th) was part of the worship.

With the triumph of 'the good old cause', Carstares did not return to his congregation in Holland. His royal chaplaincy was confirmed, with a comfortable salary attached to it and a suite of rooms assigned to him in Kensington Palace; and throughout William's reign he wielded considerable influence as the monarch's chief confidential adviser on Scottish affairs. He even received the nickname of 'the Cardinal' from those who resented his ascendancy and the means by which it had been built up. First and foremost among his achievements during the years when the Revolution was consolidated and its character determined was the winning of royal support for the disestablishment of Episcopacy in Scotland and its supersession by Presbyterianism. Despite what has often been asserted, it is by no means clear that William's own preference was for the Presbyterian cause: like James VI (and I) before him, he realised how advantageous from the sovereign's point of view an identical form of church government both north and south of the Anglo-Scottish Border might prove to be. Carstares, however, never wearied of drawing attention to the political reliability of one religious grouping (his own) and the political unreliability of the other. Though his memorandum on the subject, entitled 'Hints to the King', may in parts have been more forceful than incontrovertible, its main thesis was cogent enough, and confirmed by events throughout the period from 1688 to 1715. 'The Episcopalian party', he wrote, 'were generally disaffected to the Revolution, and enemies to the principles on which it was conducted: whereas the Presbyterians had almost to a man declared for it.' And he drew the inevitable conclusion: 'None, therefore, could think it strange that the friends of a government should enjoy all the encouragement it can afford, whilst it withheld its countenance from open and avowed enemies. . . . [It] would be very inconsistent with the end of his [William's] coming, to continue Episcopacy upon its present footing in Scotland.'[31] Such arguments carried the day. In July 1689 Episcopacy ceased to enjoy governmental recognition in Scotland,

[31] J. McCormick (ed.), *State Papers and Letters addressed to William Carstares . . . to which is prefixed the Life of Mr. Carstares* (1784), p. 39.

and in April 1690 Presbyterianism fell heir to all the advantages – and disadvantages – of establishment.

Carstares's contribution to the making of the new Scotland did not end there. He also had a great deal to do with the relative leniency of the regime which gradually emerged from the combined labours of churchmen and politicians. We are told that the draft Act for the establishment of Presbyterianism was worked over by the King and 'the Cardinal' together; and the modifications subsequently agreed upon in Edinburgh seem to represent that blend of realism and liberality (nine parts realism to one part liberality) which characterised them both. Carstares's mark is likewise to be seen on the King's oft-quoted letter recommending moderation to the first General Assembly of the Kirk that had met in Scotland since the 1650s. There were, indeed, many occasions, especially in the tense and troubled years from 1690 to 1695, when it seemed that damaging and perhaps even fatal conflict might break out between the Assembly, with its residual Covenanting fervour, its intolerance and its addiction to old battle-cries concerning the 'intrinsic power' of the Church, and the sovereign, with his predominantly secular concerns, his pragmatic approach, and his Erastian outlook. But after some dramatic near collisions, and one great moment of crisis in 1694, in which tradition has it that Carstares played the decisive role, common sense and kindliness began to tell. Thanks in large measure to Carstares and men like him, the Church which moved forward into the eighteenth century already showed some signs of that urbane reasonableness which was to be its pride in the age of William Robertson, Alexander Carlyle, and the great Evangelical leader, John Erskine.

On William's death in 1702 Carstares had no further reasons for staying in the south of England. He moved almost immediately to Edinburgh, and in May of the following year the Town Council elected him Principal of the University – an office which he held until his death in 1715. The choice was a wise one, for he had long demonstrated his interest in the Scottish universities and his concern for their wellbeing. As early as 1690 he helped to secure the appointment of his very able brother-in-law, William Dunlop, as Principal of the University of Glasgow – an example of nepotism beneficially used. Not long afterwards, he pulled off a notable *coup* by obtaining a royal grant to the four Scottish universities of £1200 sterling per annum – £300 each. At Edinburgh, this welcome increase in endowment made possible not only the provision of several theological bursaries but also the appointment of an additional member of staff. Carstares's hope that the appointee might be 'called from foreign parts'[32] (probably Holland) was not realised, but in 1702 John Cumming took up office as Edinburgh's first Professor of Ecclesiastical History, a significant addition to the body of teachers.

Even these achievements, however, pale into insignificance beside Carstares's services to the University during the years of his Principalship. At the very outset, he helped to obtain a further financial grant from the Crown. He also used his considerable reputation and exceptional diplomatic gifts to patch up a dangerous quarrel between the Town Council and the Masters of the College. His annual opening lecture to the assembled teachers and students won high praise: according to his first biographer, 'he displayed such a fund of erudition, such a thorough acquaintance with classical learning, such a masterly talent in composition, and, at the same time, such ease and fluency of expression in the purest Latin, as delighted all his auditors'.[33] And he performed the pastoral side of his duties with great acceptance, earning (it seems) the respect of the students and the affection of his colleagues.

But it was his presidency over the momentous change from instruction by regents to instruction by specialist professors that put all succeeding generations of Edinburgh students in his debt. By the beginning of the eighteenth century, the University possessed something very like a Faculty of Divinity in embryo, with a Chair of Divinity (created in 1620 to augment the theological teaching of the Principal), of Hebrew and Oriental Languages (created in 1642) and – as we have just seen – of Ecclesiastical History (made possible in the 1690s but not actualised until 1702). Under Carstares's guidance, a similar process began in what would eventually be called the Faculty of Arts. Briefly, what happened in the decisive year 1708 was the final abandonment of the old system in which four regents taught Greek, together with all the branches of Philosophy, each to his

[32] Grant, *University of Edinburgh*, vol. I, p. 230.
[33] McCormick, *Carstares*, p. 70.

own cohort of students. From that time onwards, exclusive responsibility for the teaching of Greek was assigned to one professor, while the wide field of Philosophy was divided among three others, one teaching Logic and Metaphysics, one Ethics and Natural Philosophy, and one Pneumatics and Moral Philosophy.

The implications of the change were enormous. The age of specialist scholars had come into being at a clap; Greek ceased to be a mere tool for philosophers and became a subject in its own right; Natural Philosophy obtained its release from Aristotle and (long before Cambridge carried through similar changes) began to develop under Baconian and Newtonian influences; students found themselves free to choose what they would study and in what order; and the improved quality and wider range of courses offered soon attracted a host of young men, not only from all over Scotland but also from England, the Continent of Europe and the colonies as well. Moreover, further diversification quickly followed, with the creation in 1719 of a Chair of Universal History (first occupied by Carstares's nephew, Charles Mackie, the teacher of both Robertson and Hume) and later a Chair of Rhetoric and Belles Lettres – not to mention the creation of the earliest Chairs in Law and Medicine. Edinburgh University (to be followed in course of time by Glasgow, St Andrews and Aberdeen) was poised for take-off into the modern world, and there is pretty general agreement among the authorities that no single person was more responsible than William Carstares.

Even were we to discount the academic revolution of those years, Carstares's last decade (1705–15) might well be reckoned the most important of his entire life, for it was then that he helped to reconcile his ministerial brethren to the Parliamentary Union of 1707, as well as persuading them to endure the irritations and minor disasters which followed it. Convinced as he was that such a Union was the only sure way of consolidating the benefits of the Revolution and securing them against French and Jacobite subversion, he made it his aim to quieten the fears of his co-religionists, to appeal to their best instincts as Christians and to remind them (in familiar biblical phraseology) that if sorrow endureth for a night joy cometh in the morning. He succeeded – and his reward came with the accession of the Hanoverians in 1714 and the defeat of the Jacobite rising in the following year.

Significantly enough, he who had already served as Moderator three times was once again called to preside over the General Assembly of the Kirk at its first meeting since the arrival of George I in his new kingdom. It seems only right that Carstares, that veteran of so many conflicts, should have given out the concluding psalm and then joined his fellows in the well-loved words:

> Even as a bird out of the fowler's snare
> Escapes away, so is our soul set free;
> Broke are their nets, and thus escaped we.
> Therefore our help is in the Lord's great Name,
> Who heaven and earth by his great power did frame.[34]

Appropriately for one who is often regarded as the architect of eighteenth-century Moderatism, Carstares did not wear his heart on his sleeve. But in all his adventures and intrigues, his conspiring and politicking, he seems to have retained a central core of integrity and consecration. Though laden with honours, Principal of the University and minister in succession of Greyfriars and the High Kirk (St Giles), he was known also for his kindness to the distressed clergy of Scottish Episcopalianism and his generosity to the disadvantaged of his own communion. The *Scots Courant* summed him up rather well when, two days after his death, it described him as 'a man of great worth, piety, and learning, and very charitable to the poor'.[35]

*   *   *

There is a striking little paragraph in Thomas à Kempis's *The Imitation of Christ* which runs as follows: 'Tell me now where are the lords and masters that thou knewest sometime while they lived and flourished in the schools? Now other men have their prebends and I wot not whether they once think upon them. In their lives they appeared somewhat and now almost no man speaketh of them. O Lord, how soon passeth the glory of this

---

[34] R. H. Story, *William Carstares (1649–1715)* (1874), p. 363.
[35] Dunlop, p. 145.

world.'[36] Leighton certainly knew that passage, and one suspects that he and Rollock and Carstares would all have echoed its sentiments. But if they thought, with its author, that total oblivion would soon overtake their endeavours, it is now clear that these Christian scholars of past time were – happily but entirely – mistaken.

[36] T. à Kempis, *The Imitation of Christ* (Everyman edn, 1932), p. 7.

Chapter 3

The Ecclesiastical Significance of the Revolution Settlement

When James, Duke of York, the Catholic heir to the Scottish throne, arrived in Edinburgh to preside over the Parliament of 1681, religion once more took its place (as so often in the past) at the top of the political agenda. From the very outset, two scarcely reconcilable loyalties could be seen fighting for supremacy in the minds of Scotland's legislators. While their first enactment ratified existing laws in favour of Protestantism, their second upheld the indefeasible right of hereditary succession to the throne – and this in spite of the fact that James, the heir presumptive, had repudiated the Protestant faith.[1] The highly controversial Test Act, passed a week or two later, was open to the same charge of inconsistency, as it required all office-holders in Church and State to pledge their allegiance *both* to the Protestant faith as formulated in the Scots Confession of 1560 *and* (in words that would hardly have found favour with the authors of that Confession) to the King as 'only supreme Governor of this Realm, over all persons and all causes as well ecclesiastical as civil'.[2]

James's accession some four years later only increased the likelihood of a clash between competing allegiances. On the one hand, an Act of 1685 annexing the Excise to the Crown declared the Estates' abhorrence of 'all principles and positions which are contrary or derogatory to the King's sacred, supreme, absolute power', as well as their fervent acceptance of the duty 'to own and assert the just and legal succession of the sacred line as unalterable by any human jurisdiction', and to 'assist, support, defend and maintain King James the Seventh, their present glorious

[1] *Acts of the Parliament of Scotland*, vol. VIII, pp. 238–9.
[2] *A.P.S.*, vol. VIII, pp. 243–5.

55

monarch, and his heirs and lawful successors, in the possession of their crowns, sovereignty, prerogatives, authority, dignity, rights and possessions, against all mortals.'[3] On the other hand, Scotland's supreme decision-making body, like its people generally, continued to express the fiercest possible antagonism to the religion of the one whose authority in Church and State was being so fulsomely and extravagantly extolled; and in 1686 James was even obliged to dissolve Parliament when it refused to grant the relief which he requested for his co-religionists.

By the end of 1688, a considerable number of influential Scots had come to realise just how incompatible their two great allegiances were. In the spring of 1689, prompted by the swifter and initially more robust action of their English neighbours, the revolutionary Convention at last decided to reject the totalitarian claims of monarchy by divine hereditary right in favour of the equally exclusive pretensions of embattled Protestantism – together with a cluster of interests, religious and not so religious, which had gathered around it. Three crucially important documents, the Claim of Right, the Articles of Grievances and the Oath of Allegiance, contained the sum and substance of their views.

In considering the Claim of Right, church historians have, understandably, concentrated their attention – and their criticisms – on the highly controversial clause which asserts that

> Prelacy and the superiority of any office in the Church above presbyters is and hath been a great and insupportable grievance and trouble to this Nation, and contrary to the inclinations of the generality of the people, ever since the Reformation (they having reformed from Popery by presbyters), and therefore ought to be abolished.

(Was Episcopacy always so unacceptable to the people of Scotland? And was the Reformation carried through by presbyters?) But of equal interest is the prominent place occupied in the whole manifesto by religious concerns. If arbitrary royal power is one of the evils denounced, 'Popery' is indubitably the other. 'Being a professed Papist', James has assumed the royal power and acted as King 'without ever taking the oath required by law

---

[3] *A.P.S.*, vol. VIII, pp. 459–60.

... to maintain the Protestant religion.' Having asserted his absolute right to 'annul and disable all the laws', he has used that right to subvert Protestantism. He has set up Jesuit schools, allowed the public celebration of Mass despite all laws to the contrary, and converted Protestant churches and chapels for that purpose. He has sanctioned the printing and distribution of popish books. He has sent the children of Protestant nobles and gentlemen abroad to be brought up as papists, endowed popish schools and colleges overseas, bestowed pensions on priests and bribed Protestants to apostatise by offering them places and preferment. He has employed his fellow-Catholics in 'the places of greatest trust, civil and military', while disarming and dismissing Protestants. For these and other reasons he is deemed to have forfeited his right to the Crown.[4]

Ecclesiastical offences are equally prominent in the Articles of Grievances. First and foremost, criticism is levelled against the 'Committee of Parliament called the Articles' – and of course the bishops were the linchpins of that machine. The hated Assertory Act of 1669, with its proclamation of royal supremacy 'over all persons and in all causes ecclesiastical' is denounced as 'inconsistent with the establishment of the church government now desired'. The 'commissariot courts' also come in for attack; most of the legislation of the Parliament of 1685 is condemned as being both 'intolerable' and 'impious'; and the marriage of a Scottish King or Queen to a papist should be prohibited as 'dangerous to the Protestant religion'.[5]

As might be expected, the Oath to be taken by the new sovereigns is likewise full of religious overtones. Its concluding sentence – 'we shall be careful to root out all heretics and enemies to the true worship of God' – has attracted the attention of many modern commentators, who note with approval William's admirable rejection of the incitement to persecute. But the over-all tone of what was a very solemn undertaking may be equally significant. William and Mary bound themselves to serve God in ways which accorded with the requirements of 'His most holy Word'; they accepted an obligation to maintain 'the true religion of Jesus Christ' (preaching and 'the due and right ministration of

---

[4] *A.P.S.*, vol. IX, p. 38.
[5] *A.P.S.*, vol. IX, p. 45.

the Sacraments' included); and they promised to resist all false religion, devoting their energies to the establishment of a 'true and perfect peace' for the Kirk of God and the Christian people of the realm.[6]

Taken together, these core documents of the Revolution would seem to leave its religious motivation and content in little doubt. Yet two insistent questions call for an answer.

First, how could a movement which apparently began as a revolt against Roman Catholicism – a revolt that enjoyed the support of Episcopalians and Presbyterians in almost equal measure – end in the triumph of Presbytery over Episcopacy and the emergence of a Presbyterian Establishment? To treat this problem adequately would demand examination of a host of apparently disconnected events and circumstances. Among these should be included the wisdom and folly, greed and heroism of soldiers like Dundee and Mackay, clerics like William Carstares and Bishop Rose of Edinburgh, and politicians like the Dukes of Hamilton and Atholl, the Earl of Melville, the Dalrymples and Sir James Montgomerie of Skelmorlie, together with the influence of decisions and conflicts located far beyond the frontiers of Scotland, in England, Ireland, France and the Netherlands, and (not least) the role of what looks very like sheer chance. Here, however, we must simply point, as of supreme importance, to the principled but nevertheless disastrous behaviour of the Scottish bishops, who (having wished for King James 'the hearts of his subjects and the heads of his enemies')[7] found it impossible to abjure their solemnly pledged allegiance to the Lord's anointed. Into the vacuum created by that unwitting surrender of power stepped their old antagonists, the Presbyterians; and the pendulum which had been swinging between Episcopacy and Presbytery ever since the days of Patrick Adamson and Andrew Melville came to rest, at last, on the Presbyterian side.

The other question that confronts us is this: Can we believe the revolutionaries' religious professions when we set them alongside the starkly self-serving manner in which the generality of Scottish politicians behaved throughout the critical period? The

[6] W. C. Dickinson and G. Donaldson (eds), *A Source Book of Scottish History*, vol. III (1954), pp. 208–9.

[7] R. Wodrow, *The History of the Sufferings of the Church of Scotland from the Restoration to the Revolution* (1830), vol. IV, p. 468.

most detailed recent answer can be found in P. W. J. Riley's persuasive analysis, *King William and the Scottish Politicians*, in which the following sentences are crucial:

> Just before the revolution and during its progress significant groups emerge. There were, naturally, convinced presbyterians and equally committed episcopalians. However, the majority, although they might have been averse from the political bishops of the last reigns or the prospect of over-zealous presbyterianism, did not greatly care. Some, for a variety of reasons, had moved by 1688 into a revolutionary position, which they advertised by expressing presbyterian views, it being difficult to indicate revolutionary sympathies publicly in any other way. Subsequently, they found it difficult not to be carried in the wake of zealots from whom they could not dissociate themselves even when they came to feel presbytery was being driven too far. Others, finding themselves irrevocably compromised by more or less close association with the previous administrations, chose to formalise their position either by remaining Episcopalian or by conforming only minimally with the church establishment. A man's religious allegiance, therefore, tended to be decided by his relationship to those who comprised the central administration rather than the other way round. But the foundation had been laid of the myth that Scottish political decisions were fundamentally religious.[8]

Riley's remarks are a salutary reminder of the complexity, and murkiness, of human motivation. They are also, perhaps, typical of the twentieth century in their playing down of the religious element in human activity. While not contending too strenuously for the piety of an age which was almost uniquely adept at sprinkling holy water over very unholy designs, I would suggest that Riley's own phrase about the impossibility, around 1690, of indicating revolutionary sympathies in any other way than by espousing Presbyterianism may point us to a balanced conclusion. Given the 'divine right' politics of Episcopalianism, and the deep-seated Presbyterian tradition of caution in dealing with the supreme magistrate, we can understand why things worked out as they did. And in the light of the relative dearth of sceptical views in late-seventeenth-century Scotland, as well as the possibility (open to the people of any age) of combining genuine religious convictions with the energetic pursuit of their own

8 P. W. J. Riley, *King William and the Scottish Politicians* (1979), p. 6.

59

interests, we may perhaps credit the men of 1688–90 with just about as much sincerity as we would claim for ourselves today.

Our concern so far has been with the measures which paved the way for the religious settlement of 1689–90. The settlement itself consisted largely in four pieces of legislation passed by Parliament and given the royal assent between the summer of 1689 and the summer of 1690. On 22 July 1689, one of the key Acts of the whole period called for the abolition of 'Prelacy', and – while putting nothing in place of the rejected system – intimated that the King and Queen, with the advice and consent of the Estates, would 'settle by law that church government in this kingdom which is most agreeable to the inclinations of the people'.[9] Then, after almost a year's delay, three further enactments completed the process. The first repealed the Assertory Act of 1669, with its claim that 'His Majesty hath the supreme authority over all persons and in all causes ecclesiastical within this kingdom.'[10] The second restored the so-called 'antediluvians' – ministers expelled in 1662 and still surviving – to their former parishes, whether or not those parishes were actually vacant.[11] And on 7 June 1690 the third (most important of all) established Presbyterianism as the only permitted government of the Church in Scotland. Previous laws opposing Roman Catholicism and supporting 'the maintenance and preservation of the true reformed Protestant religion' were revived or confirmed. The Westminster Confession was read out and approved. Church government and discipline through kirk sessions, presbyteries, synods and General Assemblies was restored in accordance with the celebrated 'Golden Act' of 1592 – its patronage clauses excepted. Parishes were declared vacant whose incumbents had fled, or been removed by mob action, or suffered deprivation for refusing to acknowledge the new sovereigns. And a General Assembly (the first since 1653) was appointed to meet in the October following, with authority to 'try and purge out all insufficient, negligent, scandalous and erroneous ministers'. It would hardly be an exaggeration to say that the ecclesiastical slate had been wiped clean and a new order of things substituted for the old.[12]

[9] *A.P.S.*, vol. IX, p. 104.
[10] *A.P.S.*, vol. IX, p. 111.
[11] Wodrow, *History*, vol. IV, p. 485.
[12] *A.P.S.*, vol. IX, pp. 133–4.

During the period of flux after the collapse of James VII's Scottish administration, various solutions for the religious problem had been put forward, either by William himself or by politicians like the Duke of Hamilton, Sir John Dalrymple, Viscount Tarbat and others. They included: a *real* 'comprehension' of both Presbyterians and Episcopalians within a generously defined Establishment (a proposal that might well have appealed to Robert Leighton in the previous generation); a Presbyterian Establishment conceding toleration to non-Jacobite Episcopalians beyond its pale; and even a kind of dual Establishment with Episcopalian and Presbyterian Churches, both of them State-recognised and State-subsidised, existing side by side. All ran into insuperable difficulties of one kind or another, and in the end an uncompromisingly discriminatory arrangement found its way on to the statute book.

Generations of historians have made claims and counter-claims about the true balance of religious allegiances at the time of the Revolution, but how the majority of the Scottish people really felt is still uncertain. One of the fairest modern summaries of the evidence is to be found in Dr Thomas Maxwell's Scottish Church History Society paper on 'Presbyterian and Episcopalian in 1688', where he concludes: 'Apart from the two great areas mentioned' – the largely Presbyterian south west, that is, and the largely Episcopalian north east – 'where the preponderance was clear, the issue was debatable. . . . The situation was fluid, and could be swayed either way. The convinced protagonists were determined that it would be influenced according to their principles, and set themselves to accomplish the end they desired.'[13] Behind Maxwell's judgment, of course, lies the perception that what took place in Scotland in 1689 and 1690 was a revolution – and revolutions are not made by counting heads or carefully enquiring as to the wishes of the majority. Nor, it might be added, are religious revolutions ever carried through for exclusively religious reasons: this one certainly was not.

Whatever else may be said about the Settlement, one thing is undeniable: the Presbyterians had solid grounds for satisfaction. In the years just gone by they had at best been tolerated, at worst

[13] T. Maxwell, 'Presbyterian and Episcopalian in 1688', in *Records of the Scottish Church History Society*, vol. XIII, pt. i (1957), p. 37.

excluded from influence or actively persecuted; now they were once again in the seats of power. Their satisfaction, however, was by no means unalloyed. That it was a secular body – the Estates of Parliament – which had carried through the revolution was of course inescapable. But Presbyterians could hardly avoid embarrassment when their Episcopalian antagonists argued that the best way of ascertaining the religious views of the Scottish people would be to summon a General Assembly – and to call that body *before* rather than *after* the decisive legislative steps had been taken. With the representatives – and beneficiaries – of the old Episcopalian regime in control of such an Assembly there could be little doubt as to what it would recommend. But quite apart from the responsibility of the secular power for the decisions of 1689 and 1690 (and the disquieting realisation that what Parliament had given Parliament could take away), all who cherished the Melvillian and Covenanting ideals could only deplore the Estates' studied disregard of the claims of *iure divino* Presbyterianism. Admittedly, the Establishment Act had declared its purpose to be 'the maintenance and preservation of the true, reformed, Protestant religion', and spoken of the newly recognised Kirk as 'the true Church of Christ within this Kingdom'.[14] Yet the Act which abolished 'prelacy' confined itself to describing that form of ecclesiastical government as 'contrary to the inclinations of the generality of the people', without any mention of what the Word of God had to say on the subject or any reference to the Covenants whose binding obligations had been so solemnly accepted only half a century earlier.[15] It is hardly surprising that the followers of Richard Cameron and James Renwick (though none of their ministerial colleagues) refused to enter such a vitiated Establishment, or that the ghosts of the National Covenant and the Solemn League continued to haunt the deliberations, and trouble the consciences, of Presbyterian church courts well into the nineteenth century.

To make matters worse, the Kirk's relationship with the new head of State was in some respects little better than it had been with his predecessors. If Charles II had framed his actions on the principle that the bishops should rule the ministers and

[14] *A.P.S.*, vol. IX, pp. 133–4.
[15] *A.P.S.*, vol. IX, p. 104.

the King rule both, and if James VII had clearly assumed that, in Scotland as in England, his support for the Church was conditional upon the Church's support for him, their successor was almost as difficult to deal with. No doubt William of Orange was a Calvinist and shared the Kirk's belief in predestination. But he came from a country which took a singularly lenient view of religious diversity, his grand coalition against France had involved him with Catholic allies, and south of the Anglo-Scottish Border he could not afford to alienate the Church of England by any lack of sympathy with its Scottish Episcopalian brethren. In the last resort he proved to be a pragmatist, skilled at waiting upon events; and his policy towards Scotland has been aptly described as 'non-committal opportunism'.[16]

Bombarded by conflicting reports about the religious situation north of the Border, William seems to have given different undertakings to different people; and on the eve of the Revolution his Scottish manifesto confined itself to vague assurances about 'the freeing of that kingdom from all hazard of popery and absolute power for the future' and the effective redress of 'all grievances'.[17] His broad aim, it seems, was a religious settlement which would be acceptable to as many of his subjects as possible, and so ensure the domestic peace of his new kingdoms and their willing collaboration in the fight against France and Jacobitism. As Dr Lionel Glassey has pointed out, William was attracted to begin with by the possibility of a comprehensive Church embracing both Episcopacy and Presbytery; then, more realistically, moved towards a moderate, tolerant Presbyterian settlement; and finally, when the Convention showed itself to be strongly in favour of Presbyterianism, sought (like a good 'trimmer') to make life as tolerable as possible for the hard-pressed Episcopalian clergy, thereby doing what he could to maintain a religious balance.[18] In the end, of course, he was obliged to accept the dashing of his hopes for a truly comprehensive settlement – but the Act for Settling the Peace and Quiet of the Church (1693) did admit submissive Episcopalians to a share in ecclesiastical life (by granting

---

[16] L. K. J. Glassey, 'William II and the Settlement of Religion in Scotland, 1688–90', in *R.S.C.H.S.*, vol. XXIII, pt. iii (1989), p. 322.

[17] Wodrow, *History*, vol. IV, pp. 470–2.

[18] Glassey, 'William II and the Settlement of Religion', *passim*.

them membership of presbyteries), while two years later even clergy who refused to accept the Presbyterian system were allowed to retain their livings so long as they showed themselves politically reliable.[19] In the troubled quinquennium from 1690 to 1695, however, there were many anxious moments for both the monarchy and the Church; and as one General Assembly after another clashed with the King's Commissioner and had its sittings terminated in a manner which recalled the most arbitrary behaviour of James VI or Charles I, Presbyterians with long memories must have wondered whether they had merely exchanged one form of royal despotism for another.

Nor was the attitude of the sovereign by any means the only reason for Presbyterian discontent in the aftermath of the Revolution. With the Union of the Parliaments in 1707, and the transference of political authority from Edinburgh to Westminster, the Kirk's dependence on the goodwill of the legislature became increasingly obvious. The Toleration Act of 1712 may strike the modern mind as an eminently charitable measure; but it was inspired by an intensely uncharitable High Tory (and Anglican) animosity against the sister Establishment north of the Border. It posed a real threat to the working of the Presbyterians' disciplinary system (since to be an Episcopalian was to be free from the jurisdiction of the kirk session), and in the mind of men like George Lockhart of Carnwath it marked one more welcome stage on the road to a Jacobite restoration.[20] The Patronage Act of the same year, which removed the right to choose a minister from the heritors and elders of a parish - the 1690 arrangement – and restored it to the traditional patron, was a still severer blow, inspired even more obviously than the Toleration Act by sheer anti-Presbyterian malevolence.[21] From 1712 until 1874, when it was at last repealed, this measure proved a constant source of trouble within the Kirk, and led to at least three major secessions, in 1733, in 1752 and in 1843.

In addition to all their other grievances, those who cherished the ancient ideal of a genuinely *national* Establishment could only deplore the ever-multiplying signs of the rise and sanctioning of denominationalism, and the consequent fragmentation of the

[19] A.P.S., vol. IX, pp. 303 and 449–50.
[20] *Statutes of the Realm*, vol. IV, p. 513.
[21] Ibid., pp. 522–3.

Christian community in Scotland. For many centuries, Scotsmen had assumed, almost unquestioningly, that just as the political unity of the nation found expression in a single State, so its spiritual unity called for embodiment in a single Church, *Ecclesia Scoticana*: in the cooperation and mutual support of these two powers the wellbeing of all the people would be secured. This was the ideal which underlay Knox's strivings to restore 'one face of the Kirk' in Scotland; it had inspired both the Covenanters and their royalist and Episcopalian opponents; and at the time of the Revolution it was still very much alive. The tiny Roman Catholic remnant, considerable numbers of Episcopalians and the extreme Cameronians might remain outside the religious Establishment; but the notion of one, all-embracing and authoritative National Church continued to exert its sway over the Scottish mind. Yet its days were numbered. Long before the middle of the eighteenth century all but the most conservative of churchmen were aware of its diminishing appeal, and Principal Robertson's bland acknowledgement during the 1766 schism debate that the beauty of the ecclesiastical garden consisted in the diversity of the flowerbeds was a characteristically clear-sighted recognition of the end of an era.[22]

In the remainder of this study a brief attempt will be made to answer one of the most insistent questions raised for us by the Revolution Settlement – namely, What difference did it make so far as Scottish religion was concerned? Four main areas suggest themselves for consideration: ecclesiastical polity, worship, theology and what may be called social ethos. We look at each of them in turn.

Polity

To a superficial glance, the events of 1689–90 had no more dramatic and obvious consequences than in the realm of church government, where Episcopacy was displaced by Presbytery and a hierarchy of persons by a hierarchy of courts. Yet at the local level the changeover made remarkably little difference.

'His Majesty doth allow the present administration by sessions, presbyteries and synods (they keeping themselves within

---

[22] N. Morren, *Annals of the General Assembly of the Church of Scotland, 1752–1766* (1840), pp. 331–2.

bounds and behaving themselves).'[23] That declaration was made not in 1690 but by the Restoration Parliament in 1661; and although none of the courts thus named was allowed to meet without episcopal approval such approval was invariably given. They continued to function throughout the revolutionary period.

Presbyterians after 1690 would have had no difficulty in identifying the parochial assembly, or kirk session, of the Restoration Church. Meeting weekly, it was composed of elders and deacons (both recruited by cooptation rather than by election), and presided over by the minister. Poor relief, charitable enterprises and sundry other social projects came within its purview; but its chief concern was the disciplining of the parish, including enforcement of church attendance and punishment of moral lapses – exceptionally serious cases being referred to the presbytery.[24] Every one of these matters was also the business of kirk sessions in the post-Revolution period, and there is no evidence that those who had fallen from grace were either more or less severely dealt with under the Presbyterian Establishment than under its Episcopalian predecessor.

The functioning of the presbytery also exhibits a remarkable continuity over both Episcopalian and Presbyterian periods. At its meetings, which usually took place monthly, serious disciplinary cases took up a great deal of time; but the 'exercise' (a kind of Bible study session) and theological disputations were also part of the proceedings. Delegates from the presbytery visited in rotation the various parishes within its bounds, examining minister, elders and heritors as to their diligence; and the presbytery was also responsible for 'pulpit supply', church and manse repairs, scrutiny of kirk session records and suchlike. In all this, there is nothing to distinguish the post-Revolution body from its Restoration counterpart. Two significant differences do, however, merit attention. From 1661 to 1688, elders were excluded from meetings of presbytery – presumably to eliminate the danger of disruption by a recalcitrant 'lay' element; and whereas during the Restoration period the moderator was nominated by the

[23] *A.P.S.*, vol. VII, pp. 87–8.
[24] W. R. Foster, *Bishop and Presbytery: The Church of Scotland, 1661–1688* (1958), pp. 61–70.

bishop (or, on occasion, by bishop and synod together) in Presbyterian times the members chose their own moderator.[25]

A marked difference in church polity between the Restoration period and its successor only really emerges at the level of the synod. Before the Revolution this court could not meet at all without the bishop's presence, and he always presided. Though the relationship between him and the other members doubtless depended, at least to some extent, on his character (and theirs), his wishes inevitably carried great weight because of his civil authority, his right of veto over all decisions and his wide-ranging disciplinary powers. Indeed, the stock phrase for recording synodical decisions tells its own story: they were come to by 'the bishop, with consent of the brethren'. In short, whereas in the Restoration period the synod was very much the *bishop's* court, after 1690 there was at least the possibility of a wider spread of influences.[26]

If the difference between the Episcopalian and the Presbyterian regimes is quite perceptible at synod level, it becomes a positive chasm when we compare the National Synod (to use the Episcopalian term) with the General Assembly of 1690 and afterwards. The clergy alone were entitled to attend the National Synod, while elders served alongside ministers in the Assembly; and whereas no decision of the National Synod was recognised as being valid without approval by both the Archbishop and the King, the Assembly considered itself answerable to no human authority. But in any case the National Synod remained no more than a pious hope. It was never convened, though an Act of Parliament in 1663 authorised the creation of such a body: archbishops, bishops, deans and archdeacons, the moderator and one minister from every presbytery, and representatives of the universities, all meeting under the presidency of the Archbishop of St Andrews and subject at every stage to royal approbation or disapprobation. Perhaps the outrageous behaviour of the Glasgow Assembly of 1638 was too vividly in the mind of Restoration men: as Lauderdale put it with his accustomed cynicism, 'A burnt child dreads the fire.'[27]

[25] Ibid., pp. 70–83.
[26] Ibid., pp. 83–6.
[27] Ibid., pp. 86–8. There is no similar study of the post-Revolution Church of Scotland.

In short, while at the lower levels of ecclesiastical administration the changeover from Episcopacy to Presbytery made
relatively little difference, at the highest it was of crucial
importance. In 1690, as at other moments of crisis for the post-
Reformation Church in Scotland, the General Assembly best
expressed the distinctively Presbyterian point of view, and most
clearly differentiated the Presbyterian system from any other.
'Take from us the freedom of Assemblies', cried Knox, 'and take
from us the Evangel.'[28] His successors in 1690 and subsequently
might well have amended the phrase to say, 'Take from us
Assemblies, and take from us our identity.'

Worship

The Revolution had extraordinarily little effect on worship within
the parish churches of Scotland – at least to begin with. If religious
services in the new Establishment were austere and Puritanical,
they had been almost equally so in the old one. Indeed, many
defenders of Episcopacy in the immediate aftermath of 1690 used
this fact to support their argument that nothing material had
been gained by the transition from one form of church government
to another.

Particularly striking testimony to the basic similarity of
Episcopalian and Presbyterian worship just before the Revolution
is borne by that acrimonious but apparently reliable tract for the
times, 'The Case of the Present Afflicted Clergy in Scotland',
published in 1690. There we read:

> As to the worship, it's exactly the same both in the Church and the
> Conventicle; in the Church, there are no ceremonies at all enjoined
> or practised, only some persons more reverent think fit to be
> uncovered which our Presbyterians do but by halves even in the time
> of prayer; we have no liturgy nor form of prayer, no not in the
> cathedrals, the only difference in this point is, our clergy are not so
> overbold nor fulsome in their extemporary expressions as the others
> are . . . and we generally conclude one of our prayers with that which
> our Saviour taught and commended, which the other party decry as
> superstitious and formal; Amen too gives great offence, though neither
> the clerk nor people use it, only the minister sometimes shuts up his
> prayer with it. The Sacraments are administered after the same way

[28] E. Percy, *John Knox* (1937), p. 340.

and manner by both; neither so much as kneeling at the prayers, or when they receive the elements of the Lord's Supper, but all sitting together at a long table in the body of the church or chancel. In Baptism neither party use the cross, nor are any godfathers or godmothers required, the father only promising for his child.[29]

Surprising though this state of affairs was to visitors from the South, whether Anglicans or Dissenters, it is easily enough explained. Memories of the 1637 service book died hard, ensuring that there would be no official liturgy in the Restoration Church. As one contemporary put it, orders from court forbade the bishops to introduce canons and a liturgy 'lest such things should provoke to a new Rebellion'.[30] Although reformers like Gilbert Burnet and Robert Leighton, as well as some synodical pronouncements, might indicate a lingering disquiet, there was a tendency for practices introduced or reinforced in the 1640s and 1650s to prevail. The Westminster *Directory* dictated both the form and the content of worship.

While differences in worship between Episcopalian and Presbyterian were still minimal in 1690, and no great gulf opened to divide them in the immediately succeeding years, it is nevertheless possible to glimpse some evidence of emergent change. As the Presbyterians drifted away from the *status quo* in one direction, so the Episcopalians were moving – with greater speed and perhaps more self-awareness – in another.

The Revolution Parliament having chosen not to legislate on the subject of worship, the victorious Presbyterians felt free to continue with their existing practices. The pattern they followed had been sketched out in the *Directory of Public Worship*; but with 1647 fading into the past even that palladium of Protestantism began to be neglected by the heirs of Gillespie and Henderson. Moreover, the polarisation of thought and action which took place during the later Covenanting period meant that quite a number of irreproachably Reformed ways of doing things came to be rejected as trappings of the hated Episcopalian regime. By 1690, worship was setting in an ultra-Puritanical mould, and for nigh on one and a half centuries an amalgam of Reformed traditions and Covenanting usages determined the shape and

[29] Quoted in Foster, pp. 125–6.
[30] Quoted in Foster, p. 130.

substance of religious services in the Kirk. Private baptisms and marriages became the rule rather than the exception. The Puritan importation of 'lecturing' crowded out the unadorned reading of Scripture. The custom of 'lining out' the psalms was introduced and gradually canonised. And the protracted Communion Services and seasons once favoured by the Protesters lived on into a very different age. Only in the middle of the nineteenth century did a flood of social and intellectual changes, and a revolution in taste, bring about that reappraisal and transformation of long-established liturgical practices which enthusiasts have called 'the renascence of worship' in the Church of Scotland.[31]

If near-stagnation was the chief effect of the Revolution Settlement on Presbyterian worship, among the Episcopalians it ushered in a phase of quite remarkable reassessment and innovation. A hankering after more ordered forms which developed during the Restoration period was, almost inevitably, intensified as persecution and minority status forced a return to first principles, while loss of establishment brought a freedom that had previously been unknown. Among the 'qualified' clergy (men prepared to take the oaths of allegiance to a *de facto* sovereign), the obvious development lay in worship according to the liturgy of the Church of England, that powerful sister Church whose support provided their best hope of a return to dominance. From the Revolution onwards, therefore, the popularity of the English Book of Common Prayer, sent north in cartloads by friendly bishops and Oxford dons, steadily increased – to the consternation of vigilant Presbyterians like Robert Wodrow. Among Non-jurors, on the other hand, the 1637 Prayer Book proved more attractive, partly no doubt because of its intrinsic merits, but also perhaps because it was anathema to Presbyterians of the Covenanting tradition. Its Communion office was destined to survive into modern times and become the centrepiece of Scottish Episcopalian worship. Some bishops and other clergy also devoted themselves to the study of Eastern liturgies, thereby influencing church life throughout the English-speaking world as well as in their own country. At the same time, there was much controversy over the

---

[31] Recent surveys are provided by H. Sefton, 'Revolution to Disruption' and D. Murray, 'Disruption to Union', in D. Forrester and D. Murray (eds), *Studies in the History of Worship in Scotland* (1984), pp. 65–95.

ancient 'usages' – controversy whose bitterness and obsession with minutiae parallels the disputes in Presbyterianism's Secession Churches between Burghers and Anti-Burghers, Lifters and non-Lifters. As a result of all these developments, Scottish Episcopalianism had become (in Gordon Donaldson's words) 'hardly recognisable as an heir of the Church established before 1690' – and that even before the Oxford Movement added a further impetus towards 'catholicity'.[32]

Doctrine

'Their Majesties' (so ran one of the key clauses in the Establishment Act) 'with advice and consent of the said three estates do hereby . . . ratify and establish the Confession of Faith now read in their presence and voted and approven by them as the public and avowed confession of their church.' The Confession thus referred to, the masterwork of the Westminster Assembly of Divines, had been adopted by the General Assembly of the Kirk in 1647 and by the Scottish Parliament two years later. The recognition accorded to it by the 1690 Act marks a long-lasting victory for scholastic Calvinism north of the Border. But how great a difference did that recognition actually make in the religious life of Scotland?

The Act Rescissory of 1661, which had undone the work of the Covenanting legislators of the 1640s, tacitly restored the Scots Confession of 1560 to its position as the country's theological standard, and in 1681 the Test Act required all office-bearers, both civil and ecclesiastical, to subscribe the older document. However, it is not entirely clear how effective these measures were. Bishop Burnet tells us that the bishops left Westminster 'in possession', and in 1690 another contemporary affirmed that the Scots Confession *and* the Westminster Confession were 'owned next to the Word of God by both parties' (i.e. Episcopalians and Presbyterians) 'as the standard of the doctrine of the Church'. Quite possibly *neither* Confession figured largely in the minds of established clergy during the Restoration period. (We know that the Apostles' Creed was much used in Sunday services and at

[32] G. Donaldson, *Scotland; Church and Nation through Sixteen Centuries* (1960), p. 106.

baptisms – as in the days of Knox.) What is absolutely clear is that, whether or not overt reference was made to Westminster, the Calvinistic *Weltanschauung* of which it was a notable expression continued to influence the theology and the piety of ministers and members alike.[33]

Another and very different current of thought – inclined to reject high predestinarian doctrine and emphasise the Early Fathers, the visible Church and the historic episcopate – was, of course, developing in certain quarters; and it may be that, just as pre-Revolutionary Episcopacy had begun to move towards more 'catholic' forms of worship so in doctrine it was showing signs of a reaction (which succeeding generations would carry much further) against the Reformed theology long dominant in Scotland.[34]

However that may be, the most interesting thing about the recognition accorded the Confession in 1690 is that what had originated in the heyday of Puritan enthusiasm as a vital affirmation of faith – not, so far as we can tell, designed for imposition on all and sundry – quickly came to be used not only as a doctrinal statement but also as a test of political correctness and a means of excluding Episcopalians and other undesirables from office in the Church. It is certainly not hard to trace the steady tightening of the confessional screw. In 1690, the General Assembly required all probationers and ministers just received into communion to subscribe. In 1700, *all* ministers, and elders also, were obliged to sign the Confession as the confession of their faith. In 1710, an Assembly 'Act for Preserving Purity of Doctrine' forbade the uttering of 'opinions contrary to any head or article of the said Confession and Catechisms'. And in 1711 the coping stone was placed on this edifice of enforced conformity when the Assembly produced a set of questions, together with a formula of subscription, to be put to all its servants at licensing, ordination and induction to a charge. As an example of their tenor and spirit, the following may be quoted: 'Do you sincerely own and believe the whole doctrine contained in the Confession of Faith [etc.] to be founded upon the Word of God; and do you acknowledge the same as the confession of your faith; and will

[33] Foster, pp. 155–6.
[34] Foster, pp. 157–8.

you firmly and constantly adhere thereto, and, to the utmost of your power, assert, maintain and defend the same?' (It should be noted that what was clearly expected was not mere passive acceptance but active, aggressive advocacy of every detail, 'the *whole* doctrine'.[35])

Was such authoritarian inflexibility the inevitable consequence of adopting a creed so comprehensive, so detailed and so assured? Opinions will differ on this; but historians can probably agree that there was a connection between the increasingly rigorous enforcement of the Confession and the religious and political uncertainties of the years between 1690 and 1715 – and particularly of the latter part of Queen Anne's reign. Not long after the 1707 Union of the Parliaments, resurgent English Toryism – bent upon the destruction, or at the very least the reconstruction, of the Revolution Settlement throughout the United Kingdom – was seeking by every means at its disposal to restore Episcopalian fortunes in Scotland. The Kirk felt understandably imperilled and insecure, and responded with harshly restrictive measures. What is more surprising, however, and much less excusable, is that although the worst forebodings of the period were not realised, and the Settlement of 1690 survived in all essentials, the strictest obligations to the Confession continued to be enforced from the beginning to the end of the eighteenth century – and were not finally relaxed until the last quarter of the nineteenth.

There is much in the first post-Revolution generation that strikes the modern observer as peculiarly backward-looking, unproductive and intolerant. (The horrifying execution of the teenager, Thomas Aikenhead, for sceptical blasphemous remarks is a permanent blot on its record.) Yet it is important not to exaggerate the theological immobility – or regressiveness – of the time. New men of a more open outlook were beginning to appear, even within the ecclesiastical and educational establishment. John Simson was appointed to the Divinity Chair at Glasgow in 1708, and William Hamilton went to the corresponding post at Edinburgh a year later. Simson, who underwent two heresy trials and was eventually suspended from teaching

---

[35] A. C. Cheyne, 'The Place of the Confession through Three Centuries', in A. I. C. Heron (ed.), *The Westminster Confession in the Church Today* (1982), pp. 17–20.

(though not, interestingly enough, deposed), seems to have been a slippery and self-serving character, and certainly not of martyr material. But he had a questing mind and respectable supporters, and the father-figure of the northern Enlightenment, Francis Hutcheson, who hoped to 'put a new face on Scottish theology',[36] was one of his students at Glasgow. Hamilton was much more formidable. Traditionalists like Robert Wodrow might murmur, 'It's thought he is departed from the Calvinist doctrine taught in the Church, though he keeps himself in the clouds'.[37] Yet his pupils – and they were numbered in hundreds – included William Leechman, called by one of his successors 'an improved Simson',[38] who rose to be Professor of Divinity and eventually Principal of Glasgow University; Robert Wallace, preacher in 1730 of a sermon which declared that 'it's only an impartial inquiry and free search that according to the ordinary course of things can preserve Religion in any measure of purity';[39] and the influential Wishart brothers, of whom William became Principal of Edinburgh University and George one of the capital's most highly regarded Moderate ministers. All these were less concerned with correctness of dogma than with what they considered more truly spiritual matters: in Alexander Carlyle's words, they evinced 'a turn for free inquiry, the result of which was candour and liberality of sentiment'.[40] With such men already embarked upon their careers in the first post-Revolution generation, we may be inclined to agree with that most percipient of Victorian commentators, John Tulloch, when he dates the appearance of a new mood in Scottish theology 'from about 1720'.[41] Despite the iron-clad confessionalism of the Church's official pronouncements, a very different spirit was abroad in the land even before leaders of the Revolution like William Carstares were in their graves.

[36] J. McCosh, *The Scottish Philosophy* (1875), p. 465.
[37] R. Wodrow, *Analecta*, Maitland Club (1842–3), pp. 139f.
[38] H. M. B. Reid, *The Divinity Professors in the University of Glasgow, 1640–1903* (1923), p. 261.
[39] H. Sefton, '"Neu Lights and Preachers Legal": Some Observations on the Beginnings of Moderatism in the Church of Scotland', in N. Macdougall (ed.), *Church, Politics and Society: Scotland 1408–1929* (1983), pp. 192–3.
[40] J. H. Burton (ed.), *The Autobiography of Dr. Alexander Carlyle of Inveresk 1722–1805* (1910), p. 94.
[41] J. Tulloch, 'The Church of the Eighteenth Century', in *St. Giles' Lectures*, First Series (1881), p. 263.

Social ethos

One of the most frequently quoted assessments of the balance of forces in late-seventeenth-century Scotland was made by Viscount Tarbat shortly before some of the crucial revolutionary decisions had been taken. 'The Presbyterians', he judged, 'are the more zealous and hotter; the other more numerous and powerful. The present Parliament is more numerous of Presbyterians by the new method of election of burghs, but the major part of the nobility and barons are not for Presbytery.'[42] In other words, while the Episcopalians might be outnumbered in the new-style Parliament of 1689 and 1690, and at a disadvantage (so far as enthusiasm and demonstrativeness went) when compared with their Presbyterian opponents, they were the stronger party in the country as a whole, as well as enjoying the support of most members of the upper or landed classes.

A similar estimate is to be found in a controversial pamphlet of 1690, which contended that

> There is not a falser proposition in the world than that the inclinations of the people are against Episcopacy. I can affirm with a well-grounded assurance, that if by the people you mean the commonalty, the rude illiterate vulgus, the third man through the whole kingdom is not Presbyterian; and if by the people you mean those who are persons of quality and education (whose sense, in my opinion, ought in all reason to go for the sense of the nation) I dare boldly aver not the thirteenth.[43]

While we may never know where the over-all numerical superiority lay, Tarbat's analysis nevertheless raises an interesting question. Can we distinguish between the warring factions not only in ecclesiastical polity, worship and theology, but also in social provenance and philosophy, the place each occupied in society and the views they took of social rights and duties?

In his study of the Jacobite risings between 1689 and 1746, and (still more) in his article on 'The Scottish Episcopal Clergy and the Ideology of Jacobitism', Dr Bruce Lenman gives many useful pointers towards an answer. Arguing that the restoration

---

[42] *Letters and State Papers chiefly addressed to George Earl of Melville, Secretary of State for Scotland 1689–1691*, Bannatyne Club (1843), p. 125.
[43] *An Account of the Present Persecution of the Church of Scotland in several letters* (1690).

of monarchy and episcopacy in 1660–1 was made possible by a powerfully conservative reaction among Scotland's landed classes, he contends that 'Bishops were restored as a symbol of hierarchy, order, and seemly subjection', and notes how Archbishop Sharp, for one, was always 'urbanely deferential ... to any member of the noble order'.[44] Thus was forged a kind of quadruple alliance – monarchy, episcopate, nobility and gentry – which had far-reaching implications for the Restoration Church. The bishops were dependent on the King, the clergy on both the bishops (who largely controlled the universities where ministers were trained) and the landed classes (who, as patrons, presented them to their livings). Only pastors in tune with the monarchical and aristocratic ethos of Restoration society could expect to survive or go far in it – the result being that by 1688 the parish clergy were the chief purveyors of what we now identify as Jacobite notions. Typical, for Dr Lenman, were men like Robertson of Fortingall, with his cult of the royal martyr Charles I and the royalist martyrs Montrose and Dundee, and Kirk of Balquidder, whom he describes as 'steeped in the Restoration ideology of indefeasible hereditary right and in the belief that unchallenged monarchical power was an essential condition for right order in society'.[45]

These men, and others like them, would hardly favour the attitudes expressed in the Claim of Right, the Articles of Grievances and the Establishment Act of 1690; and all the ensuing troubles of William's reign – the financially crippling war with France, the crime of Glencoe and the tragedy of Darien, not to speak of the fears aroused by the Act of Union – only served to strengthen them in their convictions and to commend those convictions to their flocks. Dr Lenman describes a sermon written at the time of the 1715 Rising by James Garden (one-time Professor of Divinity at King's College, Aberdeen) as

> rampant chiliastic Jacobitism, lambasting the peoples of Britain for breaching God's law of indefeasible hereditary right; holding up the disasters of famine and war as God's scourge against the unrighteous; adding a heady dash of Scottish nationalism with the assertion that

[44] B. Lenman, 'The Scottish Episcopal Clergy and the Ideology of Jacobitism', in E. Cruickshanks (ed.), *Ideology and Conspiracy: Aspects of Jacobitism, 1689–1759* (1982), p. 38.
[45] Ibid., p. 43.

the Act of Union was yet another act incurring the wrath of God; and crowning it all with the triumphant assertion that only the restoration of the legitimate sovereign could bring peace and prosperity and happiness to the three distracted realms.[46]

In view of teachings such as these it becomes a little easier to appreciate the watershed in Scottish attitudes represented by the Revolution's transfer of power from Episcopacy to Presbytery.

What then of the Presbyterians? Dr Mason has drawn our attention to the following indictment of the Covenanting preachers by that distinguished seventeenth-century antiquary, Sir James Balfour: 'In lieu of obedience and conformity to government [they] did teach and obtrude to the people . . . nothing more than Christ's cause, religion, liberty and privilege of the subject, whereby they have not only embittered the affection of the vassals but in effect quite poisoned them against their native sovereign and prince.'[47] That which Balfour deplored – regard for 'liberty and privilege of the subject' – was transmitted by the Covenanters to their chastened but hardly submissive descendants, and never entirely died out. What can only be called the more popular and democratic spirit of Presbyterianism may be seen above all in its approach to the crucial matter of ministerial appointments. Back in 1561 the *First Book of Discipline* laid down that 'it appertaineth to the people, and to every several congregation, to elect their own ministers'. Although the revolutionaries of 1690 did not go as far as that, they did desert the patronage system which had prevailed since the Restoration, and instead gave to heritors and elders the privilege of proposing a minister to the whole congregation. Of course, this abolition (or at least transference, as Gordon Donaldson preferred to call it) of patronage endured only until 1712, when English Tories combined with Scottish Episcopalians and Jacobites to restore the traditional rights of patrons. Yet a faint hint of Presbyterianism's more egalitarian spirit still survived in the eighteenth-century Kirk – even when conformism and 'influence' apparently reigned supreme and when the perfections of the 'Glorious' Revolution became an excuse to block every move towards change or improvement. 'God's

[46] Ibid., p. 46.
[47] R. Mason, 'Aristocracy, Episcopacy, and the Revolution of 1638', in T. Brotherstone (ed.), *Covenant, Charter, and Party* (1989), p. 22.

promise of guidance', cried Ebenezer Erskine in his sermon to the synod of Perth and Stirling in 1732, 'is given not to heritors or patrons, but to the Church, the body of Christ. . . . And shall we suppose that ever God granted a power to any set of men, patrons or heritors or whatever they be, to impose servants on His family without their consent, they being the freest society in the world!'[48] Unobtrusively but powerfully, that libertarian leaven never ceased to work, until in the age of the American and French Revolutions it took hold even of resurgent Evangelicalism and brought about the upheaval of the Disruption.

A brief final comment. As a member and minister of the Church of Scotland, the present writer may be regarded as belonging in some sense to the party which triumphed in 1690. But he is well aware that none of those who now bear the religious labels which aroused so much acrimony three hundred years ago can be easily identified with the attitudes and actions, admirable or reprehensible, of their ecclesiastical forebears. The Presbyterian of today is *not* indistinguishable from the Presbyterian of yesterday, nor are contemporary Scottish Episcopalians identical with those who bore that name at the time of the Revolution. Moreover, while we have been guilty of many injustices to each other, many misrepresentations, we are also – in innumerable ways – each other's debtors. To our mutual indebtedness even the embattled partisans of 1690 no doubt made their own substantial contribution. As T. S. Eliot has put it,

> We cannot revive old factions
> We cannot restore old policies
> Or follow an antique drum.
> These men, and those who opposed them
> And those whom they opposed,
> Accept the constitution of silence,
> And are folded in a single party.[49]

Perhaps it is not necessary for us to postpone our recognition of an underlying unity with those who were once, conceivably, our antagonists until time and the hour have imposed that ultimate constitution upon us.

---

[48] A. R. MacEwen, *The Erskines* (1900), p. 71.
[49] T. S. Eliot, *Four Quartets* (1944, 1949), p. 41.

Chapter 4

Thomas Chalmers: Then and Now

In his own day, and for some decades thereafter, the greatness of Thomas Chalmers seems to have been well-nigh universally acknowledged. Karl Marx, it is true, referred to him, in a phrase which was presumably meant to be uncomplimentary, as 'the arch-parson';[1] and Thomas Carlyle, at his sourest, could avow that 'such an intellect, professing to be educated, and yet so ill-*read*, so ignorant, in all that lay beyond the horizon in space or time, I have almost nowhere met with'.[2] They may be seen as anticipating the less adulatory verdict of a subsequent age. At the other end of the scale, many contemporary estimates strike us today as excessive or even ludicrous. 'Bury me beside Chalmers' was the death-bed plea of that 'earnest student', the hero-worshipping John Mackintosh;[3] while John Cairns of Berwick (the only nineteenth-century representative of the Seceding tradition who came anywhere near Chalmers in stature and influence) dared to compare him with Plato, Descartes, Pascal, Leibnitz and Kant as combining 'an intellect essentially and characteristically scientific' with 'that intuition of moral genius which sounds the depth of human nature and the destinies of human society'.[4]

Most assessments, though more moderate than those just quoted, were considerably nearer panegyric than denunciation. Even Carlyle once remarked that 'It is not often that the world

---

[1] K. Marx, *Capital*, trans. S. Moore and E. Eveling, ed. F. Engels (3rd edn, 1896), p. 630 n.
[2] T. Carlyle, *Reminiscences*, ed. C. E. Norton, intro. I. Campbell (1972), p. 216.
[3] N. MacLeod, *The Earnest Student, being Memorials of John Mackintosh* (pop. edn, 1863), p. 476.
[4] J. Cairns, *Thomas Chalmers* (n.d.), p. 5.

has seen men like Thomas Chalmers, nor can the world afford to forget them', and supposed that 'there will never again be such a preacher in any Christian Church'.[5] If Melbourne, Peel, Sir James Graham and (latterly, at least) Lord Aberdeen were not among his admirers, some eminent statesmen certainly were. According to the eighth Duke of Argyll, he was one of the best and greatest men he had ever known;[6] according to Mr Gladstone, 'an admirable man . . . one of Nature's nobles';[7] according to Lord Rosebery, 'the most illustrious Scotsman since John Knox'.[8] The acidulous John Morley referred to 'mighty Chalmers'.[9] Lord Cockburn spoke of 'four men who in my time have made Scotland illustrious – Dugald Stewart, Walter Scott, Thomas Chalmers, and Francis Jeffrey'.[10] Sydney Smith exclaimed, 'He was not one man; Dr Chalmers was a thousand men.'[11]

Perhaps less remarkably, churchmen over several generations united to honour him. That patron saint of modern Evangelicalism, Charles Simeon, observed of Chalmers with characteristic portentousness, 'Truly I regard him as raised up by God for a great and peculiar work';[12] while the Scottish Episcopalian Dean Ramsay remarked that 'His highest praise, but, at the same time, his *just* eulogium is, that his fervency of spirit, his sensibility, and his energy, were all exercised and called forth in the one great and magnificent cause – promoting the glory of God and the welfare of Mankind.'[13] Again, whatever post-Disruption Auld Kirkers might make of other dignitaries of the Free Church, they united to honour the man whom Norman MacLeod referred to

[5] G. D. Henderson, *Heritage* (1943), p. 113; D. A. Wilson, *Carlyle Till Marriage (1795–1826)* (1923), p. 134.

[6] A. T. Innes, *Studies in Scottish History, Chiefly Ecclesiastical* (1902), p. 184.

[7] J. Morley, *The Life of William Ewart Gladstone* (1905 edn), vol. I, p. 110.

[8] Lord Rosebery, *Miscellanies, Literary and Historical* (1921), vol. I, p. 238.

[9] Morley, *Gladstone*, vol. I, p. 169.

[10] Henderson, *Heritage*, p. 109.

[11] I. Henderson, 'Thomas Chalmers, 1780–1847', in R. S. Wright (ed.), *Fathers of the Kirk* (1960), p. 130.

[12] A. Philip, *Thomas Chalmers, Apostle of Union* (1929), p. 21.

[13] E. B. Ramsay, *A Biographical Notice of the late Thomas Chalmers, DD, LLD* (1850), p. 46.

as 'dear old Chalmers';[14] while from the rival denomination Robert Rainy, Chalmers's late-Victorian successor in the leadership of both Church and Assembly, spoke for nearly all when he described him quite simply as the greatest man he had ever met.[15] And the note of admiration continued to echo – in Scotland, at any rate – far into our own iconoclastic century. 'He had', wrote James Denney, 'the greatness of the nation in him as well as that of the Church, and it is a great gain to a churchman when he has such an interest in the State as keeps his ethics from becoming ecclesiastically narrow in range';[16] and this view was apparently shared by the author of a delightful little essay which appeared as late as 1960. 'It is easy to criticise', wrote Professor Ian Henderson in a compilation entitled *Fathers of the Kirk*, 'not so easy to think of many since his day who have conceived for our country a pattern of life at once so Scottish and so permeated by spiritual values.'[17]

How do we account for the unique place which Chalmers won for himself among his contemporaries and his immediate successors? The basis of his reputation, in an age whose appetite for the spoken word seems almost incredible today, was an oratorical power that verged on wizardry. John Brown the essayist (who left a memorable account of one of Chalmers's sermons and the impression it made on some youthful hearers) reported that 'His eloquence rose like a tide, a sea, setting in, bearing down upon you, lifting up all its waves – "deep calling unto deep"; there was no doing anything but giving up yourself for the time to its will.'[18] After hearing him in the Assembly, Francis Jeffrey of the *Edinburgh Review* exclaimed that there was 'something altogether remarkable about that man'.[19] Hazlitt, testifying to Chalmers's 'prophetic fury' in the pulpit, told how he 'never saw fuller attendances or more profound attention' than at St John's, Glasgow, in 1822: 'It was like a sea of eyes, a swarm of heads, gaping for

[14] D. MacLeod, *Life of Norman MacLeod*, vol. 1 (1876), p. 63.
[15] P. C. Simpson, *The Life of Principal Rainy* (1-vol. edn, 1909), p. 92.
[16] Philip, *Chalmers*, p. 16.
[17] Henderson, 'Thomas Chalmers', p. 140.
[18] J. Brown, *Horae Subsecivae*, 2nd series (3-vol. edn, 1908), p. 133.
[19] D. Masson, *Memories of Two Cities: Edinburgh and Aberdeen* (1911), p. 57.

mysteries and staring for elucidations.'[20] What happened during one of Chalmers's early visits to London, in 1817, was only a slightly exaggerated version of the normal course of events wherever he went to preach or to lecture. 'All the world wild about Chalmers', noted Wilberforce in his diary, and went on: 'Sunday, 25th [May]. Off early with Canning, Huskisson, and Lord Binning to the Scotch Church, London Wall, to hear Dr Chalmers. Vast crowds . . . Lords Elgin, Harrowby, etc. . . . I was surprised to see how greatly Canning was affected; at times he was quite melted into tears.'[21] That was in the morning. Of the afternoon service in the Scots Church, Swallow Street, another enthusiast reported: 'I never witnessed the place so full in my life, pews, passages, pulpit stairs, windows, etc., etc., all crowded to excess; and some noblemen, members of Parliament, and even some most beautiful young ladies of distinction hauled through the vestry window. . . . The carriages stood from the head of Vigo Lane to near Sackville Street in Piccadilly.'[22]

Such an extraordinary impact is hard to explain. Neither originality of thought nor grace of style could be claimed for the speaker: the content of his preaching differed scarcely at all from that of much less gifted colleagues (though he was perhaps more indifferent than they to the subtler nuances of Calvinist orthodoxy), and of its form it has been said that 'he trampled underfoot every accepted canon of pulpit success'.[23] Hazlitt took refuge in a quotation, 'There's magic in the web':[24] and maybe we should leave it at that. But presumably the secret lay in the cumulative effect of a great variety of things. We think of his fertile imagination and his skill at creating atmosphere. We note his fondness for vivid and arresting phrases: 'moonlight preaching ripens no harvest', 'the expulsive power of a new affection', 'rather save a single soul than deliver an empire from pauperism', 'a house-going minister, a church-going people', 'who cares for any Church, but as an instrument of Christian good?' and so on. We

[20] W. Hazlitt, *The Spirit of the Age, or Contemporary Portraits* (4th edn, 1894), p. 63 n.
[21] W. Hanna, *Memoirs of the Life and Writings of Thomas Chalmers* (1849–52), vol. II, p. 102.
[22] H. Watt, *Thomas Chalmers and the Disruption* (1943), p. 48.
[23] Ibid., p. 49.
[24] Hazlitt, *Spirit of the Age*, p. 75.

recall his ability to surpass all his contemporaries at dressing up a single idea in a dozen different guises without ever wearying his audiences, as well as his occasional willingness to challenge accepted notions. We cannot overlook his unequalled force of conviction and (as important as anything) the indefinable charisma of a personality which, though genial and benign, was at the same time strangely elusive and inaccessible. Or are we perhaps to ground Chalmers's appeal not so much in his own outstanding gifts as in the psychology of his hearers: their need to find some stable foothold amid the torrent of revolutionary change, their hopes of escape, in spirit if not in flesh, from the crowding horrors of social convulsion, their tendency to transpose the economic struggle into a religious key, their search for entertainment – and the divine – in a dreary world? There is still room here for worthwhile speculation, and the outcome still remains doubtful.

Whatever our verdict upon it, Chalmers's preaching never constituted his sole title to fame. As an administrator he had something which verged on genius, combining (in John Cairns's phrase) 'absorption in great principles' with 'interest in the minutest details'.[25] Examine the record of his dealings with the Town Council of Glasgow before and during the so-called 'St John's experiment', as well as the multitude of injunctions and memoranda which he drew up for his beloved 'agency' of co-workers; consider the depth and the range of his enquiries into poor law administration, not only in Scotland but also throughout Great Britain; study his reports to the General Assembly as convener (from 1834 to 1840) of its Church Extension Committee, discerning behind the statistical tables in the appendices the driving force of a superb organiser – the father, surely, of the modern committee system of the Kirk. Remember, finally, how even in his last years, when sick and old and sometimes dispirited by the collapse of so many cherished enterprises, he was capable of conceiving and bringing to maturity the wonderful Sustentation Fund which made possible the continued existence of the Free Church and entitles him to be called Scotland's first and greatest advocate of Christian stewardship. Do all that, and you will have gone a long way towards accounting for the spell he cast on both his own and subsequent generations.

[25] Cairns, *Chalmers*, p. 6.

There is yet more to be said, however. To his outstanding gifts as orator and administrator he added a quite exceptional breadth of interests. He began his academic career by holding an assistantship in mathematics; the greatest sensation of his Glasgow ministry was caused not by ordinary sermons but by the *Astronomical Discourses* and the *Commercial Discourses*, which together sought to relate the Faith to contemporary intellectual concerns. He was competent in chemistry, physics and botany, and keenly interested in geology; he held a university chair in Moral Philosophy; and although his hopes of achieving recognition as an economist were hardly realised, John Stuart Mill remarked of his *Political Economy* that at least he always had the merit of studying phenomena at first hand.[26] And, as an attractive little story from his old age would seem to suggest, he never lost a certain openness and generosity of mind. Dean Stanley, meeting him just eleven days before his death, discovered that Chalmers had recently finished reading Gibbon's *Decline and Fall*, and later told how 'the old man's face, Evangelical devout Scotsman as he was, kindled as he spoke of the majesty, the labour, the giant grasp displayed by that greatest and most sceptical of English historians'.[27]

Over and above all these things, we must reckon with a character – sometimes domineering, often unpredictable, nearly always compellingly intense and vital – which impresses by its unusual combination of dynamism and charm. The dynamism comes home to us when we consult Professor Hugh Watt's descriptive list of *The Published Writings of Dr Thomas Chalmers*, a whole volume devoted to recording the titles of some two hundred separate publications (sermons, tracts, lectures, reports and numerous lengthy treatises), which poured from his pen between 1805 and 1847;[28] when we realise that beyond this printed material there lies the vast repertory of manuscript letters lodged in New College Library, Edinburgh, whose cataloguing occupied several years; and when – to select only one example from many such relationships – we read David Keir's history of *The House of*

---

[26] J. Shield Nicholson, Preface to G. C. Wood, *The Opinions of Dr Chalmers Concerning Political Economy and Social Reform* (1912), p. 5.

[27] Philip, *Chalmers*, p. 73.

[28] H. Watt, *The Published Writings of Dr Thomas Chalmers (1780– 1847): A Descriptive List* (1943).

Collins, and observe how even a man of William Collins's superb business ability could find himself driven almost to the limits of endurance by his greatest author's never-ending flow of new projects, his vigilant attention to detail (not least where profits were concerned), and his invariable assumption that what seemed central to him must seem central to everybody.[29]

The magnetic charm is equally undeniable, as Collins's long-suffering fidelity bears witness. He was only one of many, famous and not so famous, who felt its influence. John Anderson heard Chalmers preach in Edinburgh during the early summer of 1815, and, like Boswell with Johnson, was enslaved for ever. His *Reminiscences of Thomas Chalmers* are the fruit of a sedulous, life-long garnering of the great man's utterances, public and private, important and less important.[30] Contemporaries of stature such as David Stow the educationalist and Robert Story the minister of Rosneath (friend of Edward Irving, Thomas Erskine of Linlathen and John McLeod Campbell) clung to his friendship through many vicissitudes. Generations of students, including Alexander Duff the missionary pioneer and Robert Murray M'Cheyne the influential Evangelical preacher, acknowledged him to be one of the shaping influences (in quite a few cases, *the* shaping influence) in their lives. Professor David Masson, whose *Memories of Two Cities. Edinburgh and Aberdeen* contains a lively introduction to Chalmers, was not unrepresentative of all these when, telling of the unforgettable impression made by the famous preacher on a raw lad from Aberdeenshire, he wrote:

> Till he flashed casually before me in that perambulation of benevo-lence which led him into our bleakish parts, never had I felt such power, never had I conceived the possibility of such prodigious-ness of energy in human form. He answered all one's young notions, and more, of what 'greatness' might be; and from that day the whole of that part of our island to which my vision was as yet pretty much bounded, seemed to me full of him, and almost of him only. Scotland was but a platform to and fro on which there walked a Chalmers.[31]

[29] D. E. Keir, *The House of Collins: The Story of a Scottish Family of Publishers from 1789 to the Present Day* (1952).
[30] J. Anderson, *Reminiscences of Thomas Chalmers* (1851).
[31] Philip, *Chalmers*, pp. 19–20.

Perhaps Dr John Brown the essayist got even nearer than that to Chalmers the man. 'There was', he tells us,

> no separating his thoughts and expressions from his person, and looks, and voice. How perfectly we can at this moment recall him! Thundering, flaming, lightening, in the pulpit; teaching, indoctrinating, drawing after him his students in the lecture room; sitting among other public men, the most unconscious, the most king-like of them all, with that broad leonine countenance, that beaming, liberal smile; or on the way out to his home, in his old-fashioned great-coat, with his throat muffled up, his big walking-stick moved outwards in an arc, its point fixed, its head circumferential, a sort of companion and playmate, with which doubtless he demolished legions of imaginary foes, errors and stupidities in men and things, in Church and State. His great look, large chest, large head, his amplitude every way; his broad, simple, childlike, in-turned feet; his short, hurried, impatient step; his erect royal air; his look of general good-will; his kindling up into a warm yet vague benignity when one he did not recognise spoke to him; the addition, for it was not a change, of keen speciality to his hearty recognition; the twinkle of his eyes; the immediate saying something very personal to set all to rights, and then sending you off with some thought, some feeling, some remembrance, making your heart burn within you; his voice indescribable; his eye – that most peculiar feature – not vacant but asleep – innocent, mild, and large; and his soul, its great inhabitant, not always at his window; but then, when he did awake, how close to you was that vehement, burning soul! how it penetrated and overcame you![32]

So Brown's appreciation (written, be it remembered, only a few years after Carlyle had published his *Heroes and Hero-worship*) reaches its memorable climax:

> Dr Chalmers was a ruler among men: this we know historically; this every man who came within his range felt at once. He was, like Agamemnon, a native ἄναξ ἀνδρῶν, and with all his homeliness of feature and deportment, and his perfect simplicity of expression, there was about him 'that divinity that doth hedge a king'. You felt a power in him, and going from him, drawing you to him in spite of yourself. He was in this respect a *solar man*, he drew after him his own firmament of planets. They, like all free agents, had their centrifugal forces acting ever towards an independent, solitary course,

[32] Brown, *Horae Subsecivae*, 2nd series, pp. 122–3.

but the centripetal also was there, and they moved with and around their imperial sun – gracefully or not, willingly or not, as the case might be, but there was no breaking loose: they again, in their own spheres of power, might have their attendant moons, but all were bound to the great massive luminary in their midst.[33]

Such, then, was the man who stood so near the centre of our country's secular and religious life during the first half of last century. His prominence cannot be questioned. But what of his effectiveness? There would seem to be good grounds for arguing that, despite the talents he possessed, the influence he wielded, the respect bordering on veneration generally accorded him, the story of Chalmers's life is in the last analysis a story of failure, failure in the matters which concerned him most, failure of a kind that may well cast doubt upon the soundness of the principles which shaped his ministry and perhaps still shape the ministry of the Kirk. Let me explain. When the word 'failure' is used in connection with Chalmers, one's immediate reaction is probably to think of the Disruption and of what it implied for his vision of a popularised Church of Scotland, allied with the State but independent of it, evangelical, national and free. The events of 1843 were indeed a tragedy, for Chalmers as well as Scotland, but they are not what I have chiefly in mind. I am thinking rather of what happened, even before the Disruption, to the ideals which had more to do with shaping his churchmanship than Non-Intrusion, and as much even as Spiritual Independence: I mean, of course, his devotion to the parochial system and to the principle of Establishment, the great hinges on which all his thinking and acting turned.

First, Chalmers and the parochial system. Chalmers believed that the two great evils of his day were irreligion and poverty. He also believed that the two were intimately connected, the former being the root cause of the latter. And he contended that the only way of eliminating either was: the revival, within the context of modern industrial society, of the ancient virtues of rural and small-town life in Scotland; recognition of a providential ordering, perhaps we should say stratification, of society; unselfconscious philanthropy on the part of the rich, and grateful but never subservient acceptance of it by the deserving poor; family loyalty; sturdy independence; hard work; thrift; temperance; and of course piety – all of them, it may be, somewhat idealised in retrospect.

But how was the much-needed recovery of these desirable characteristics to be achieved? For his answer, Chalmers turned to the territorial parish as he had known it in the Anstruther of his boyhood and the Kilmany of his first ministry. A manageably small area housing a community of some two thousand souls who lived, worked and worshipped together, with a church and a school at its centre and a minister and a kirk session to attend to both its spiritual and its temporal necessities: here, he argued, was the basic – he would even have said the redemptive – unit of Scottish society. Here was the means of national regeneration. Admirably suited to coping with the traditional problems of country life, it also (in his opinion) constituted the only remedy for the horrifying conditions created during his lifetime by industrialisation, the population explosion and the rise of large towns: the destitution, crime, squalor and disease, all on an immense scale, which not only defied moral and sanitary control but even seemed to be undermining the very foundations of civilised life and Christian faith in Glasgow, Edinburgh, Dundee and the Central Lowlands of Scotland generally.

Broadly understood, Chalmers's profound regard for the parochial system may be said to underlie all the major interests and activities of his long ministry. It was a close ally of his devotion to 'the Establishment principle'. It strengthened his enthusiasm for Church Extension, his antipathy to pluralities, his emphasis upon the need for improvement in the training of ministers. It was not unconnected with his adherence to the Non-Intrusion movement and his (belated) support for the abolition of patronage. But if Chalmers's advocacy of the parochial ideal extended over almost his entire adult life, his practical demonstration of its effectiveness was concentrated in two relatively brief periods: one near the beginning of his career as a national figure, the other at its close. These were, of course, the 'St John's experiment' from 1819 to 1823 and the 'West Port operation' from 1844 until his death in 1847. Whether or not he made his case must depend largely upon the success or otherwise of those two great-hearted but very diversely regarded enterprises. The earlier was much the more important of them, and attention here may be confined to it, leaving those who are interested to consider the later by means of Professor S. J. Brown's definitive article in the *Records of the Scottish Church History Society*.[34]

The news of Waterloo was only a few weeks old when Chalmers was inducted to the charge of Glasgow Tron. Four years later, having attained a fame which, at least in some quarters, almost rivalled that of the great Duke himself, Scotland's most celebrated preacher was ready to provide a dramatic and (as he believed) utterly cogent demonstration of the adequacy of the parish system to meet even the fiercest challenges that urban life could offer to the Christian Faith and the Christian Church. All that he demanded for the achievement of his purpose was an area of operations as representative as possible of the worst that 'slumdom' could do, together with freedom to tackle things in his own way, untrammelled by any interference from either civic or ecclesiastical authorities. Both were granted him, and in the late summer of 1819 he entered upon his labours as minister of the newly created parish of St John's. Carved out for him by the Council from three overgrown East End parishes, and crowded with some ten thousand exceptionally poor people, it presented all the difficulties – and all the opportunities – which even he might have desired. The great experiment could begin.

The distinctive thing about Chalmers's ministry at St John's was that it took the traditional features of parochial administration – spiritual oversight, education and poor relief – more seriously, and dealt with them more efficiently, than had perhaps ever been done before.

The task of spiritual supervision, which was quite beyond the minister's own unaided powers, was addressed by adopting the simple expedients of sub-division and devolution. Chalmers parcelled out the territory in twenty-five districts or 'proportions', containing from sixty to one hundred families apiece; and to each he assigned an elder, charged with the oversight not only of St John's members but of every household not effectively connected with some other congregation, Seceding or Roman Catholic, within the city. These men went where he could not find time to

[34] S. J. Brown, 'The Disruption and Urban Poverty: Thomas Chalmers and the West Port Operation in Edinburgh, 1844–47', *Records of the Scottish Church History Society*, vol. xx, pt. 1 (1978), pp. 65–89.

go, 'ministering', as he put it, 'from house to house in prayer and in exhortation and in the dispensation of spiritual comfort':[35] helping to keep alive the people's contact with their local church and its activities, informing the minister of problems as they arose, and binding the whole parish together by innumerable filaments of spiritual and social intercourse. Through their labours, it was hoped, some sense of individual worth and significance might be restored to the bewildered and degraded inhabitants of an overgrown city; and certainly there is nothing far fetched in seeing the 'proportion' as a kind of successor to the intimate parish community of earlier days. (The scheme, incidentally, was more than just a successful exercise in the delegation of duties and the deepening of Christian fellowship. It also pioneered what would now be called the training of the laity; for the congregation of St John's learned to regard itself as being less an assemblage of hearers than a body of workers, its mission to the parish planned and directed by the clergy but managed and carried through by a subordinate band of elders, deacons, Sunday and day school teachers, and others – the NCOs, as it were, of a Christian army.) All in all, no part of Chalmers's work in Glasgow was more impressive than what he did in this matter of spiritual supervision.

High priority was also given to the task of education. At St John's, as formerly at the Tron, the religious instruction of every child in the parish was enthusiastically promoted: each 'proportion' had at least one Sunday school, and some had two or even three. But this did not satisfy Chalmers. He often pointed out how great an obstacle illiteracy or semi-literacy could be to a true understanding of the biblical message, and in any case he firmly believed that a measure of elementary education was the best possible defence against the wiles of political agitators. As early as September 1819, therefore, he set about providing his new parish with modestly endowed day schools after the pattern which he most admired: the parochial schools of the Scottish countryside, where, to quote his own words, 'the education is so cheap as that the poor may pay, but at the same time . . . so good as that the rich may receive'.[36] The effects were soon evident. An education committee was formed in the congregation; the

[35] Hanna, *Memoirs*, vol. II, p. 508.
[36] Ibid., pp. 239–40.

immediate construction of two schools and two masters' houses was agreed upon; and within about two years four salaried teachers were in charge of over four hundred pupils. By the time of his departure from Glasgow in 1823 the number of scholars had risen to nearly eight hundred.

Most difficult and controversial of all Chalmers's activities at St John's was his handling of the vast, mind-boggling problem of poverty. Conditions in early nineteenth-century Glasgow were more like those now obtaining in Calcutta or Mexico City than anything we know in the West; and most onlookers were baffled or terrified or driven to despair by the abject misery and degradation of the new urban proletariat. An increasingly popular response (imported, it seems, from the South) was to levy a poor-rate on the city's property owners and distribute the proceeds as 'indoor' (poorhouse) or 'outdoor' relief to the needy. In Chalmers's eyes, however, this was an altogether deplorable expedient – a palliative, not a cure, undermining the traditional self-respect and self-sufficiency of the Scottish people, and leading in the long run to an increase rather than a diminution of the distress. In opposition to it, he advocated what we might call 'the Anstruther solution', and what he himself described as 'the principle of locality'. This involved reliance, within the parish, and under the supervision of the minister and kirk session, upon the self-help of the poor, the assistance of relatives, the kindness of neighbours and the discriminating charity of the rich to achieve what could never be looked for from a compulsory national scheme with its multiplicity of officials, its impersonality and its tendency to demoralise the beneficiaries.

Central to Chalmers's scheme was the revival of the ancient office of the diaconate; and the instructions which he issued for the guidance of the new deacons clearly indicate how he hoped to reduce a huge problem to manageable proportions. 'When one applies for admittance through his deacon upon our funds', ran the memorandum,

> the first thing to be inquired into is, if there be any kind of work that he can yet do so as to keep him altogether off [the poor roll] or as to make a partial allowance serve for his necessities; the second, what his relatives and friends are willing to do for him; the third, whether he is a hearer in any dissenting place of worship, and whether its session will contribute to his relief. And if after these previous inquiries

it be found that further relief is necessary, then there must be a strict ascertainment of his term of residence in Glasgow, and whether he be yet on the funds of the Town Hospital, or is obtaining relief from any other parish. If upon all these points being ascertained the deacon of the proportion where he resides still conceives him an object for our assistance, he will inquire whether a small temporary aid will meet the occasion, and state this to the first ordinary meeting. But if instead of this he conceives him a fit subject for a regular allowance, he will receive the assistance of another deacon to confirm and complete his inquiries by the next ordinary meeting thereafter, at which time the applicant, if they still think him a fit object, is brought before us, and received upon the fund at such a rate of allowance as upon all the circumstances of the case the meeting of deacons shall judge proper.[37]

Impostors had little chance of obtaining relief under such conditions, while the genuinely distressed were unlikely to become destitute.

For a time at least the scheme seemed to be highly successful. The burden of assistance borne by the parish was reduced from £1400 to £280 per annum; after only two years it became possible to relieve the Town Hospital (or poorhouse) of responsibility for any St John's parishioners who were still on its books; and such confidence had been generated that a supplementary place of worship, paid for by loans raised on the security of its seat-rents, was built to carry still further the 'principle of locality' and the practice of self-help. As Professor L. J. Saunders commented in a classic study, 'even if the secular rulers of Glasgow refused to spend money on churches and schools, a way seemed open for a self-supporting and limitless church extension; if the state continued indifferent or hostile, the Church would attempt to fulfil its national mission by its own enthusiastic effort'.[38] In 1823, however, Chalmers was appointed to the Chair of Moral Philosophy at St Andrews, and thence, five years later, he migrated to the Chair of Divinity in Edinburgh. The great St John's experiment – or at least his intimate association with it – was over.

What verdict are we to pass upon it? His own and subsequent generations seem pretty well convinced that Chalmers's attempt

[37] Ibid., p. 299.
[38] L. J. Saunders, *Scottish Democracy, 1815–1840: The Social and Intellectual Background* (1950), p. 216.

to revitalise the parochial system produced commendable results in the area of pastoral oversight and the instruction of the young; though they are serious criticisms that the fees charged in the schools excluded the poorest children and that the integrity of the parish (on which he always laid great stress) was constantly threatened by an influx of pupils from outside. But in the crucially important matter of poor relief, the number one issue of the day, judgments have on the whole been unfavourable, and that despite Chalmers's patent conviction that failure there meant failure all along the line.

Even in the early years, with their undoubted triumphs, the current of opinion probably tended to go against Chalmers. On a fairly superficial level, it was argued (by Carlyle, for example) that such success as his methods did enjoy was due not to their intrinsic excellence but to their deviser's quite exceptional gifts: the oratory which attracted huge crowds and so ensured substantial offerings for the poor fund; the charm and dynamism which recruited and organised a host of able and wealthy officebearers to administer the St John's experiment; the masterfulness which overbore all resistance; and the optimism which made light of tremendous difficulties. More searchingly, men like Professor W. P. Alison of Edinburgh University suggested that Chalmers did not understand, or take sufficient account of, the environmental factors in early nineteenth-century poverty, factors which called for Christian compassion rather than the somewhat censorious moralism which he sometimes displayed.[39] And of course the verdict of events (doubtless not unaffected by such strictures) was equally unfavourable. In 1837, St John's ceased to be an enclave within the Poor Law administration of Glasgow. In 1843, the Disruption – in which, ironically, Chalmers played a central part – extinguished all hope that official support would ever be given to an implementation of his ideas throughout the country. In S. J. Brown's

[39] cf. O. Checkland, 'Chalmers and William Pulteney Alison: A Conflict of Views on Scottish Social Policy', passim, in A. C. Cheyne (ed.), *The Practical and the Pious: Essays on Thomas Chalmers (1780–1847)* (1985), pp. 130–40; also S. J. Brown, *Thomas Chalmers and the Godly Commonwealth in Scotland* (1982), pp. 289–96, and R. A. Cage, *The Scottish Poor Law, 1745–1845* (1981), pp. 126–30.

words, 'By assuming a leading role in the Disruption of the Church of Scotland, he had helped to deprive the nation of perhaps the only institution capable of mobilising sufficient resources for organising an effective national, social and educational structure based upon his parochial idea.'[40] In 1845, the Poor Law Amendment Act finally took responsibility for the care of the poor out of the Church's hands. Britain had begun its journey away from 'the ideal of parish communities and church-directed social services'[41] towards the social welfare state, and the valorous experiment had failed.

Today, over one hundred and fifty years later, the criticisms directed against the St John's project and against Chalmers as a social reformer are many and various. His plans have been called 'speculative and over-confident'.[42] His concentration on the individual and the family, though praised as an anticipation of the 'family casework' approach of our own time, is seen as blinding him to the wide interdependence – impersonal but nonetheless real – of all citizens in a great commercial centre like Glasgow. He is accused of failing to reckon with the new facts of social and geographical mobility (Dr Lee of Edinburgh's Old Kirk and later Principal of the University first made this accusation in the 1830s),[43] of encouraging, through the inquisitorial methods which he recommended to his deacons, the concealment rather than the discovery and relief of poverty, and of discriminating with undue rigour between the 'deserving' and the 'undeserving' poor. He is dismissed because of his attachment to a view of economic relations which did not reckon with the emergent world of strikes, lock-outs, booms and slumps; he is denounced for his coolness towards Trade Unions, his paternalism, his amateurism and his *petit-bourgeois* sentiments and sympathies. His dependence on *laissez-faire* theorists and the sombre harshness of Malthusian economics is noted and deplored. 'It may be surmised', wrote one modern scholar, 'that others, neglecting his example and

---

[40] Brown, 'The Disruption and Urban Poverty', p. 66.
[41] Ibid., p. 88.
[42] Saunders, *Scottish Democracy*, p. 217.
[43] Dr. Lee's *Refutation of the Charges brought against him by the Rev. Dr. Chalmers and Others in reference to the Questions on Church Extension and University Education* (1837).

concentrating on his economic teachings, derived from them a positive discouragement to active effort for social betterment.'[44]

Perhaps most serious of all, a strange heartlessness is discerned as underlying the treatment of poverty worked out by Chalmers and his supporters. That in itself may sufficiently explain the lack of enthusiasm now shown for the great man's social teaching (though its profoundly clerical flavour may also be partly responsible). And if Professor Saunders is right it probably also accounts for the massive reaction against all that he stood for which set in long before his death in 1847. At the close of an invaluable discussion of 'The Christian and Civic Economy', Saunders remarks:

> In his understanding of industrial conflict and industrial failure alike Chalmers seemed to exhibit such a contrast between principle and application that many turned away from what seemed to them too much a 'business Christianity'. . . . Some sought out more satisfying forms of social faith or were caught up by utopian enthusiasms. Others, in hope or bitterness, adopted a secularism that seemed a blasphemy to the orthodox. . . . It was only as a workingman achieved success and emerged from his class that Chalmers's rhetoric began to carry with it something of the conviction of experience.[45]

Alongside Chalmers's enthusiasm for the parish must be set his equally great devotion to the Establishment principle and the ideal of a National Church. But just as the parish was being subjected to unprecedented pressures and strains during his lifetime, so the age-old notion of an Established Church was also coming under increasing criticism.

That there should be one Scottish Church just as there was one Scottish State, and that the former had a right to all the economic and political assistance it might require from the latter, seems to have been something like an axiom for John Knox and his reforming associates. Inherited from medieval times, it was acted upon in the 1560s, survived all the vicissitudes of Stewart rule, and commanded general support in the country down to the Revolution Settlement. From then on, however, it underwent a process of slow but almost unceasing erosion. The continued

---

[44] S. Mechie, *The Church and Scottish Social Development, 1780–1847* (1960), p. 57.
[45] Saunders, *Scottish Democracy*, p. 221.

survival of the Roman alternative had always been an embarrassment to those who held that there should be only 'one face of the
Kirk' in Scotland; but it was even more disturbing when all
Protestants could not be gathered within the fold of the Established
Church. In 1690, the Cameronians held themselves aloof from
an uncovenanted Kirk. In 1712, the British Parliament's grant of
toleration to the Episcopalians meant the official acceptance of
religious dissent. Thereafter, the decline of the old 'one State –
one Church' ideal was accelerated by the Presbyterian secessions
of the mid-eighteenth century and the rise (during the Moderate
hegemony) of what might be called a 'live and let live' attitude
within the Establishment itself. Even more important, towards
the close of the century the Seceding heirs of Ebenezer Erskine
gradually abandoned their original respect for the idea, if not the
actuality, of Establishment. Joining hands with the spiritual
descendants of Thomas Gillespie, the founder of the voluntarist
Relief Church, they manifested increasing hostility to the very
idea of a National Church and, in particular, to the special
pretensions and privileges of the Church of Scotland. (Chief among
the influences which brought about their change of heart were
the continuing difficulties created by patronage, the American
example of freedom from State control, the liberating effects of
the French Revolution and the intellectual ferment which eventually led to political and social reform in the 1830s.) This new
attitude came violently to the surface in the so-called Voluntary
Conflict, touched off in 1829 by Andrew Marshall's famous
sermon, 'Ecclesiastical Establishments Considered'.

Marshall, who was a United Secession minister in Kirkintilloch,
called for the abolition of every form of religious Establishment
throughout Great Britain, employing arguments which were to
be repeated again and again during Chalmers's lifetime. The
starting point of his case was the situation then confronting the
churches, a situation where the authorities were generally favourable to the Christian mission but where most of the common
people remained unaffected and unresponsive. What was to be
done? He asked:

> Shall we have recourse to the secular arm? Shall we solicit the aid of
> the law – not only placing ourselves under its protection but arming
> ourselves with its force? Shall we repair to our unenlightened brethren
> with the imposing apparatus of a religious Establishment – showing

them our Confession of Faith which they are henceforth to adopt – showing them the act of the legislature sanctioning that Confession – telling them that, by the orders of a paternal government which cares for their best interests, they are distributed into parishes – that by the order of government provision is made for erecting churches among them, and endowing clergymen – and that by the same order each particular division of them is to receive a minister, whom some-one will send them and whose business will be to teach them the way of salvation?[46]

To all these questions Marshall's answer was a resounding negative, which he supported with a perfect battery of arguments.

The Lord of the Church, he reasoned, had not set up a religious Establishment, nor did the early Christians know anything resembling one. Such an institution fosters religious exclusiveness, leads almost inevitably to persecution, nourishes dissatisfaction among those excluded from its benefits, secularises the Church and discourages Christian liberality. It is almost inevitably inefficient, and has been shown to be so by the superior vigour of American Voluntaryism. As for a line of reasoning much used in defence of establishments by Chalmers and others, Marshall had this comment to make:

It is said that unless we send the Gospel to men they will never seek it; it is none of the things they naturally desire, none of the things they are apt to deem essential to their comfort, or which, of their own accord, they will endeavour to provide. Means must therefore be employed to continue it among them; and what means are so suitable or promise to be so efficient as a national establishment? To this argument we reply by admitting the premise but denying the conclusion. We admit that the expense of sending it, and in all probability of preserving it among them for a time, must be defrayed; but we deny that the interposition of the civil power is either necessary for the purpose or to be desired. Let the gospel emanate from those who have been put in trust with the gospel; let it emanate from the church to which the Lord Jesus has given the commission; and if the ministers of the church require assistance in the work, pecuniary assistance or assistance of any other kind, let them look for that assistance, let them confidently expect it, from their Christian brethren.[47]

[46] A. Marshall, *Ecclesiastical Establishments Considered. A Sermon* (1829), pp. 15–16.

[47] Ibid., pp. 41–2.

Needless to say, there was no dearth of apologists for either
the Church of Scotland or the Establishment principle which was
its foundation. Among them Chalmers figured prominently. Of
his many writings on the subject three are particularly significant:
his treatise, *On the Use and Abuse of Literary and Ecclesiastical
Establishments*, first printed as early as 1827; his sermon, 'On
Ecclesiastical Endowments', preached just after Marshall's in
1829; and his *Lectures on the Establishment and Extension of
National Churches*, delivered in London at the height of the
controversy in 1838. The treatise, which was written in defence
of university endowments (then under attack) argued against those
who would leave the provision of schools and colleges – and
churches – to the operation of the laws of supply and demand,
and contended that the remedy for ignorance and impiety alike
was a national Establishment, with a schoolmaster and a minister
in every parish: only thus would people become conscious of
their real needs, and find the means of satisfying them close at
hand. The sermon concerned itself with two of Marshall's chief
allegations against Establishment: that it was a corruption of the
Church, unknown before Constantine, and that it involved State
control and the secularisation of religion. In reply, Chalmers
argued that, just as the supporters of a missionary society may
give it their financial assistance without exercising any control
over its message or its ministers, so with the State's relation to
the Church. 'For the sake of an abundant gospel dispensation we
are upheld in things temporal by the State. For the sake of a pure
gospel dispensation we are left in things spiritual to ourselves.'[48]
The celebrated London lectures have a special, almost melancholy,
interest for the historian in view of the comment which events
were soon to pass on optimistic phrases like the following:

> It should never be forgotten that, in things ecclesiastical, the
> highest power of our Church is amenable to no higher power on
> earth for its decisions. It can exclude, it can deprive, it can depose at
> pleasure. . . . There is not one thing which the State can do to our
> independent and indestructible Church but strip her of her
> temporalities. *Nec tamen consumebatur*, she would remain a Church
> notwithstanding.[49]

[48] *The Works of Thomas Chalmers* (1835–1842), vol. XI, p. 150.
[49] Hanna, *Memoirs*, vol. IV, pp. 45–6.

At the time, however, the most impressive aspect of the lectures was their central contention that pure Voluntaryism (Voluntaryism *ab intra*, as Chalmers liked to call it) was incapable of reclaiming the heathenised masses for Christianity, and that only an adequately endowed State Church could do so.

In drawing attention to this point we really move from the Voluntary Controversy, properly so called, to the great debate about Church Extension which grew out of it. From the Middle Ages almost until Chalmers's lifetime the ecclesiastical map of Scotland had changed very little, at least so far as the number of parishes, their boundaries and the size and location of the parish churches were concerned. But now it was being transformed by the population explosion and the growth of large towns which accompanied the Industrial Revolution. How were the churches to react? The Dissenting bodies were happily free to respond to demand – if not to need – whenever it arose: they grasped the opportunity with both hands and called many new congregations into being. But their flexibility was not possible for the Establishment, which had to tackle its problems without contravening the numerous regulations imposed by the State in order to safeguard the interests of existing parishes and the rights of heritors. One device which enjoyed official approval was to increase the number not of parishes but of ministers in a hard-pressed area: St Andrew's in Edinburgh, for example, became a collegiate charge in 1800, and so provided two pastors instead of one for the rapidly developing New Town. Another was to find stipends for new charges by uncollegiating old ones in less populous districts, an idea which encouraged the city fathers to erect some of the capital's handsomest churches in the decades immediately after 1815.

Despite their attractions, however, collegiating and uncollegiating proved to be mere palliatives of the situation. Especially favoured by those who wished to extend the Church's influence was the provision of 'chapels of ease', sanctuaries erected and supported by the people in the hope of their incorporation, sooner rather than later, into the regular parochial system. Unfortunately, the suspicious attitude of Moderate Assemblies baulked this hope for many years. Only a few dozen chapels were admitted between 1707 and 1833, whereas Presbyterian Dissent erected 500 places of worship in the same period; and even when a chapel was accorded recognition the status of its minister remained markedly lower than that of his colleagues. In Hugh Watt's words, 'Though trained in the same University Faculty as the average parish minister, licensed by the same presbytery, called by a congregation of considerable numbers, and regularly ordained to the ministry, he had not only no defined field of labour, and no seat in any Church court, he had not even a kirk session of his own.'[50] To Evangelicals like Chalmers this was an intolerable situation; and one of the earliest consequences of their attaining an Assembly majority (in 1834) was the passage of the Chapels Act, which sought to remove all the disabilities just referred to. Church Extension on a large scale was now a real possibility, and it became a certainty with Chalmers's appointment that same year as Convener of the Church Accommodation Committee.

In his first address to the members of the committee the new Convener expressed his enthusiasm for the assignment. 'I can truly affirm', he declared, 'that had I been left to make a choice among the countless diversities of welldoing, this is the one office that I should have selected as the most congenial to my taste.' He then went on to describe the aims of Church Extension as he conceived them:

> I trust the Committee will not relax its exertions, and not relinquish them, even though it should require the perseverance of a whole generation, till we have made it a sufficiently thick-set Establishment, and brought it into a state of full equipment – till the churches have been so multiplied, and parochial charges so sub-divided that there will not one poor family be found in our land who might not, if they will, have entry and accommodation in a place of worship and religious instruction, with such a share in the personal attentions of the clergyman as to claim him for an acquaintance and a friend.[51]

'A sufficiently thick-set Establishment': that (in Chalmers's quaint phraseology) was the target which he set himself and his committee, and only the even more remarkable record of Church Extension under his leadership in the period after 1843 has dimmed the lustre of the great campaign which followed. Appeals of a kind previously unknown in the Kirk were directed to both

[50] Watt, *Chalmers*, p. 137.
[51] Hanna, *Memoirs*, vol. III, pp. 451–2.

individuals and congregations; collections were made, and congregational associations of penny-a-week contributors formed; a programme of special meetings nationwide was organised; and in his report to the Assembly of 1838 the Convener was able to intimate that in four years over £205,000 had been raised and 187 churches added to the strength of the Church of Scotland.[52]

It was an astonishing achievement, and most men would have been inclined to rest on their laurels at that point. Not so Chalmers. To have built the churches was, in his estimation, only a beginning. Ministers must now be provided for them, and although recruitment would present no problems (there was a glut of candidates at the time) payment was a different matter. The clergy already at work in Scottish parishes were mainly provided for out of the ancient teinds (tithes) or, in larger towns, out of seat rents; but there was little likelihood of the old endowments being stretched to cover the new livings, and it ran counter to Chalmers's deepest convictions to charge for accommodation in such a way as to exclude poor parishioners from worship. The only way forward, it seemed, was to take the fact of Establishment seriously and turn to the State for assistance. Nor was there an absence of precedents for so doing. As recently as 1818 the sister Establishment south of the Border had benefited to the extent of £1 million from a government grant for church building; and another £500,000 had been made available six years later. At that very time, moreover, the Kirk itself received £100,000 towards the construction and endowment of some forty 'Parliamentary churches' (as they came to be called) in the remote Highlands. It was therefore decided to make application to the Whig ministry of Lord Melbourne for another such grant, and in July 1834 the first of several Scottish deputations visited London. The friendly reception accorded them made hopes run high; but the parliamentary session was too far advanced for anything to be done immediately, and the Kirk's envoys returned home with nothing to show save 'good words and comfortable promises'.[53]

[52] *Fourth Report of the Committee of the General Assembly of the Church of Scotland on Church Extension, Given in and read on the 22nd of May 1838 by Thomas Chalmers, DD, Convener* (1838), p. 12.
[53] N. L. Walker, *Robert Buchanan, DD. An Ecclesiastical Biography* (1877), p. 47.

Before the opening of the next session the Whigs had fallen from power and been succeeded by Sir Robert Peel and the Tories; yet even that turn of events was hardly discouraging. The Tories were more of a Church party, and more friendly to Church Extension, than their opponents; and Chalmers received positive encouragement to renew the application for aid. In February 1835 the King's speech, which was, of course, a statement of government policy, foreshadowed imminent legislation in the Church's favour. Success seemed to be within its grasp.

And then the blow fell. The announcement of the Government's intentions had been greeted with 'a veritable tornado of protest',[54] in which the Voluntaries of both England and Scotland took the lead. They accused the General Assembly, and Chalmers in particular, of blatant deception. Their real aim, surely, was not the evangelisation of the poor and the unchurched but the annihilation of every religious body in Scotland except the Kirk. If their schemes were fully realised, Dissent could not possibly survive; and, in any case, was the Church of Scotland even making adequate use of its existing endowments? Such statistics as were available suggested that it was not! Bombarded by allegations of this kind, the Government (friendly though it was) hesitated; and while it hesitated another turn of fortune brought Melbourne, the very antithesis of Chalmers in politics and religion alike, back to office. By this time, some measure of a temporising kind was almost inevitable; and despite the pleas of another Scottish delegation at Westminster the appointment of a Royal Commission to investigate the whole situation was soon announced.

The disappointment and alarm of the Kirk were only increased when the names of those who would serve on the Commission became known. They included several outspoken and aggressive Voluntaries. 'A restless, locomotive, clamorous minority', commented Chalmers,

> by the noise they have raised, and by the help of men irreligious themselves, and therefore taking no interest, but the contrary, in the religious education of the people, have attained in the eyes of our rulers a magnitude and an importance which do not belong to them – while the great bulk of the population, quiet because satisfied, are by an overwhelming preponderance on the side of the Establishment.[55]

[54] Watt, *Chalmers*, p. 146.
[55] Hanna, *Memoirs*, vol. II, p. 483.

(An early reference, this, to the 'silent majority' so familiar to politicians in the following century!) He did not refuse, however, to collaborate in the inquiry, for it was his belief that a sufficiently rigorous investigation would reveal the Church's aims to be exactly as he had always described them: not clerical enrichment and enhancement of status, and certainly not the diminution or elimination of Dissent, but simply the uplift of the neglected poor and the betterment of the nation's life as a whole.

The Commission, which had also been asked to report on religious facilities within the Dissenting churches, made its various reports in due course. From the Establishment's point of view they proved to be somewhat more favourable than might have been expected. Despite all that the Secession and the Relief had done, church accommodation in the great cities was revealed as having fallen far behind the increase in population: in Edinburgh, for example, there was room for only 48 per cent of the people. On the other hand, this was not to say that all the available sittings were let: far from it. In Edinburgh alone, 11,000 – mostly the cheapest – had not been taken up at all. Over one-third of the inhabitants of the capital, and an even higher proportion in Glasgow, were living in entire neglect of religious ordinances. The opponents of Establishment drew their own conclusions from such evidence; but in Chalmers's eyes it served only to underline the clamant need for government help so that the Church, properly endowed at last, might be empowered to enter upon that 'aggressive' evangelism which only an Established Church could perform.

Unfortunately for the Kirk and its spokesmen, the ambiguous findings of the Commission – inadequate accommodation insufficiently utilised – failed to move Lord Melbourne's Government in the desired direction. Whatever else the agitation of the last few years had done, it had certainly convinced the Prime Minister and his colleagues that this was not the time to alienate their valuable supporters, the Dissenters of England and Scotland. The most they would do, therefore, was to bring in a bill which was quite unsatisfying so far as the Church Extension Committee was concerned. Yet another official deputation from the Kirk failed to alter things. To the complaint that the proposed legislation would inflict a grievous wound upon the Church of Scotland, Melbourne replied 'That, gentlemen, is your inference.

You may not be the better for our plan, but – hang it – you cannot surely be worse.'[56] There was no guarantee that the Tories, though full of promises while out of office, would be any more generous; and in any case, by the time they had a chance to do something the Ten Years' Conflict over patronage and ecclesiastical independence (by 1841 in its last stages) had irretrievably blurred the issues. The chances that the Church would obtain what it considered an adequate addition to its endowments had become slight indeed. During the next few years, Church Extension enthusiasts were obliged to rely, like their Dissenting antagonists, on the freewill offerings of the faithful; in the early spring of 1843 the lawcourts' belated condemnation of the Chapels Act deprived the new Church Extension charges of their hard-won status; and a month or two later the Disruption finally put an end to Chalmers's surviving hopes.

Just as Chalmers's faith in the parochial system had scarcely been upheld by the crucial experiments at St John's and the West Port, so now his advocacy of the Establishment principle was rebuffed, and his reliance on a Christian government to support the missionary outreach of the Church disappointed, by the fate of the great endowment appeal. At both the local and the national level it is difficult not to see him – despite all the many successes which attended his exertions – as being, in the last analysis, something of a failure: a magnificent failure, admittedly, but a failure nevertheless.

That this was so may be explained in part by the character and convictions of the man himself, in part by the circumstances of the time. With all his endearing qualities, he alienated not a few by his overbearing manner and his almost monomaniacal obsession with whatever happened to be the scheme of the moment. His personal relationships (at least outside the family) can be presented as a sad succession of conflicts and misunderstandings: from the early confrontations with local landowners in the East Neuk of Fife, the gentleman in the Arbroath area to whose children he was briefly a tutor, the professor of mathematics and the University Senate at St Andrews, and the presbytery of Cupar,[57] to the

[56] Ibid., vol. IV, p. 23 n.
[57] Cf. J. McCaffrey, 'The Life of Thomas Chalmers', in Cheyne, *The Practical and the Pious*, pp. 31–64 (38–9), and Brown, *Chalmers and the Godly Commonwealth*, chs 1 and 2.

appallingly bitter controversy with Dr Lee over the Moderatorship in the 1830s, the breach with Lord Aberdeen at the height of the Ten Years' Conflict, and the animosities which he aroused in many of the politicians with whom he had to negotiate over endowment.[58] He could be disturbingly illogical: failing, for example, to see the possible incompatibility of Non-Intrusion and the Establishment principle. In his social philosophy, as a man like Patrick Brewster of Paisley realised, he was frequently more bourgeois than Christian, more indebted to Adam Smith and Malthus than to the humanitarian insights of the Gospels and the Epistles. At two crucial moments in his career he was revealed, once by Professor Alison and once by Dr Lee, to be doctrinaire and lacking in both realism and compassion. He was by no means untouched by the fanaticism which could be so disturbing a characteristic of some embattled Evangelicals. Above all, perhaps, he failed his country and his Church by presenting them both with an anachronistic ideal – of Scotland as an aggregation of Anstruthers, meeting the problems of the nineteenth century with the solutions of the sixteenth.

At the same time, however, we should remind ourselves of the well-nigh overwhelming problems which confronted him and his beloved Scotland in that tragic generation. Changes perhaps greater than any known to Western man since the fall of Rome – changes for which there is still no satisfactory answer – were putting an almost intolerable strain on Church and society alike; and if Chalmers failed to retrieve the situation, at least he helped to minimise some of the difficulties as well as putting heart into many thousands of those who had to contend with them. More than two centuries after his birth we can salute him as a true genius, if a flawed one. And we (who are small failures only because we have never attempted anything very big) may apply to him the wise words used by Carlyle at the close of his essay on Burns: 'Granted, the ship comes into harbour with shrouds and tackle damaged; the pilot is blameworthy; he has not been all-wise

---

[58] Cf. I. F. Maciver, 'Chalmers as a "Manager" of the Church, 1831–1840', passim, in Cheyne, *The Practical and the Pious*, pp. 84–97, and I. Muirhead, 'Chalmers and the Politicians', passim, in Cheyne, *The Practical and the Pious*, pp. 98–114; also Brown, *Chalmers and the Godly Commonwealth*, esp. chs 5 and 6.

and all-powerful; but to know *how* blameworthy, tell us first whether his voyage has been round the Globe, or only to Ramsgate and the Isle of Dogs.'[59]

---

[59] T. Carlyle, *Critical and Miscellaneous Essays* (Centenary edn, 1899), vol. I, p. 318.

Chapter 5

The Ten Years' Conflict and the Disruption: An Overview

The Disruption drama of 1843 was played out against a background of astonishing change, profound and many-faceted, which left few areas of Scottish life untouched.

Socially, the country was in course of transformation by the rise of mechanised industry, the helter-skelter growth of large towns, and a population explosion which tripled the size of Glasgow between 1780 and 1815. Politically, the revolutionary Reform Act of 1832 had begun Britain's long march to universal suffrage, arousing high hopes among those who longed for a truly democratic form of government. Ecclesiastically, momentous developments were taking place both inside and outside the Church of Scotland, the state-recognised, state-supported religious 'Establishment'. Inside it, the balance of power between parties was undergoing drastic alteration. The Moderates – reasonable men, accommodating and down-to-earth, the lesser descendants of those eighteenth-century giants, William Robertson and his friends, who had made Edinburgh one of the centres of the enlightened world – no longer dominated the counsels of the General Assembly, and were fast losing both prestige and influence throughout the nation. The reinvigorated Popular party, on the other hand, strong in the enthusiasm, demonstrative piety and crusading spirit of the religious revival associated with the names of Wesley, Whitefield and Wilberforce, had already annexed the challenging title of 'Evangelical' and was now poised to take over the direction of religious affairs from its allegedly effete, reactionary and worldly-minded adversaries. Outside the Church of Scotland, the Presbyterian Dissenters (United Secession and Relief, soon to come together in the United Presbyterian Church) were growing in numbers, confidence and aggressiveness. Calling for the disestablishment of the Auld Kirk in the interests of 'voluntary' religion, they embarrassed it not a little by drawing attention to their own superior generosity, to the ease and speed with which they could respond to the needs of an increasingly mobile population, and – most important of all – to their vastly more democratic method of appointing ministers

The conflict that ended in the Disruption began ten years earlier, when the General Assembly of 1834 passed two Acts which sought to take account of the social, political and ecclesiastical circumstances just indicated. One was the Chapels Act, the other the more famous Veto Act.

The aim of the Chapels Act was to bring about the full incorporation, within the existing ecclesiastical structure, of the new extension charges (or 'chapels') that had sprung up, especially in the Central Lowlands, as a result of the staggering increase and movement of population experienced there since the closing decades of the eighteenth century. Pushed through by the Evangelical party (from whose ranks most chapel ministers were drawn), this crucially important piece of legislation elevated the chapels to equality of status with the ancient parish churches of the land – spiritual equality, at any rate. They were assigned parish areas, clearly delimited; their government was to be by kirk sessions with full authority; their ministers became entitled to sit in all the Church courts. It is difficult to exaggerate the significance of what was a truly revolutionary measure. It consolidated the Evangelical ascendancy. It facilitated the return of Dissenting congregations to the Established Church. It gave a tremendous fillip to Church Extension, with over 200 new congregations being brought into existence by 1843. There were only two snags about it. For one thing, it increased the tension between the Church of Scotland and the Dissenters, whose clothes it might be said to have stolen. For another, some critics objected that only Parliament could create new parishes. In 1834, these objections were brushed aside; but by 1843 the second in particular had become a formidable problem.

If the Chapels Act may be regarded as embodying the Church's response to social change, the Veto Act was even more obviously its answer to the transformation of the political scene. By opening the door to democratic practices in secular life, the Great Reform Act highlighted their absence in the ecclesiastical realm. More and more people were being allowed to choose their political leaders: why was it only Dissenters of the Secession and Relief Churches who could choose their religious leaders? – The focus of concern here was, of course, the patronage system. Ever since the Parliament of the United Kingdom had passed the Patronage Act in 1712 (against fierce Scottish resistance), the appointment of parish ministers rested mainly in the hands of the country's landed proprietors, though the Crown had the right of presentation to some three hundred livings and quite a number of others were in the gift of urban corporations or the universities. Opposition to the system was not much in evidence during the late eighteenth and the early nineteenth century, but from about 1830 it became increasingly vocal, especially among Evangelicals. Prominent individuals like Andrew Thomson of St George's, Edinburgh, called for its complete abolition; but the majority, who were no radicals, preferred with Thomas Chalmers to retain the system while introducing a popular element into it. This they sought to do by means of the Veto Act (1834), which grafted the principle of 'non-intrusion' – that is, the assertion of the inviolability of congregational freedom against all outside interference – onto the old procedure. What resulted was as follows. The patron still presented; the presbytery still examined the person named and, if he passed the test, inducted him to the pastoral charge; but now an equally important role was assigned to the congregation. If they could neither initiate the process nor complete it, they *could* terminate it. According to the new Act, if a majority of the 'male heads of families' who were communicants recorded their opposition to the patron's nominee, the presbytery were obliged to reject him without further ado. In other words, a congregational 'veto' would henceforth block the 'intrusion' of an unpopular presentee. The rights of the people were at last to be given appropriate weight.

Needless to say, not everyone was happy with the Veto Act. Some (as has already been indicated) desired the total abolition of patronage. Others preferred a more gradual approach, rejecting a single piece of Assembly legislation in favour of a whole series of judicial decisions by the Church courts. All objections, however, were overborne. The Lord Chancellor, no less, expressed his approval of the proposed Act, while the Government – patron, on behalf of the Crown, in one-third of all parishes – undertook to follow the procedure which it laid down. All seemed to be set fair.

One cloud nevertheless appeared on the horizon – a cloud presaging storms of totally unexpected violence. The Moderate party in the Church, who were still a considerable body, disapproved of the Veto. Among other things, they pointed out that popularity was not always the best indicator of a minister's worth; that the new Act would almost inevitably cause friction in the parishes; that the only really significant objections to a presentee – those relating to his intellectual or moral inadequacies – could already be dealt with in the course of his 'trials for licence' by the presbytery; that it was a regrettable innovation to substitute the negative veto for the positive 'call' by the congregation (which still survived, though in a somewhat shadowy form, from earlier days); and that what the Non-intrusionists proposed came perilously near to replacing a Presbyterian with a Congregational polity, since presbyteries would in future be bound to accept the will of congregations on the subject of ministerial appointments. Most ominously of all, disgruntled Moderates observed that the new measure would certainly impinge upon property rights – which were a civil, not a religious, matter – and so do much to alienate the most important classes in the community.

These objections, disregarded in 1834, soon returned to plague the Church. As we can see more clearly today, triumphant Evangelicalism had not faced up with sufficient realism to the awkward question: what would happen if a vetoed presentee or a thwarted patron rebelled against the operation of the Veto Act and challenged its legality in the civil courts? The answer to that question was quickly forthcoming, and an exceedingly unpleasant answer it proved to be.

In October 1834, the patron of the parish of Auchterarder in Perthshire, the Earl of Kinnoul, issued a presentation in favour of one Robert Young, a recently licensed probationer-minister. Young preached twice in the vacancy, but at the crucial meeting of the congregation only two parishioners signed the 'call' while a huge majority – 287 male heads of families out of 330 – registered their dissent as provided for by the Veto Act. In due course, therefore, the presbytery rejected Mr Young; and there the matter should have rested. What actually happened was very different. Encouraged by one of the most eminent lawyers of the day, John Hope, Dean of the Faculty of Advocates, Young appealed to the Court of Session (Scotland's supreme civil court) against what he believed to be the illegal behaviour of the presbytery. Eventually, in March 1838, that Court sustained his appeal, agreeing with him that 'The said Presbytery are bound and astricted to receive and admit the pursuer as minister of the church and parish of Auchterarder, according to law.'

What could the Church do now? Meeting a few weeks later, the General Assembly made what was to prove a fateful decision. After passing an unrepentant 'resolution on spiritual independence' which harked back to similarly embattled pronouncements that had been made in the sixteenth century by Andrew Melville and in the seventeenth by the authors of the Westminster Confession of Faith, they appealed to the ultimate judicial authority in the United Kingdom, the House of Lords. A year later, they got their answer. On 4 May 1839 the two supreme Law Lords, Lord Brougham and Lord Cottenham, ruled that the patron's rights were absolute, that no objections by parishioners were relevant, and that in examining a presentee presbyteries should concern themselves only with his 'life, literature and doctrine', and not with his acceptability to the congregation. In a phrase, the Veto Act was illegal, and if the Church did not accept that fact its office-bearers would meet with the full rigour of the Law – interdicts, fines, even imprisonment. As F. W. Maitland said of an equally famous judgment in 1904, 'The cold hand of the Law fell on the living body of the Church with a resounding slap.'

A fortnight later, the General Assembly made a reply which combined intransigence with some indications of willingness to negotiate. It refused to ordain Mr Young, adducing the principle of 'non-intrusion'. But it accepted the Lords' ruling so far as the temporalities (manse, stipend, etc.) of Auchterarder parish were concerned; and it appointed a special committee to treat with the Government for a resolution of the problems then emerging – problems which threatened both the privileges of Scotland's religious Establishment and a harmonious relationship between Church and State.

At this point in the narrative it may be advisable to pause for a moment and summarise the chief points at issue, not only between churchmen and their legal and political adversaries but also among churchmen themselves. The Moderate party in the Kirk, together with the civil courts, held that in an Established Church even ordination was not a purely spiritual matter: it involved civil concerns as well. They also contended that the congregational 'call' was no more than a courteous convention, and that the only essential qualifications of a minister were sound theology, adequate educational attainments and a good character – all of which were looked into by the presbytery at his 'trials'. The Evangelicals and the General Assembly, on the other hand, argued that ordination is an entirely spiritual affair, altogether separable from admission to a 'living'. Moreover, the 'call' (whose pedigree they traced back to Reformation times) was for them of fundamental importance; and they were convinced that acceptability to his people must be included among a minister's essential qualifications.

But even more profound differences than these can be discerned. One side stressed the supreme duty of civil obedience, their favourite biblical text being Romans 13:1: 'The powers that be are ordained of God.' Without submission to the secular authorities, they argued, it would make no sense to talk about 'national recognition of religion', which was at the heart of Establishment. They added that only the civil courts could adjudicate impartially between Church and State. And they called for repeal of the illegal Veto Act, abandonment of emotive references to Christ's Headship over the Church (despite their current popularity in Non-Intrusionist circles) and recognition that there is no greater ecclesiastical evil than schism. The other side were concerned above all with spiritual freedom, and not infrequently quoted Acts 6:29: 'We ought to obey God rather than men.' They owed much to Andrew Melville's 'Two Kingdoms' theory of Church–State relations, developed during his celebrated controversy with King James VI. Church and State, they averred, have each their prescribed sphere of operations, but in early nineteenth-century Scotland the State (personified by lawyers and politicians) is encroaching – with devastating results – upon the Church's territory. In order, therefore, to maintain its God-given privileges the latter must stand firm – even, if necessary, at the cost of losing the benefits of Establishment.

Political theorists have sometimes contrasted the two views under the headings of Erastianism and Theocracy. To contemporaries in 1840 they must have looked more like the classic instance of an irresistible force meeting an immovable object.

We return now to the chronological sequence of events. Happenings similar to those that had occurred in the parish of Auchterarder took place elsewhere (in Lethendy, for example, and Culsalmond); but it was at Marnoch, in Banffshire, that the gravity of the problems confronting the Church was most clearly revealed. The details need not be gone into, fascinating though they were. What should be noted is that at this time the presbytery concerned – the presbytery of Strathbogie – had not an Evangelical but a Moderate majority. These men, soon to be famous as 'The Strathbogie Seven', reluctantly decided that in the clash between Church courts and civil courts they must, like dutiful citizens, obey the law of the land and induct a rejected presentee. For so doing they were eventually deposed from office by the General Assembly of 1841, a measure which shocked many, even within the Evangelical camp, and led to the rise of a 'Middle Party' who feared that the Non-Intrusion leaders, Robert Candlish and William Cunningham in particular, were steering the Church onto the rocks. Another, equally ominous, consequence of the Marnoch imbroglio was that by the spring of 1842 there were two con-gregations, two ministers and two kirk sessions (as well as two churches and two manses) within the parish, each claiming to be the true representative of the Church of Scotland!

One conceivable way out of the impasse still remained. Parlia-ment had made the law which the civil courts were administering: could it be persuaded to alter what it had once enacted? With this hope in mind, and under the leadership of the venerable Thomas Chalmers himself, the Non-Intrusionists turned from the lawyers to the politicians and sought help at Westminster. Unfortunately for them, the situation there could hardly have been less favourable. The Whigs (in power until the late summer of 1841) happened to be largely dependent on the support of Radicals and Dissenters, neither of whom had any love for Established Churches. And as if that was not enough their leader, Lord Melbourne, evinced a deep distrust of Dr Chalmers, remarking, on one occasion: 'He is a madman, and all madmen are rogues.' Little could be hoped for from that quarter. But among the Tories the prospect was equally unpromising. Still recovering from the shock of the Reform Act, they were intensely suspicious of all democratic or pseudo-democratic movements – among which Non-Intrusionism might well be included. The consequences of undermining the Patronage Act and recognising popular rights in the parishes appalled them; and their most influential figure, Sir Robert Peel (soon to become Prime Minister), had been known to speak of the Non-Intrusionists as 'the Popish-Presbyterian party'. In the end, neither Whigs nor Tories were prepared to respond positively to the Church's pleas; and although several distinguished individuals – Lord Aberdeen, the Duke of Argyll, Sir George Sinclair and the future Lord Dalhousie among others – tried to find a solution, none was successful. The ultimate disappointment came as late as March 1843, when a long debate in the House of Commons ended with a decisive rejection of the call for a special parliamentary enquiry into the state of affairs in Scotland. (Scottish Nationalists, incidentally, will not be unduly surprised to learn that a majority of MPs from north of the Border was on the losing side. Had there been a parliament in Edinburgh the Disruption might never have occurred!)

Meanwhile, outside Parliament, events moved towards their denouement. In May 1842 the General Assembly did what they had shrunk from doing in 1834, and expressed their support for the total abolition of patronage. They also gave their approval to the 'Claim of Right', an assertion in elevated – and controversial – terms of the Church's spiritual independence. In November of the same year a 'Convocation' of several hundred Non-Intrusionists met in Edinburgh to stiffen resolve and finalise plans for their forthcoming rejection of Establishment as it had been known and valued in Scotland since 1690. In January 1843 came the Government's answer to the pleas and warnings of the previous Assembly: a firm refusal either to repeal the Patronage Act or to grant the demands of the Claim of Right. That same month, another legal decision made things even worse. Giving judgment in the Stewarton case, the Court of Session repeated what they had done a few years previously with the Veto, and declared the Chapels Act to be illegal. Their ruling in this instance had peculiarly baneful implications for the Non-Intrusion cause, since it meant that chapel-of-ease ministers were no longer entitled to sit in the courts of the Church, and consequently that the Evangelicals would almost certainly lose the dominance over the General Assembly which they had enjoyed since 1834. An

Assembly vote in favour of Disruption (a formal severing of the traditional alliance between Church and State) was suddenly rendered much less likely. As they considered the various choices now open to them, the Non-Intrusionist leaders therefore came to the conclusion that what today's military would call a pre-emptive strike was their best hope of snatching victory out of almost certain defeat. The time for debate was in any case past. The time for solemn affirmation and sacrificial action had come – affirmation and action which would not only forestall, but also cast into the shade, anything which their adversaries might subsequently decide or do. The dramatic events of 18 May 1843 in Edinburgh were the result.

When the Assembly met that afternoon in St Andrew's Church the retiring Moderator, Professor David Welsh (a leading Non-Intrusionist), broke with routine. Instead of making up the roll of members and installing his successor, he read out a lengthy Protest against the conditions being imposed on the Church by the State – conditions which made it impossible for him and his associates to accept the privileges of Establishment any longer. He then left the chair and the building, followed by some two hundred ministers and elders who shared his views. Through an excited crowd, and joined by many sympathisers, they processed to the Tanfield Hall in Canonmills, where they constituted themselves 'The Church of Scotland – *Free*', and signed a Deed of Demission renouncing the many benefits of Establishment. The long-heralded Disruption had at last taken place, and the Free Church – the most vital and thrusting of nineteenth-century Scotland's religious bodies – was launched upon its remarkable career.

There can be little doubt that what had just taken place was the most important event in Scotland's religious history since the establishment of Presbyterianism in 1690. For the ministers who 'went out' (some 450, eventually, out of a total of around 1200), it involved very considerable sacrifices: the renunciation of churches, manses, glebes, stipends – and social standing. For the members who accompanied them (between one-third and one-half of the whole) it meant facing up to financial demands greater than any the Church had previously made upon them. For the entire nation, it meant an accelerated movement into an ordering of things where the State rather than the Church presided over such essentials of community life as poor relief and education.

For true religion, it brought both loss and gain. Loss, because of the slow extinction of the ancient ideal of the Church as the focus of unity and service in every parish, and because of the bitter animosities that divided Auld Kirk and Free Kirk over several decades. Gain, because of the flood of energy, enthusiasm and generosity which was released in the youthful Free Church, leading (at home) to the building of hundreds of new churches, manses and schools, as well as theological colleges of international repute, and (abroad) to the development of missionary endeavour on a scale and of a quality hardly surpassed by any other communion in the English-speaking world.

The historiography of the Disruption is a study in itself, and can hardly be entered into here. But it may be worth noting that most scholars of the present generation are much less inclined than their predecessors were to concentrate on the religious aspects of the story. Today's favoured approach is through sociology; and if its exponents have not said the last word on the subject they must certainly be credited with contributing much that is stimulating and persuasive. Foremost among them is Dr Allan MacLaren, author of *Religion and Social Class: The Disruption Years in Aberdeen* (1974). Ignoring theological questions altogether, MacLaren concentrates on the social circumstances which made possible the emergence of the Free Church in the provincial capital of the North-East and largely explain its subsequent development. In particular, he highlights the conflicting interests of two groups within the city: the old dynasties of top families (lawyers and merchants for the most part, quite often with landed connections) and the emergent, entrepreneurial middle class (men of obscure origins but increasing wealth, socially and geographically mobile, who 'having been denied accommodation by their social superiors increasingly sought confrontation with them'). It was this latter group who, according to MacLaren, found their way into the Non-Intrusionist camp, and after the Disruption 'were to direct the new Church along its initial dynamic course, shape its organisation, make it a success as a denomination, and having achieved their own ambition and proved their ability, leave it with unsolved problems such as its role as a twin to the Established Church'.

To balance MacLaren's work with a contribution of a much more theological flavour, the late Professor Ian Henderson's *Power without Glory: A Study in Ecumenical Politics* (1967) is well worth examining, and equally provocative. Discussing the run up to the events of 1843, Henderson points to what he considers a fatal error on the part of early nineteenth-century Evangelicalism. It had, he suggests, 'a perfectly legitimate and indeed laudable central political object, the abolition of the 1712 breach of the Act of Union' (the Patronage Act). But in order to gain its ends the Evangelical party 'transposed its activities into a theocentric key. By taking to itself the great name of the Evangel, and not some colourless designation like that of the Moderates, its rival party, it successfully conveyed the idea that to oppose it was to oppose the Gospel.' He therefore concludes: 'The will of God was thus once again in the saddle of the Church of Scotland. And as in the sixteen-forties the result was disaster', since 'any ecclesiastical party which identifies its policy with the will of God has got a hold of the right formula for breaking the Church of Scotland. For it is a formula which precludes discussion, and makes possible lovelessness and even prayer against one's brother in Christ.'

Incidentally, Henderson's remarks point us to a notable – and perhaps somewhat overlooked – aspect of the Disruption period: that is, the general unwillingness of the participants to conciliate or mediate or concede anything. One thinks not only of leading Non-Intrusionists like Robert Candlish, William Cunningham and Hugh Miller, but also (on the other side) of John Hope, Lord Brougham and the Tory Home Secretary, Sir James Graham. Their bellicosity seems to mirror the confrontational attitudes of an entire society. It was an age of crusades and campaigns – not only the Voluntary Controversy and the Ten Years' Conflict, but also Chartism and Owenite Radicalism and the Anti-Corn Law League as well, an age in which claims tended to be pitched at their highest, and the language of denunciation stretched to its limits. That Scotland was not unique even in the realm of ecclesiastical warfare is demonstrated by the early history of the Oxford Movement, whose leaders used language not unlike that which came from the lips of Chalmers and his colleagues – as when, in his famous sermon of July 1833 on 'National Apostasy', John Keble exclaimed: 'How many [Church members] continue their communion with the Church *established* (hitherto the pride and comfort of their lives) without any taint of those Erastian principles on which she is now to be governed? What answer can we make henceforth to the partisans of the Bishop of Rome when they taunt us with being a mere Parliamentary Church?' If the Ten Years' Conflict split the Church of Scotland, the Tractarians' war with liberal thought and State interference tore Oxford apart, sorely divided families like the Wilberforces, and if it did not split the Church of England in the 1840s has come near to doing so in the 1990s. The whole sad tale of early-Victorian bellicosity does not excuse the virulence of pamphlets, sermons and Assembly speeches which afflicted (and excited) the Scottish public between 1834 and 1843; it may at least persuade us to view them with a little more understanding.

Before concluding, there is one question to which we must attempt an answer: was Non-Intrusion a worthwhile cause, and can the Disruption be justified?

Almost simultaneously with the walk out of 1843, Sir William Hamilton, the distinguished Edinburgh philosopher, addressed the would-be secessionists in a pamphlet entitled, 'Be not Schismatics, be not Martyrs by Mistake'. His argument was that Non-Intrusion had never been a Calvinist or Presbyterian principle, and that religious believers should be grateful to the civil magistrate, whose worldly wisdom was capable of checking the aberrations of over-enthusiastic divines. More than a century later, another eminent Edinburgh academic, Professor Gordon Donaldson of the chair of Scottish History, bade fair to flutter the ecclesiastical dovecotes in like manner. The essay on 'Church and Community' in his *Scottish Church History* (1985) is an attack on the Melvillian 'Two Kingdoms' theory which underlay the Non-Intrusionists' programme. In characteristically forthright language, Donaldson remarks that 'The frequent assertion that "Christ is the sole King and Head of the Church", settles nothing. The Kingship of Christ over His Church is acknowledged by all. What is at issue is not the Kingship of Christ but the agencies on earth through which the heavenly Kingship is exercised.' And he goes on to contend that 'preoccupation with the Kingship of Christ over His Church may actually be dangerous', as it is 'apt to lead to a view of the State as purely secular': 'The One-Kingdom theory, on the other hand, sanctifies the State as well as the Church, seeing them both as alike subject to the Kingdom of Christ.' Professor Donaldson (we may presume) would not have 'gone out' in 1843;

and when we recall how speedily the Disruption led to secularising measures like the withdrawal of Poor Law administration from Church control in 1845, and of education from Church control in 1872, we cannot but acknowledge that he has a point.

But there is much – very much – to be said on the other side. It is an impressive fact that two of the most learned and penetrating political theorists of the twentieth century, the left-wing Socialist, Professor Harold Laski, and the Anglo-Catholic divine, Father Noel Figgis, should agree in commending the Disruption as a prime example of the defence of ecclesiastical freedom against the encroachments of State power. For Figgis's closely argued thesis, reference must simply be made to his *Churches in the Modern State* (2nd edition, 1914). Laski, however, is irresistibly quotable. His *Studies in the Problem of Sovereignty* (1st edition, 1917) contains the assertion that 'The Presbyterians of 1843 were fighting the notion of a unitary State,' and goes on to observe that 'If the State, theoretically, were in the event victorious, practically it suffered a moral defeat. And it may be suggested that its virtual admission in 1874 [when patronage was abolished] that the Church was right is sufficient evidence that its earlier resistance to her claims had been mistaken.' And he concludes: 'A State that demands the admission that its conscience is supreme goes beyond the due bounds of righteous claim. It will attain a theoretic unity only by the expulsion of those who doubt its rectitude. It seems hardly worthwhile to discuss so inadequate an outlook.'

The leading Church historian of the present generation in Britain, Sir Owen Chadwick, comes down – in the end – on the same side. Admittedly, he deplores the fact that Chalmers and his companions could not wait. 'Legal systems', he writes, 'are always more flexible than they look; even lawyers have hearts beneath their waistcoats of chain-mail; quietness and patience and persuasion are no less Christian virtues than is the heroic sacrifice of stipends on high principle.' Yet his final words on the Ten Years' Conflict are much more positive: 'Nevertheless the headship of Christ is that without which churches may as well be swept aside into heaps of rubble or converted into gymnasia. In all the span of Christian history one can find no clearer demonstration of the sacred appeal to that headship, in the realm of ecclesiastical polity, than in the events of 1842–43 and the leadership of [Thomas Chalmers].' ('Chalmers and the State', in A. C. Cheyne (ed.), *The Practical and the Pious* (1985).)

A final observation. When the broken parts of Scottish Presbyterianism came together again, in the Union of 1929, they did so on the basis of an agreed statement – the so-called Declaratory Articles – which discussed, along with various other topics of fundamental importance, the relationship between Church and State. It included the following carefully chosen words:

> This Church, as part of the Universal Church wherein the Lord Jesus Christ has appointed a government in the hands of Church office-bearers, receives from Him, its Divine King and Head, and from Him alone, the right and power subject to no civil authority to legislate, and to adjudicate finally, in all matters of doctrine, worship, government and discipline in the Church, including the right to determine all questions concerning membership and office in the Church, the constitution and membership of its Courts, and the mode of election of its office-bearers, and to define the boundaries of the spheres of labour of its ministers and other office-bearers. Recognition by civil authority of the separate and independent government and jurisdiction of this Church in matters spiritual, in whatever manner such recognition be expressed, does not in any way affect the character of this government and jurisdiction as derived from the Divine King and Head of the Church alone, or give to the civil authority any right of interference with the proceedings or judgments of the Church within the sphere of its spiritual government and jurisdiction.

That momentous statement, to which the Parliament of the United Kingdom gave its carefully considered assent, was only made possible (it may with confidence be asserted) by the trials and tribulations, the struggles and the sacrifices, of the men and women of the Disruption.

NOTE

There is a simple but perceptive introduction to the subject in G. D. Henderson, *Heritage: A Study of the Disruption* (1943), which was published as part of the centenary commemoration.

General Church histories such as A. L. Drummond and J. Bulloch, *The Scottish Church, 1688–1843* (1973) are still useful; and much detail, as well as impressions of the divergent views of contemporaries and near-contemporaries, may be found in three classic studies – J. Bryce, *Ten Years of the Church of Scotland, 1833–1843*, 2 vols (1850), R. Buchanan, *The Ten Years' Conflict*, 2 vols (1849), and A. Turner, *The Scottish Secession of 1843* (1859).

Two collections of essays point the way to further study: A. C. Cheyne (ed.), *The Practical and the Pious: Essays on Thomas Chalmers (1780–1843)* (1985) and S. J. Brown and M. Fry (eds), *Scotland in the Age of the Disruption* (1993).

C. Brown, *The Social History of Religion in Scotland since 1730* (1987) contains many valuable insights. And of course no student of the period can ignore the authoritative biography by S. J. Brown, *Thomas Chalmers and the Godly Commonwealth in Scotland* (1982).

Chapter 6

The Bible and Change in the Nineteenth Century

Like all their spiritual forbears since the Reformation, Scottish Protestants at the outset of the nineteenth century shared John Knox's conviction that 'Faith hath both her beginning and continuance by the Word of God.'[1]

Identifying that Word with the Scriptures of the Old and New Testaments, they regarded the Bible as the supreme rule of faith and life, both personal and national, whose divine authority very few were disposed to question. During the age of Enlightenment, admittedly, sceptical views and the tentative beginnings of an interest in the sources and literary methods used by the biblical writers (the so-called 'higher criticism') had made their appearance; but the average minister and his parishioners were scarcely affected by them, and there is little evidence that they attracted much attention from the sophisticated urban intelligentsia either. Whether in the Established Church or in the various Dissenting bodies which had hived off from it in the decades after the Revolution Settlement of 1690, the Bible was indeed the *Holy Bible*, and the entire life of the people was profoundly affected by it.

In days when a high proportion of the total population were regular church attenders, a major part of every service of worship was given over to the reading and exposition of the sacred text. The principal object of parish school education was to enable children to read the Bible for themselves, and it seems virtually certain that most of them were more familiar with the history and literature of ancient Israel than with that of their native land. Common speech was shot through with biblical language and biblical allusions, and in many homes the opening and closing of

[1] D. Laing (ed.), *The Works of John Knox*, vol. IV (1855), p. 133.

123

the day found the whole family gathered around the Word. When the young Thomas Carlyle left Ecclefechan for Edinburgh University in 1809, his mother gave him a two-volume Bible to keep him company;[2] and on his death-bed in 1832 the great Sir Walter Scott, when asked what book should be read to him, replied, 'Need you ask? There is but one' – and could be heard, even in delirium, repeating fragments from Job, Isaiah and the Psalms.[3] It would not be a very great exaggeration to say that Scotland, as she stood on the threshold of the Victorian age, was indeed the country of a Book.

The reason why her attitude to the sacred volume, and her use of it, was not essentially different in the 1830s from what it had been in the days of Knox, or the Covenanters, or the original Seceders, was due in large measure to the Evangelical Revival and its conservative – not to say reactionary – influence. As the spiritual temperature rose in the years immediately after the Napoleonic Wars, there was a quite conscious return to the things which, in the estimation of Evangelical leaders like Andrew Thomson (minister of St George's, Edinburgh, from 1814 to 1831) and Thomas Chalmers (Professor of Divinity at Edinburgh University from 1828 until the Disruption of 1843), had laid the foundations of national greatness; and supreme among these were the Holy Scriptures. But along with the exuberance and ardour of resurgent Evangelicalism went an intransigence and acrimony which ushered in a more embattled age; and the bitter Apocrypha Controversy was one of the earliest manifestations of this. It began in 1821 when Robert Haldane, an outstanding Evangelical activist of Baptist principles, was horrified to discover that the British and Foreign Bible Society (BFBS) (a body with many subscribers in Scotland) had covertly been distributing Bibles contaminated by the inclusion of the 'Apocryphal' books.[4] He and his numerous supporters agreed with the original leaders of Protestantism – though not with the early Christian Fathers or the authorities of medieval and post-Reformation Catholicism – that 1 and 2 Esdras, Ecclesiasticus, 1 and 2 Maccabees and the other 'uncanonical'

[2] F. Kaplan, *Thomas Carlyle: A Biography* (1983), p. 28.
[3] E. Johnson, *Sir Walter Scott: The Great Unknown*, vol. II, *1821–1832* (1970), pp. 1266 and 1275.
[4] A. Haldane, *The Lives of Robert Haldane of Airthrey, and of his brother, James Alexander Haldane* (8th edn, 1871), pp. 484–5.

works associated with them had no place in the corpus of truly inspired literature, the Christians' Bible. They set about rectifying the situation, and campaigned against the Apocrypha with passion and skill. But their stance did not go unchallenged, even inside the Evangelical camp, and a furious battle raged throughout the 1820s. It saw the emergence of Haldane as 'the founding father of Fundamentalism',[5] and resulted in the large-scale withdrawal of Scottish support from the BFBS. It was also responsible for the introduction of a new edginess into theological debate throughout the English-speaking world. It raised, in more pressing form than ever before, questions about the nature and even the reality of biblical inspiration which were never very far from the centre of religious concern and debate during the remainder of the century. And (of particular importance for the present study) it led to the formulation of what would long remain the typical conservative answer to a whole constellation of biblical problems.

Scrutiny of that answer reveals one outstandingly important feature. While it was worked out in relation to a widely diverse range of antagonists – typical early eighteenth-century rationalists like Toland and Woolston; later Socinians like Joseph Priestley; more compromising spirits like Philip Doddridge the eminent English Dissenter, who professed to find different degrees of inspiration within the covers of the Bible; forerunners of modern liberalism like Schleiermacher and Coleridge; and of course the defenders of the Apocrypha – it inclined more and more to opt for the unequivocal, neck-or-nothing assertion of a uniformly divine authorship throughout the sacred volume. The biblical writers were increasingly cast in the role of amanuenses of the Almighty. This development stands clearly revealed in the works of four influential writers, all from the opening decades of the century: George Hill, Professor of Divinity at St Andrews from 1788 to 1819, possibly the most distinguished theological teacher of the unreformed Establishment; John Dick, occupant of the only professorial chair in the United Secession Church from 1820–33; Robert Haldane (1764–1851), a man of great stature in the Evangelical world, whom we have already met; and Thomas Chalmers, who dominated the ecclesiastical scene for a generation

---

[5] A. L. Drummond and J. Bulloch, *The Church in Victorian Scotland, 1843–1874* (1975), p. 251.

before his death in 1847. In all their writings on the subject we can detect the same tendency to make the highest possible claims for Scripture, as well as more or less the same predilection, when speaking of it, for words like 'infallible', 'inerrant', 'perfect' and 'immaculately pure' – words destined to be at the centre of even more intense debate in the later decades of the century.

The discussion of biblical authority to be found in these men's writings, and others like them, tended (when not directly concerned with the status of the Apocrypha) to focus upon the question of whether or not different degrees of inspiration could be found in Holy Scripture. Might it be said that at one level – the lowest – God so superintended the minds of the biblical writers as to obviate the possibility of errors occurring in their work; that at another he 'elevated their conceptions beyond the measure of ordinary men'; and that at the highest level he actually suggested the thoughts they were to express and the words they were to employ? Of our four authorities, only George Hill was prepared to give an affirmative answer. Dissenting from those apologists for the Faith who held that the highest form of inspiration was at work throughout the Bible, he contended (in his *Lectures in Divinity*, the first edition of which, dealing almost exclusively with the New Testament, was published posthumously in 1821) that

> this opinion, which is probably entertained by many well-meaning people, and which has been held by some able defenders of Christianity, is now generally abandoned by those who examine the subject with due care. . . . It is not only unnecessary to suppose that the highest degree of inspiration was extended through all the parts of the New Testament, but the supposition is really inconsistent with many circumstances that occur there.

In so saying, however, he disclaimed any desire to undermine the doctrine that the writers of Holy Scripture were divinely inspired in all things, and their works the infallible standard of Christian truth.

> We do not say that every thought was put into the mind of the apostles, and every word dictated to their pen, by the Spirit of God. But we say, that by the superintendence of the Spirit they were at all times guarded from error, and were furnished upon every occasion with the measure of inspiration which the nature of the subject required.

He therefore felt able to summarise his conclusions in language which was as assured and even uncompromising as that of his most dogmatic contemporaries:

> His [Jesus'] apostles ... received ... such a measure of the visible gifts of the Spirit as attested their commission, and such a measure of internal illumination as render their writings the infallible standard of Christian truth. From hence it follows, that everything which is clearly contained in the gospels and epistles, or which may be fairly deduced from the words there used, is true.[6]

Hill's careful phraseology may have left room for greater flexibility in certain respects than some of his contemporaries would have liked; but his old-style orthodoxy can hardly have been in doubt. Dick, Haldane and Chalmers were much more intransigent. The first of them, whose *Essay on the Inspiration of the Holy Scriptures* was originally published in 1800, would (like Haldane and Chalmers after him) have no truck with the notion of degrees of inspiration.

> Few writers [he lamented] who now undertake to defend the cause of revelation, hold the plenary inspiration of the Scripture. That idea has become unfashionable ... and he only is supposed to entertain rational sentiments on the subject, who looks upon the sacred books as partly human and partly divine; as a heterogeneous compound of the oracles of God, and the stories and the sentiments of men. There are even some, by whom this partial inspiration is denied [he was probably thinking of Priestley] and the Scriptures are regarded as the writings of faithful but fallible men, who had nothing to preserve them from error but the accuracy of their information, and the integrity of their hearts. The spirit of infidelity is working among Christians themselves.

Against any such flirting with faithlessness the old Seceder reminded his public that a supernatural revelation surely requires a supernatural record. After all,

> to those who admit that miracles are wrought to attest revelation, it will not seem incredible that there should have been one miracle more, so obviously necessary, as the inspiration of the persons by whom it was committed to writing.

[6] G. Hill, *Lectures in Divinity*, vol. 1 (1821), pp. 368–9, 373–4.

Yet in the last resort he put his trust not in reasoning but in the Scriptures' own claim to divine authority: 'We appeal to their own testimony, and might produce many passages in which it is explicitly asserted, or plainly implied.'[7]

Haldane, as might have been expected of one never deficient in pugnacity, showed even less inclination to compromise. In his *Evidence and Authority of Divine Revelation* (volume I, 1816), he declared that the Holy Scriptures themselves give 'no countenance whatever' to the notion of differing degrees of inspiration. There is but one kind of inspiration, and that the highest, for God communicated to the biblical writers the very 'ideas and words [sic] which they have engrossed in that sacred book'.[8] Chalmers likewise would have nothing to do with 'superintendence' or 'suggestion'. But in his lectures *On the Inspiration of the Old and New Testaments* (delivered in the 1830s, but republished as late as 1879 during a subsequent phase of the Bible debate) he went his own distinctive way in refusing point-blank to discuss what he called 'the act of inspiration'. For him, all that mattered was 'the product of inspiration': the Bible as we have it, whose language God has made His own, and through which He speaks to us now. Over and above the Scriptures' own claims to divine authority and complete reliability, moreover, we must reckon with the unanimous verdict of Christian tradition over many centuries, which has always held that the Bible 'is not a medley of things divine and things human; but is either throughout a fallible composition, or throughout, in all its parts, the rescript of the only wise and true God'. His conclusion, therefore, though reached by a somewhat different route, agreed in all essentials with Haldane's, and even matched it in belligerency.

> We know that the anti-apocryphalists of the day have been accused of too fiercely resenting the encroachments that have been attempted on the canon and inspiration of Scripture, and that on the plea of the encroachments being small ones. We shall say nothing of the resentment; but however slight those encroachments may have been, they could not be too strenuously or too energetically resisted ... It is the part of Christians to rise like a wall of fire round the integrity

[7] J. Dick, *An Essay on the Inspiration of the Holy Scriptures* (4th edn, 1840), pp. x–xi and 236.

[8] R. Haldane, *The Evidence and Authority of Divine Revelation*, vol. I (1816), pp. 135 and 137.

and inspiration of Scripture; and to hold them as intact and inviolable as if a rampart were thrown around them, whose foundations are on earth and whose battlements are in heaven.[9]

The conservatism of pronouncements such as these was only reinforced by the Ten Years' Conflict and the Disruption, and reached its apogee in the mood of the Free Church during the first decades of its existence. At the opening of the new denomination's theological seminary in Edinburgh in 1850, lectures were delivered which can be seen as a kind of manifesto for the traditional views; and the same message comes through in subsequent publications by Free Church teachers. 'What are we to understand by the inspiration of the Bible?' asked Robert Candlish, minister of Free St George's, Edinburgh, and Principal of New College (1861–73), in a lecture given in 1851. He answered:

> I hold it to be an infallible divine guidance exercised over those who are commissioned to declare the mind of God, so as to secure that in declaring it they do not err. What they say, or write, under this guidance, is as truly said and written by God, through them, as if their instrumentality were not used at all. God is in the fullest sense responsible for every word of it.[10]

James Bannerman, who taught at New College from 1848 to 1868, brought out his *Inspiration: The Infallible Truth and Divine Authority of the Holy Scriptures* in 1865. Hailed as the definitive defence of orthodox doctrine on the subject, it contained this summary appreciation of the Scriptures:

> In *the first place*, they contain a communication of truth supernaturally given to man; and in *the second place*, they contain that truth supernaturally transferred to human language, and therefore free from all mixture or addition or error.[11]

Supremely formidable was the celebrated William Cunningham, who succeeded Chalmers as Principal of New College in 1847 and taught there from 1843 until his death in 1861. His *Theological Lectures* (not actually published until 1878) probably

---

[9] T. Chalmers, *On the Inspiration of the Old and New Testaments, with introductory note by Professor Smeaton* (1879), pp. 21, 35–6.

[10] R. S. Candlish, *The Authority and Inspiration of the Holy Scriptures* (1851), p. 6.

[11] J. Bannerman, *Inspiration: The Infallible Truth and Divine Authority of the Holy Scriptures* (1865), pp. 149–50.

constitute the ablest – certainly the most learned and subtle –exposition of traditional views by any Scottish theologian in modern times. His arguments cannot be easily summarised, but the following sentence may serve as a not unrepresentative indication of his stance: 'The Holy Spirit not merely superintended the writers (of the Bible) so as to preserve them from error, but suggested to them the words in which the communication was to be conveyed.'[12]

Alas! for Cunningham and his friends: scarcely had the conservative doctrine of scriptural authority been formulated in such unyielding terms when a very different view began to infiltrate scholarship in Scotland as elsewhere. Within the span of a single lifetime, attitudes were revolutionised; and by the end of the century, still more by 1914, the older approach barely survived in universities and colleges and was visibly in retreat on the parochial front as well. Perhaps the Free Church 'fathers' themselves had something to do with the change. As has been recently pointed out, they not only provided the hard doctrine for their successors to react against, but also accelerated the process they deplored by raising crucial questions without always returning satisfactory answers.[13] Even Evangelicalism's encouragement of Bible reading may have introduced some Scottish believers to inaccuracies and inconsistencies – not to mention scientific or ethical anomalies – in the sacred text of which they would otherwise have been unaware. Nor did the spirit of reform, abroad during the 1830s, leave the scholarly world untouched: a Royal Commission set up to inquire into the state of the universities drew attention, *inter alia*, to the lamentable provision then made for the study of the biblical languages and text as compared with the resources devoted to systematic theology. 'A system', remarked one campaigner, 'ought not to supersede the study of the sacred record itself';[14] and in due course the foundation of new chairs of Biblical Criticism redressed the balance a little in favour of textual rather than purely dogmatic study. Account should likewise be taken of the heightened moral sensitivity of the Victorian age, which made it difficult to maintain that every part of the Bible

[12] W. Cunningham, *Theological Lectures* (1878), p. 346.
[13] R. Riesen, 'Higher Criticism in the Free Church Fathers', in *Records of the Scottish Church History Society*, vol. XX, pt. 2 (1979), p. 120.
[14] W. M. Gunn, *Hints on the Study of Biblical Criticism in Scotland* (1838), p. 20.

was equally authoritative. A new spirit of tolerance and tentativeness which, along with a growing preference for the apologetic as opposed to the dogmatic spirit, rendered the hard-line orthodoxy of the traditionalists increasingly uncongenial, was also a factor. Most important of all was the scientific revolution associated with the writings of Lyell and Darwin, which provided a picture of man and his environment difficult to reconcile with the statements of Scripture if literally understood.

But there can be no doubt that what really transformed the situation was the emergence, in the wake of Enlightenment and Romanticism, of a new *historical* way of looking at life, and the rapid development of the attitudes and techniques of historical scholarship. Students of the Bible were encouraged thereby to regard it not so much as a quarry of texts easily removable from their peculiar setting or as a compendium of theological propositions, but as the record of a particular people – its history and its literature – over many centuries: to ask questions about the original context of each narrative or pronouncement as well as about its author's distinctive concerns and purposes, to appreciate the diversity of materials and viewpoints that it contained, to be aware of possible inconsistencies and inaccuracies, to seek the early sources behind the later compilations, and to steer clear, as much as possible, of a priori assumptions and harmonisations. They came to recognise that the whole great literature might not everywhere attain a uniformly high moral religious level. They rejoiced to discover that they were conceivably reviving a view not unknown to the original Reformers: in Robertson Smith's words, 'Just as the principle of a personal faith is the foundation of all the fresh life of the Reformation, so the principle of a historical treatment of Scripture is at bottom the principle of the whole Reformation theology.'[15] And in all their labours they were guided less by the traditions of the Church and the demands of dogmatic theology than by what the text actually said to the well-informed, candid and sensitive mind. There were, of course, some disadvantages in the new approach. It could encourage the view that the Bible was a book for literary and historical experts. It could be vitiated by naturalistic or positivist presuppositions, or represented as coming 'in paper

[15] Cited by T. M. Lindsay, 'Professor Robertson Smith's Doctrine of Scripture', *Expositor*, 4th series, vol. X (1894), pp. 241–64.

parcels from Germany'.[16] It could reduce 'the impregnable rock of Holy Scripture'[17] to shifting sands. But to those who adopted it there came a sense of liberation and a conviction that the riches of Holy Scripture were being opened up in a way scarcely conceivable under the old ordering of things.

The story of the revolution is inextricably bound up with the career of William Robertson Smith. A pupil of Scotland's first great biblical critic, A. B. Davidson, Smith completed his studies at New College in 1870, when – such was his precocious distinction – the Free Church appointed him Professor of Hebrew and Old Testament at its Aberdeen College. His inaugural lecture bore the title, 'What history teaches us to seek in the Bible', and was in essence a plea for the historical rather than the dogmatic approach. 'We must', he told his hearers, 'let the Bible speak for itself. Our notion of the origin, the purpose, the character of the Scriptural books must be drawn, not from vain traditions but from a historical study of the books themselves.'[18] Smith's pursuit of this ideal soon led him to adopt positions that were unlikely to commend themselves to Free Church traditionalists. An article he contributed to the *Encyclopaedia Britannica* in 1875 assumed that the Scripture narratives we now possess are later, edited versions of accounts dating from various periods in Jewish history, assigned the so-called 'Mosaic' legislation to a period hundreds of years after Moses, suggested that most of the psalms were of non-Davidic origin, eliminated much of the predictive element in the prophets, and denied authorship of the Gospels to the persons whose names they bear. Horrified, the conservatives took action in the courts of the Church, accusing him of teaching that was 'of dangerous and unsettling tendency' and constituted (whether by direct contradiction or subtle disparagement) a threat to 'the doctrine of the immediate inspiration, infallible truth, and divine authority of the Holy Scriptures'.[19] In 1881 – despite all his

---

[16] John Kennedy of Dingwall, cited by J. S. Black and G. W. Chrystal, *The Life of William Robertson Smith* (1912), p. 401.

[17] Title of a series of articles by W. E. Gladstone, published in *Good Words*, March–November 1900.

[18] J. S. Black and G. W. Chrystal (eds), *Lectures and Essays of William Robertson Smith* (1912), p. 233.

[19] 'The Draft Form of Libel', in Black and Chrystal (eds), *Lectures and Essays*, Appendix B, p. 582.

learning and his forensic brilliance – Smith was removed from his Chair as unworthy to be trusted with the training of candidates for the Free Church ministry. Soon moving to Cambridge, he spent the rest of his tragically brief career as University Librarian and Professor of Arabic there. His deposition was a major blow to the new scholarship in Scotland. But it is noteworthy that the Assembly had contrived to get rid of the heretic without specifying – far less condemning – his heresies; and that on the morrow of the great debate a number of his supporters boldly declared their determination 'to pursue the critical questions raised by Professor W. R. Smith' and 'to protect any man who pursues these studies deliberately'.[20] No one called them to account, and it soon became evident that the Assembly's action had been powerless to undo Smith's work of educating Scotland in the new views.

Three further 'heresy trials' followed in the course of the next twenty-five years. In 1890, Professors Marcus Dods and A. B. Bruce fell foul of the conservatives for their espousal of views not vastly different from Smith's. Dods's inaugural lecture at New College in 1889 revived suspicions aroused as early as 1877 by a sermon of his on 'Inspiration and Revelation'. His offences included speaking of 'mistakes and immoralities' in the Old Testament, as well as asserting that the doctrine of verbal inspiration was 'a theory . . . which is dishonouring to God, and which has turned inquirers into sceptics by the thousand'.[21] But despite the provocation the Free Church Assembly decided to proceed no further with the case. Most significantly, its leader, Robert Rainy of New College, opined that a man should not be deemed unsuitable for the Christian ministry because he had detected 'inaccuracies' in Holy Writ – so long as he also took it to be everywhere the Word of God.[22] Bruce's errors had been expressed in a book, also published in 1889: *The Kingdom of God: Christ's Preaching according to the Synoptic Gospels*. He was said to have imputed untrustworthiness to the Gospel writers, and in the course of his defence he certainly declared that they were not objectively reliable. He was also accused of presenting Christ as a poet, a mystic, even a schemer, rather than a divine

---

[20] Black and Chrystal, *Life*, p. 450.
[21] M. Dods, 'Recent Progress in Theology' (1889), p. 30.
[22] *Proceedings and Debates of the General Assembly of the Free Church of Scotland, 1890* (1890), pp. 111–15.

figure. But in his very able defence Bruce argued that (however infelicitous his expressions) he had as an apologist to deal with difficult topics, that he merited indulgence for tackling a new field of study, and – above all – that, though his view of inspiration might differ from the conservatives', he was like them absolutely convinced of the unique, divine character of Holy Scripture.[23] Once again, the case was dropped. Twelve years later, in 1902, came the last of the great heresy trials. George Adam Smith, Professor of Old Testament in the United Free Church College, Glasgow, had published a volume of lectures, *Modern Criticism and the Preaching of the Old Testament*, which contained assertions that Jewish religion before the eighth century BC was polytheistic in character, that the early chapters of Genesis were unhistorical, and that the lives of the patriarchs had their 'fanciful' elements. The Church's College Committee, however, refused to indict him. Their report agreed with much of what he had written, and contended that to assign a late date to the 'Mosaic' legislation of the Pentateuch was not to cast doubt on the divine inspiration and authority of the Bible. In the end, the Assembly dismissed the case, though Smith's views were neither accepted nor rejected and scholars were warned to be careful what they said.[24] Clearly, the atmosphere had greatly changed since 1881.

In the decades immediately before the First World War the traditional view of Scripture had been driven to the remote fringes of ecclesiastical and academic life. A host of well-respected scholars was at work applying the new principles and methods to every part and aspect of Holy Scripture, converting ministers and members to agree with them, and publishing a flood of commentaries, translations and dictionary articles. The allegedly 'assured' results of literary and historical criticism were confidently spoken of. A developmental account of Israel's religion was becoming the rule rather than the exception, and the inerrancy of the biblical narratives found fewer and fewer defendants. The kind of assertions for which Robertson Smith was condemned had lost their power to shock. More and more frequently, open

[23] Ibid., pp. 169–73.
[24] *Proceedings and Debates of the General Assembly of the United Free Church, 1902* (1902), pp. 87–118, and College Committee's Special Report xi A, p. 9, *Reports to the General Assembly of the United Free Church of Scotland* (1902).

acknowledgement was made of the diversity of attitudes found among the New Testament writers; and the 'quest of the historical Jesus' came to be pursued as eagerly in Scottish as in German universities. Yet despite all the activity, and the confidence, biblical scholarship in Scotland seldom manifested unbalanced or excessive enthusiasm for the new ideals. If A. B. Bruce adopted ever more radical views, his colleague James Orr moved steadily in the opposite direction; and James Denney, one of the ablest biblical scholars his country ever produced, pursued a notably middle-of-the-road course. Only the most prescient observer, however, could have foreseen the counter-revolution due to be effected in the 1940s and subsequently by the disciples of Karl Barth and the devotees of American fundamentalism.

The prevailing attitude to Scripture at the close of the period under review may be found conveniently expressed in Marcus Dods's *The Bible: Its Origin and Nature* (1905). In it he made the following points. On revelation: 'Those books which form our Bible are all in direct connection with God's historical revelation which culminated in Christ.' Consequently, 'If anyone wishes to know what God is in His relation to men . . . it is to the Bible appeal must be made. And therefore the Bible may itself legitimately, if loosely, be called the revelation.'[25] On inspiration: all preconceived notions of what it ought to be or accomplish must be rejected. It cannot mean inerrancy, for 'Had verbal accuracy been required for our saving use of the Bible, it would have been secured. It has not been secured, therefore it was not required.' Nor are we to think of it as present in some parts of the Bible and absent from others. What we *can* say is that it is not the *ipsissima verba* of Scripture that were inspired but the writers themselves. Inspiration 'enables its possessor to see and apprehend God and His will, and to impart to other men what he himself has apprehended'; and if Scripture gives us a trust-worthy account of the divine self-revelation (as it does) we have no need to claim that every phrase or word has God's authority behind it.[26] On infallibility: this does not mean inerrancy, for criticism, 'with a virtually unanimous voice', has ruled that out in the case of either Testament. What it does mean is complete

[25] M. Dods, *The Bible: Its Origin and Nature* (1905), pp. 23 and 95–6.
[26] Ibid., ch. 4, esp. pp. 112 and 127.

reliability in conveying to us 'a sufficient knowledge of Christ' and of the divine self-revelation which was consummated in Him. In the end of the day, therefore, it is Scripture's 'self-evidencing power' which persuades us to accept it as the Word of God – and which enables Dods to assure his readers that 'if it is spiritual guidance . . . man is in search of then you may refer him absolutely to the Bible'.[27]

Throughout our period, opponents of criticism nearly always linked it with unbelief. In actual fact, however, one of the most arresting facts about Scottish biblical scholarship between, say, 1860 and 1914 was its leaders' success in combining critical practice with a fervently expressed Christian faith and deep involvement in the life of the Church. Of A. B. Davidson, criticism's true founding father in Scotland, his biographer tells us that 'He never put Historical Criticism first. To him it was only the handmaid of religion.'[28] The arch-heretic (according to some reckonings), Robertson Smith, was equally affirmative, and in one of his earliest controversial writings stated a conviction from which he never departed:

> I receive Scripture as the Word of God and as the only perfect rule of faith and life . . . because in the Bible alone I find God drawing near to men in Christ Jesus and declaring to us in Him His will for our salvation. And this record I know to be true by the witness of His Spirit in my heart, whereby I am assured that none other than God Himself is able to speak such words to my soul.[29]

One of Smith's most enthusiastic supporters, Professor J. S. Candlish of Glasgow Free Church College, made his standpoint sufficiently clear in the title of a pamphlet he issued during the trial: *The Authority of Scripture Independent of Criticism*. A. B. Bruce delivered a like message: 'This', he told the Assembly in 1890, 'is a book by itself, the literature of a very real revelation which God has made to mankind through the Hebrew race. Whatever differences there may be among us . . . we are all at one on the main question.'[30] And Marcus Dods agreed. 'The affir-

[27] Ibid., ch. 5, esp. pp. 135, 152 and 162.
[28] J. Strahan, *Andrew Bruce Davidson* (1917), p. 249.
[29] Quoted from 'Answer to the Form of Libel', p. 21, in Lindsay, 'Professor Robertson Smith's Doctrine', p. 250.
[30] *Proceedings and Debates* (1890), p. 175.

mation of inaccuracy in certain details', he informed the College Committee in 1905, 'has assuredly a bearing on one's theory of inspiration; but it does not, on my part, involve the slightest hesitation as to the divine authority of Scripture, the pervading influence which makes it God's Word.'[31]

This belief in the compatibility of faith and criticism, which had sustained many Scottish scholars throughout the century of change, remained a dominant influence in the life and work of their immediate successors – as the writings of H. R. Mackintosh and James Moffatt (to name only two) bear ample witness. The former, Scotland's finest systematic theologian between James Denney and John Baillie, believed, like T. M. Lindsay before him, that the new approach to Scripture realised some basic insights of early Protestantism; and he transmitted that message with an eloquence which revealed his own heart-felt agreement. Writing in 1924, he recalled how the Reformers, while clearly distinguishing between the Bible and the Word of God, nonetheless 'never lost sight of the cardinal point that it is only in and through the Bible that God's word of mercy and judgment reaches us'. And in the same article he united a commendation of criticism with a summons to faith.

> The whole Reformation view of Christianity is bound up with a historical treatment of Scripture. But that is only a half truth. The other half, of still greater importance, is that nothing but the Spirit of God in the heart of the believer enables him to realise that in very truth it is God, and none else, who is seen in the history.[32]

Moffatt, then probably the world's best-known New Testament scholar, argued in his *Approach to the New Testament* (1921) that the obvious drawbacks of literary and historical criticism were either 'incidental defects' or 'temporary pains of growth', whereas 'What the historical approach means, is that a truer estimate of the writings is put forward than could be reached so long as they were regarded as equally and verbally inspired.'[33] And in the introduction to his pioneering translation

[31] Quoted from College Committee's Special Report, in H. F. Henderson, *The Religious Controversies of Scotland* (1905), p. 239.

[32] H. R. Mackintosh, 'The Reformers' View of Scripture' in C. Gore, *The Doctrine of the Infallible Book* (1924), pp. 56–7.

[33] J. Moffatt, *The Approach to the New Testament* (1921), pp. 235 and 206.

of the whole Bible (1926), after quoting the preface to the Authorised Version of 1611, he commented: 'These words put nobly the chief end of reading the Bible, and the object of any version' (might he have added, of all critical study as well?): 'it is to stir and sustain present faith in a living God who spoke and speaks.'[34] With such testimonies this survey of biblical scholarship in Scotland's century of change may be brought to a not inappropriate close.

RECOMMENDED FURTHER READING

Black, J. S. and G. W. Chrystal, *The Life of William Robertson Smith* (1912)

Cheyne, A. C., *The Transforming of the Kirk: Victorian Scotland's Religious Revolution* (1983)

Drummond, A. L., and J. Bulloch, *The Church in Victorian Scotland, 1843–1874* (1975)
The Church in Victorian Scotland, 1874–1900 (1978)

Greenslade, S. L. (ed.), *The Cambridge History of the Bible: The West from the Reformation to the Present Day* (1963), esp. chs 7 and 8.

Johnstone, W. (ed.), *William Robertson Smith: Essays in Reassessment* (1995)

McFadyen, J. E., *The Approach to the Old Testament* (1926)

Moffatt, J., *The Approach to the New Testament* (1921)

Riesen, R., *Criticism and Faith in Late Victorian Scotland: A. B. Davidson, William Robertson Smith and George Adam Smith* (1985)

---

[34] J. Moffatt, Introduction to *The Moffatt Translation of the Bible* (1957), p. xlv.

Chapter 7

Church Reform and Church Defence: The Contribution of John Tulloch (1823–86)

Nineteenth-century Scotland gave at least four incontestably great men to ecclesiastical history: Thomas Chalmers the church leader, John McLeod Campbell the theologian, David Livingstone the missionary explorer and William Robertson Smith the biblical scholar and pioneer of what used to be called comparative religion. While hardly ranking with them, there was a second cohort of able and devoted figures – Edward Irving, Alexander Duff, Hugh Miller, Norman MacLeod, John Cairns, Robert Rainy and George Macdonald spring to mind – who played important parts in the nation's life, its religion, literature and learning. Among these must be included Principal John Tulloch of St Mary's College, St Andrews.[1]

Born in 1823 in the Perthshire village of Dron, where his father was parish minister, young Tulloch went to the University of St Andrews for the study of Arts and Divinity. Although his academic performance was hardly outstanding, the authorities must have glimpsed his potential, for he spent only a short time in parish work, first in Dundee and then in Kettins (Angus), before being selected by the government of the day for the much-sought-after dual appointment of Principal of St Mary's and Professor of Theology in his old university. There he remained from 1854 until his death in 1886. While frequently lamenting the meagre financial provision made for himself and his family, and sometimes tempted by the ampler opportunities which chairs at Glasgow and Edinburgh seemed to offer, he nevertheless found much to delight him in the quiet but sociable East Neuk of Fife; and almost

---

[1] There is a good, if typically Victorian, biography by Margaret Oliphant, *A Memoir of the Life of John Tulloch, D.D., L.L.D* (1888).

the only shadow upon his enjoyment of academic office, its duties and its privileges, was cast by the mysterious and desolating attacks of nervous depression which dogged him from early manhood to the very brink of old age.

He travelled far during the incredibly long vacations of that halcyon age, poured out a stream of articles and books (most important being *Rational Theology and Christian Philosophy in England in the Seventeenth Century*, his *magnum opus*, and the St Giles Lectures for 1885 on *Movements of Religious Thought in Britain during the Nineteenth Century*), dabbled not unhappily in university politics, and lectured with acceptance to his small but admiring classes. He served as one of the Commissioners of the Board of Education set up in 1872, and played an active part in the negotiations for university reform which bore fruit in the Acts of 1858 and 1889. For a short time at the end of the 1870s, he was editor of *Fraser's Magazine*; and his friendships came to include some of the best-known literary personalities of the day. He eventually acquired a standing with Scottish church folk – and with their queen – similar to that enjoyed a little earlier by Norman MacLeod and a little later by John Caird. In 1878 he was called to the Moderatorship of the General Assembly of the Church of Scotland.

Such a story enables us to understand how Tulloch's death in 1886 seemed to many like the end of an era. Within his lifetime the Auld Kirk, recovering from the shock administered to it by the Disruption (which took place towards the close of his training for the ministry), gradually acquired some expertise in dealing with the challenges of urban, industrialised society, forged new evangelical weapons and refurbished old ones, discarded many of the constraints imposed upon it by seventeenth-century Puritanism, refashioned its worship on more catholic lines, and set about redefining its relationship to the system of doctrine whose best-known formularies are the Shorter Catechism and the Westminster Confession of Faith; and few, if any, of the Church's servants could claim a greater responsibility for the transformation brought about in the Scottish religious scene by all that than John Tulloch. One of the most eminent and influential representatives of Scotland's 'Broad Church' school – and, incidentally, a staunch friend and admirer of his opposite number in England, Dean Stanley of Westminster – he led the way in the revolutionising of the Presbyterian *Weltanschauung* which took place between 1850 and 1900; and towards the end of his life he came, rightly, to be regarded as the very embodiment of the liberal churchmanship of the Victorian period.

In seeking to summarise the characteristic beliefs and attitudes of Tulloch the church reformer (the first part of this study), we may conveniently focus our attention on four quite short addresses which he gave to academic and other audiences during the first twenty or so years of his teaching career: the inaugural lecture, 'Theological Tendencies of the Age', delivered at St Andrews in 1854; an introductory (opening-of-session) lecture, without a title, delivered there ten years later; an address on 'Theological Controversy' given to Edinburgh University Theological Society in 1865; and 'Religion and Theology: a sermon for the times', preached in Crathie parish church in 1875. The following themes occur and recur in these highly personal yet, at the same time, carefully considered programmatic statements:

1. *Devotion to 'inquiry' and an intense dislike of 'dogmatism'*

Tulloch was always well aware, particularly in the middle years of his life, that the spirit of unbelief – of 'anti-supernaturalism' and 'subjective criticism' – was abroad in Victorian Britain. 'There is', he once remarked, 'much of a negative and doubtful character in the mere literary atmosphere we are all breathing.'[2] But he differed from many of his contemporaries in maintaining that against such a foe ecclesiastical condemnation was of little avail, and could in fact do much positive harm. 'I must venture to say', he told his young hearers in 1864,

> that the most ominous and saddening signs I can see on the religious horizon are not the spirit of inquiry, whether within the church or without it, but the unreasoning dogmatism with which in many cases this spirit has been met. The spirit of inquiry may be harmful . . . but it is not necessarily either injurious or dangerous; while one has only to open any page of the New Testament, or study any century of Christendom from the beginning, to see that a blind and angry dogmatism is no weapon of spiritual warfare, and can never advance the cause of truth.[3]

[2] Introductory Lecture (no title, 1864), p. 11.
[3] Ibid., p. 10.

Moreover, the type of unbelief at work in the fifties and sixties was such as to render violent dogmatism peculiarly inappropriate. 'The assailants of the old views of Christianity', he observed, 'are for the most part of philosophical temper, and of quiet thoughtfulness. They can only be met with any success in a corresponding spirit, with the weapons of a higher thoughtfulness, a more conspicuous moderation, and a fairer learning.'[4] Quoting the advice of one of his heroes, John Hales, that 'If it be the cause of God which we handle in our writings, then let us handle it like the prophets of God, with quietness and moderation, and not in the violence of passion, as if we were possessed rather than inspired,' Tulloch continued:

> There is no higher task for the Christian reason in every age than to vindicate the eternal basis of Christianity as a truth for the reason no less than for the conscience and the heart, as the highest philosophy no less than the highest expediency To abdicate this rational ground of defence is to confess the Gospel to be a superstition – to acknowledge a hopeless schism between reason and conscience, between philosophy and religion. . . . No doubt the Church has its rights of utterance – its power to condemn as well as its duty to inquire and defend – but none the less true is it that men no longer heed utterances which are not weighty in argument as well as in tone, nor bow before a condemnation which is not reasoned as well as authoritative.[5]

Gentle and level-headed inquiry, dialogue rather than denunciation, are what Tulloch admired and was ever seeking to commend.

2. Conviction that neither undiluted Traditionalism nor undiluted Rationalism is the way to Truth

The greater part of Tulloch's inaugural lecture in 1854 was devoted to a discussion, and rejection, of two prominent tendencies in theology and religious life which he believed to be characteristic of his time. There was, in the first place, what he called traditionalism, by which he meant 'not merely the recognition of an element of traditional authority in theological investigations . . . but the exclusive supremacy of this element in some shape or another'.[6] One of its chief manifestations was in the Anglo-

---

[4] Ibid., pp. 10–11.
[5] Ibid., p. 14.
[6] 'Theological Tendencies of the Age' (Inaugural Lecture, 1854), pp. 6–7.

Catholic school, for whom (he contended) 'the great question in matters of doctrine was not "What saith Scripture, under the scrutiny of reason or the Christian consciousness?" but "What saith the Church?"'[7] Tulloch was not insensitive to the virtues of the Oxford Movement, as he shows in the closing pages of his chapter on it in *Movements of Religious Thought*; and the Inaugural also contains a glowing tribute:

> The genuine earnestness of the men who first engaged in it, and the depth of sacred conviction from which it has sprung, will not be denied by any who have given it their candid attention; and we must no less acknowledge the consummate scholarship, the range and subtlety of intellect, the fine and beautiful comprehension often of the real import of the Church's history ... especially, perhaps, the exquisite literary skill displayed in the writings which it has called forth.

At the same time, however, he rejected Anglo-Catholicism as being 'utterly opposed to our sympathies', and used the phrase 'purely disastrous' to describe its effects on Christian theology.[8]

The other manifestation of traditionalism, which Tulloch found even less congenial, was old-style Evangelicalism as he encountered it in his own country. It too (according to him) rejected the claims of reason and conscience, this time in the interest of a narrowly confessional interpretation of Holy Scripture; and once again the consequences were devastating.

> The general evidence of this traditional tendency [he wrote] ... is a slavish adherence to certain religious formulae – a timid cowering from the glance of Reason as something which it is felt somehow ought to be acknowledged, but which it is not known how to acknowledge. . . . However it may profess to acknowledge the right of private judgment, there is nothing less known, and nothing less tolerated by the adherents of this school than any free and fruitful exercise of this right. Authority, in fact, has here, in certain cases, established itself in a far more inflexible, as in a far less dignified and impressive form, than in Catholicism. And as irresistible evidence of this, we find this school, of all, the most utterly destitute of a living and learned theology.[9]

One can understand why Tulloch, having condemned Evangelicalism for its basic irrationality, would sympathise with men

[7] Ibid., p. 8.
[8] Ibid., p. 9.
[9] Ibid., pp. 10–11.

like Irving and Erskine of Linlathen and McLeod Campbell (all of whom had run up against it) and with F. W. Robertson (who had thrown it off after a struggle). His frank enthusiasm for Coleridge also becomes comprehensible, for it was Coleridge – he believed – who 'once more in his age made Christian doctrine alive to the Reason as well as the Conscience – tenable as a philosophy as well as an evangel'.[10]

But if Tulloch eschewed traditionalism he felt equally unhappy with the most obvious alternative to it, namely rationalism. In each and all of its many forms (he himself referred to the 'positive', the 'intellectual', the 'intuitional' and that associated with the name of Friedrich Schleiermacher) its aim seemed to be 'to find the determining element of theological truth in some purely inward or subjective standard'; and with this he could not agree.[11] If the original revelation of Reason is not to be rejected,' he told his students, 'the later objective revelation in Scripture must withal remain the standard and arbiter of Truth. . . .The Bible must be acknowledged as not only co-ordinate with Reason, but as forming, in all points of religious truth, the ultimate *determining* authority.'[12] And although by the end of his life Tulloch had somewhat modified his hostility to Schleiermacher, his favourable comments in *Movements of Religious Thought* on Julius Hare and Connop Thirlwall and other disciples of the great German theologian imply no fundamental change in his position.[13] That, as his criticisms of John Stuart Mill and others also reveal, remained to the end what it had been in the 1850s.[14] In the words of his Inaugural, he opposed rationalism 'not because it embraces a subjective element of determination in Theological Science, but because in different forms it embraces nothing else', setting up 'the shifting standard of the human spirit' as the sole arbiter of Christian truth and science.[15] And his conclusion on the whole matter was as follows:

---

[10] *Movements of Religious Thought in Britain during the Nineteenth Century* (Victorian Library re-issue, 1971), p. 19.
[11] 'Theological Tendencies', p. 13.
[12] Ibid., p. 30.
[13] *Movements of Religious Thought*, pp. 34–8, 75–9.
[14] Ibid., ch. 6, passim.
[15] 'Theological Tendencies', p. 27.

On the one hand, we can have no fruitful and vigorous Theology without the continual, ever-renewed inquest of free criticism – practical religion, even, perishes under its decay: on the other hand, the Bible must ever limit and bind all such progressive inquiries, for here we have no longer the word of man but the word of God. . . . Its light, therefore, must at once guide and circumscribe our onward course.[16]

3. Historical approach to all credal formulations

As an appendix to the published version of his 1865 lecture to Edinburgh University Theological Society on *Theological Controversy, or the Function of Debate in Theology*, Tulloch printed some notes on the Westminster Confession of Faith which are of interest as condensing his views on a subject which exercised the Scottish mind throughout the greater part of the century. Observing that the propriety of confessions of faith would soon become a crucial question for Christian people, he called for historical and philosophical study of the Church of Scotland's 'subordinate standard'. 'The Confession of Faith in its origin and in its principles', he claimed, 'was the manifesto of a great religious party which, after a fierce conflict, gained a temporary ascendancy in England and Scotland.' And he went on:

> Indeed, the same thing could be said of every Protestant Confession of Faith. . . . They are one and all historical monuments, marking the tides of religious thought as they have swelled with greater fullness in the course of the Christian centuries; and none of them can be understood aright simply by themselves, or as isolated dogmatic utterances, but only in connection with their time and the genius and character of the men who framed them.

The consequences of such a view were far reaching. In Tulloch's words:

> The popular ecclesiastical notion of creeds and confessions as in some sense absolute expressions of Christian truth – *credenda* to be accepted very much as we accept the statements of Scripture itself – is a notion . . . which every student deserving the name has long since abandoned. Those creeds and confessions are neither more nor less than the intellectual labours of great and good men assembled for the most part in synods or councils, all of which, as our Confession

[16] Ibid., p. 32.

itself declares, 'may err, and many have erred'. They are stamped with the infirmities no less than the nobleness of the men who made them. They are *their* best thoughts about Christian truth as they saw it in their time – intrinsically they are nothing more; and any claim of infallibility for them is the worst of all kinds of Popery – that Popery which degrades the Christian reason while it fails to nourish the Christian imagination.[17]

Tulloch's historical approach to all credal statements is, of course, only one aspect of his tendency to view a very wide range of questions, and particularly biblical ones, from the historical angle. In this he revealed himself as sharing in – and helping to spread – a mood which had begun to establish its ascendancy over the cultivated intellect of Britain round about the middle of last century. It was a mood which (to quote a historian from our own time) inclined to view Truth 'no longer as absolute, philosophically static, revealed once for all, but as relative, genetic and evolutionary';[18] and for theology its implications were tremendous. If Tulloch did not see all of them, he at least saw some; and his teaching was the more valuable in consequence.

4. Hatred of 'bibliolatry', and a cautious confidence in the methods of biblical criticism

Few things annoyed Tulloch more than what he called 'subjective criticism' – meaning by that an essentially unsympathetic and hypercritical attitude to the Bible. Such criticism, he averred in his introductory lecture at St Andrews in 1864, 'partakes of the very spirit of unbelief – the spirit, namely, which refuses to recognise a divine revelation at all – sets its own light against the light of God, its own reason against the divine reason in Scripture'.[19] Yet even here his essential moderation shows itself, for he never falls into the opposite error of 'bibliolatry', never asserts the absolute identity of the Bible with the Word of God. Although he can affirm that 'The facts of an objective revelation, and that Scripture contains such a revelation, are primary and constitutive facts of Christianity,' he nevertheless also contends that 'not only

---

[17] 'Theological Controversy' (1865), pp. 26–7.
[18] N. Annan, 'The Strands of Unbelief', in *Ideas and Beliefs of the Victorians* (1949), p. 151.
[19] Introductory Lecture (1864), pp. 14–15.

does Christianity not dread – it demands, as a condition of its higher intelligent life, that the several books of Scripture, as the successive media of divine revelation through a long series of ages, should be minutely investigated, tested and proved by all the aids of criticism, and by all the growing light of the Christian consciousness.'[20] He counsels us, moreover, to learn to distinguish between the Divine revelation in Scripture on the one hand and our inherited beliefs, prejudices and conceits on the other. This relaxed attitude towards the literary and historical approach to Scripture – this belief, as he put it, that 'the Christian reason must have room to work'[21] – is clearly evident throughout Tulloch's writings. It appears not only in the approval given to Coleridge's liberal views on the subject but also in the complimentary references made to the exegetical labours of Arthur Stanley and Benjamin Jowett. 'From this time,' he once wrote of the year 1855, when both these men published commentaries on Pauline epistles,

> has greatly advanced that profounder study of the New Testament, which looks beyond its traditional to its real aspects and its organic relation to contemporary usage and opinion – which sees in it a living literature, and not a mere repertory of doctrinal texts. . . . The text of Scripture has been studied in its own meaning, and not in support of dogmas which were the growth of long after centuries, and would have been wholly unintelligible to the writers credited with them. The spirit has been liberated from the letter, and the very form and pressure of divine truth as originally presented to the world brought near to us.[22]

Crudities and even inconsistencies notwithstanding, this is a view which would still, nearly a century later, commend itself to a high proportion of theological scholars – which suggests that in reading Tulloch we not only survey the religious thought of a bygone period but also glimpse the shape of theologies yet to come.

5. Desire to distinguish between theology and religion

Tulloch's Crathie sermon of 1875 on 'Religion and Theology' makes a distinction which appears repeatedly in his writings. He

[20] Ibid., p. 16.
[21] Ibid., p. 17.
[22] *Movements of Religious Thought*, p. 332.

would not (so he tells his hearers) have them despise or disparage theology. But he wishes them to remember that the welfare of the soul is not determined by theology and its answer to such problems as 'the antiquity of man, the age and genesis of the earth, the origin and authority of the several books of Scripture'. These matters have to be dealt with, admittedly, and in dealing with them there is available to us 'no light but the dry light of knowledge'; yet the satisfaction of our spiritual requirements need not await their solution.

> Because I cannot be sure [he wrote] whether the Pentateuch was written, as long supposed, by Moses, or whether the Fourth Gospel comes as it stands from the beloved apostle, am I less in need of the divine teaching which both these Scriptures contain? Surely not. That I am a spiritual being, and have spiritual needs craving to be satisfied, and that God is a spiritual power above me, of whom Christ is the revelation, are facts which I may know or may not know, irrespective of such matters. The one class of facts are intellectual and literary. The other are spiritual if they exist at all. If I ever know them, I can only know them through my own spiritual experience; but if I know them . . . I have within me all the genuine forces of religious strength and peace.

Better than all theological definitions, therefore, is 'the honest and good heart' which (in the Gospel phrase) 'having heard the Word, keeps it, and brings forth fruit with patience'.[23] And so Tulloch's last word on this matter is a summons to rigorous inquiry on the theological level, together with quiet receptivity on the religious level. As he told the congregation at Crathie:

> I have no ready answers to your questions, no short and easy method with modern scepticism. Inquiry must have its course in theology as in everything else. It is fatal to intelligence to talk of an infallible Church, and of all free thought in reference to religion as deadly rationalism to be shunned. . . . You must examine your own hearts; you must try yourselves whether there be in you the roots of the divine life. If you do not find sin in your hearts and Christ also there as the Saviour from sin, then you will find Him nowhere. But if you find him there . . . then you will accept difficulties and doubts, and even the despairing darkness of some intellectual moments, when

[23] 'Religion and Theology' (1875), pp. 10–13.

the very foundations seem to give way, as you accept other trials; and, looking humbly for higher light, you will patiently wait for it, until the day dawn and the shadows flee away.[24]

There are echoes here not only of Tulloch's beloved Caroline Divines, but also of the views of Coleridge and F. D. Maurice and (still more) of F. W. Robertson and Scotland's Thomas Erskine.

To sum up what has been discovered so far, I think we can say that Tulloch's message as a church reformer was, above all else, a summons to humility of spirit and receptivity of mind. Change, he constantly asseverated, is always at work in human affairs, even where the most apparently immutable attitudes or systems are concerned, and in the world of the intellect to be immobile is to be dead. Let us, therefore, be prepared to abandon old shibboleths and to welcome new insights; and let dogmatists – especially Scottish ones! – never forget that God's truth is larger than their imperfect notions of it and that 'the movements of Christian thought are for this very end, that we may prove all things and hold fast that which is good'.[25] And, as he puts it in the closing sentences of his last book:

> What we perhaps all need most to learn is not satisfaction with our opinions – that is easily acquired by most – but the capacity of looking beyond our own horizon; of searching for deeper foundations of our ordinary beliefs, and a more sympathetic appreciation of the beliefs of others. While cherishing, therefore, what we ourselves feel to be true, let us keep our minds open to all truth, and especially to the teaching of Him who is 'the Way, the Truth and the Life'.[26]

Tulloch's 'broad church' convictions eventually won through to respectability, and even acclaim, within his own denomination and beyond it. He was (as we have seen) elevated to the Moderatorship in 1878, and during the closing years of his life he was accorded a virtually unique status in academic and other circles. To him, along with Norman MacLeod and John Caird, was chiefly due the markedly liberal character of their denomination in late-Victorian times. But no sooner had he weathered one storm than another – politico-ecclesiastical, this

[24] Ibid., pp. 21–2.
[25] *Movements of Religious Thought*, p. 335.
[26] Ibid., pp. 335–6.

time, rather than theological – burst upon him; and the last ten or fifteen years of the Principal's life were largely spent in battling not for the liberalisation of the Church of Scotland but (at least in his understanding of things) for its very survival.

*   *   *

Percipient observers are nowadays inclined to think that danger lights had been flashing for the Auld Kirk ever since the extension of the franchise in 1867 and the formation of Gladstone's crusading first ministry soon afterwards. But it seems to have been the disestablishment of the Irish Church in 1869 which really gave the signal for Scotland's Presbyterian Dissenters – virtually all the United Presbyterians, and a very high proportion of Free Church men – to launch a campaign for the disestablishment and disendowment of the Church of Scotland, a campaign that came within an ace of success on more than one occasion during the next two or three decades. At the very time when the Auld Kirk, at last on the way to recovery from the trauma of the Disruption, was trying to persuade Parliament to free it from the age-old incubus of patronage and so to pave the way for a reunification of Scottish Presbyterianism within the walls of the national Zion, the United Presbyterian Church (led by Principal John Cairns) and the Free Church (led by Principal Robert Rainy) began to speak with one voice in favour of the destruction of that same establishment.

On 6 May 1872, in Edinburgh, Cairns fired the first great salvo in the campaign with a long and careful lecture on dis-establishment. It would, he argued, advance the cause of Christian truth and sound doctrine, for (alluding to the rationalism and latitudinarianism within the Church of Scotland) 'the whole tendency of Established Churches is to greater and greater latitude'.[27] It would also promote Christian freedom: '[The Auld Kirk] has practically enjoyed a great deal of liberty; but, like a ship swinging by a lengthened cable, has been liable at any moment to be drawn up to the anchor of State jurisdiction.'[28] It would, furthermore, serve as a much-needed encouragement to financial

[27] 'Disestablishment of the Church of Scotland' (1872), p. 13.
[28] Ibid., p. 15.

liberality among the members of the Established Church; and in Cairns's opinion it was the only sure path to the reunion and reconstruction of Scottish Presbyterianism. Principal Rainy soon came to the same conclusion. He told the Free Church General Assembly of 1872 that 'his conviction was growing day by day that the only solution was Disestablishment';[29] and when, with the return of the Conservatives in 1874, Parliament finally acceded to the Church of Scotland's wish for the ending of patronage as traditionally understood, the consequent legislation did little more than push Rainy and the Free Church across the thin dividing line between unease with the Establishment and outright antipathy to it. At a crowded meeting in Edinburgh, Rainy was openly critical of the Government's recent action, commenting:

> They resolved to transfer the existing rights of patrons, rights older than the Reformation, to a broader constituency. But it has been made perfectly clear in the process that they will not look at the question on which the Disruption turned. They have altered, in one respect, the constitution of the Church of Scotland, but they will not contemplate the possibility of an Establishment on any other principle than that principle of subjection which the lawcourts declared and the State confirmed in 1843.[30]

In other words, no radical change had taken place – and a mitigated evil is still an evil. Recalling Chalmers's appeal for 'an independent jurisdiction in things ecclesiastical', 'a comprehensive measure of adjustment', and his assertion that nothing less would satisfy, Rainy expressed regret that 'Nothing of that kind is in view now . . . State and Church, on a fresh consideration of the whole case, join together to make their rearrangement on the footing that the independence which we [i.e. the secessionists of 1843] claimed for Christ's Church, and for the sake of which we separated from the State, is quite unreasonable and ought not to be thought of.'[31] The only solution, therefore, was Disestablishment; and Chalmers's successor in the leadership of the Free Church boldly affirmed his belief that 'the termination of the existing connection with the State will do no harm to the

---

[29] P. C. Simpson, *The Life of Principal Rainy* (1909), vol. I, p. 267.
[30] R. Rainy, Speech in Music Hall, Edinburgh, Dec. 1874 (1874), p. 8.
[31] Ibid., pp. 9–10.

ministers of the Establishment, no harm to the people, no harm to the country, no harm to the cause of Christ'.[32]

As early as May 1872, the Synod of the United Presbyterian Church set up a Disestablishment Committee; two years later, the Free Church did the same; and in 1877 its General Assembly definitely pronounced in favour of disestablishment. For at least twenty years thereafter the Church of Scotland was under fairly continuous threat, though circumstances looked less menacing while the Conservatives held power at Westminster between 1874 and 1880. How was the danger to be met? It may be said that the Auld Kirk's leaders – Tulloch conspicuous among them – decided on a three-fold strategy, each part of which was pursued in close connection with the others. First, they developed what might be called a philosophy of establishment in answer to the criticisms of the Voluntaries; second, they alerted their fellow-churchmen to the baneful potentialities of the situation, as well as acquainting them with the arguments that could be proffered in the Church's defence; and third, they exerted pressure upon the politicians (especially Liberal ones, whose links with Dissent created many problems) to dissuade them from responding favourably to the increasingly vociferous calls for disestablishment that were addressed to them. Our next task, therefore, is to examine Tulloch's part in the execution of this programme, paying special attention to his defence of establishments in general and of the Church of Scotland in particular. And our reliance will be placed in the main upon the speeches which he made in the General Assemblies of 1878 (as Moderator), 1882, 1883 and 1885 (the last two as convener of the Church Interests Committee, for whose creation he had been largely responsible), together with the 1885 'Address to the People of Scotland' (of which he was the chief signatory), and his final utterance on the subject, the posthumously published St Giles Lecture of 1886 on 'National Religion in Theory and Fact'.

One of the Principal's main concerns at this time is to highlight the various misconceptions on which – in his estimation – the disestablishment case is based.

a. There are, to begin with, the related notions that the National Church is a mere creation of the State (or, at best, the

32 Ibid., p. 16.

beneficiary of a concordat with the State), and that any connection between Church and State is inevitably harmful to spiritual interests. The former is a distortion of history:

> The Church of Scotland as it now exists is no doubt, in its civil rights and privileges, a parliamentary institution. The act of the first Scottish parliament of William and Mary, in the spring of 1690 (April 25), established the Presbyterian creed, church government, and discipline. In other words, established and ratified, in its present form, the Church of Scotland. But not only was the reformed church already in existence as the religion of the people, but the reformed church itself was only a new outcome of Scottish religious faith which, from the beginning, had been one of the most powerful elements of the national civilisation. At no period of Scottish history, many as are its transformations, can religion be said to have been formally adopted by the government and set up for its own purposes.[33]

The latter notion (on the harmfulness of the Church–State connection) errs even more seriously in that it disjoins the spiritual and the natural, the sacred and the secular.

Tulloch contends:

> The truth is that nowhere can the spiritual be isolated and caught by itself. . . . The Church is distinct from the world in idea, but never in fact. . . . To suppose a Church to be more spiritual because it has clothed itself, so to speak, with a body of its own, instead of having fitted itself to the national organisation and order, is simply an imagination without any true meaning when analysed. The Voluntary theory, therefore, or the theory of a radical divorce in the nature of things between Church and State is not only unhistorical, but essentially unveracious. There can be no such divorce. Every church, by its mere existence, entwines itself more or less with the State, and incurs legal relations and obligations. The higher attributes of the State . . . imply the working of Christian principles within it, or in other words, an incorporate religious life; and again the Church, by its simple activities, by the fact that it is a body and constitution as well as a soul, touches the State, with its complex machinery of law and order, at every point. Instead of being separate, or tending to separate, they tend to merge at every point, and to run up into the same magnificent ideal.[34]

[33] 'National Religion in Theory and Fact' (1886), pp. 42–3.
[34] Ibid., pp. 64–6.

b. Another favourite contention of the Voluntaries was that the very existence of an Established Church violated the great principle of 'equality'. But in the appeal 'To the People of Scotland', which was issued in the run up to the elections of 1885, Tulloch sees this 'dubious' word as summarising 'all in the shape of general argument that is put forward for the destruction of the Church', and counters with the dictum that 'What is called "religious equality" becomes, when fairly looked at, a gross injustice.'

> 'What is required', it is said, 'is *religious equality* in the eye of the law for every denomination of Christians.' But are not all denominations – Protestants and Catholics, Presbyterians, Free Church, United Presbyterian, Episcopalian – already equal in the eye of the law? Each and all are equally free to worship God according to their conscience. Free Churchmen and United Presbyterians are certainly not repelled from the parish church by any difference of creed, worship, or government. They simply prefer their own Church. But why should they on this account wish to destroy the parish church as a national institution? What is this but to say – We do not differ from you in creed or worship, but because we don't go to the parish church you shall not have it to go to. Of our own will we refuse a share in the old endowments, and we will not let you have a share, however content you may be with your portion.... any property we have is our own, but the property of the parish church is 'national' – ours as much as yours; and we intend to take it from you, and from the poor who have so long enjoyed it. Is there anything Christian in such an argument as this?

And so his contentions reach their forceful conclusion:

> No equality can be violated where no rights are invaded. *There are no rights of Dissenters affected by the existence of the parish church.* If I am entitled equally with others to a share of anything of which I am deprived, my rights would be invaded. But if I am offered my share and decline to have it, preferring something else, what right have I to complain? That I should not only decline my own share, but insist that others on my account shall have no share, is surely the height of absurdity and injustice.[35]

c. As the above makes abundantly clear, on the Voluntaries' agenda for Scottish reconstruction disendowment was almost

---

[35] 'Address to the People of Scotland' (1885), pp. 6–8.

indissociably connected with disestablishment. It is hardly surprising, therefore, that Tulloch devoted a good deal of attention over the years to the argument that the teinds were either an unjustifiable tax on the people or a gift from the State which could at any time be removed from the Church's possession and devoted to other – secular – purposes. Of his many trenchant remarks on the subject, what he had to say towards the very end of his life is particularly worth noting.

In the Church Interests Committee's address 'To the People of Scotland' in 1885 he declared:

> It cannot be too clearly borne in mind that the teinds, which are the support of the Church, are in no sense a tax upon the community. They do not cost the people anything. They are an ancient property belonging to the Church, for the religious benefit of the people. . . . The opponents of the Church are driven to sad shifts when in this, as in other instances, they are compelled in the face of facts to misrepresent Scottish history.[36]

And he develops the same theme at greater length in his St Giles Lecture of 1886 on 'National Religion in Theory and Fact', where he remarks:

> There can be nothing less true to the facts of the case or evidence of history, than to suppose that what is called the 'State Church' in either country [England or Scotland] has been called into being merely by State legislation, and endowed by State funds, and that it is equally competent for the State to withdraw what is called its support as it was originally to bestow it. What was never bestowed may, no doubt, be withdrawn by legislative power, because this power is in a certain sense omnipotent in relation to all privilege and property; but certainly there is no ordinary sense in which it can be said that the revenues of the Church were created and allocated by the State. They were the gifts of individuals, for the spiritual benefit of the people, and in a true sense, therefore, the property of the Church so long as used consistently with their original gift. Any wanton interference with the property of the Church is as unjustifiable, therefore, as interference with any other species of property. . . . The revenues really belong to the parishes in which they are gathered, for a definite purpose, and they can only be alienated by repudiating, not merely ancient law and usage, but considerations of moral equity and government.[37]

[36] Ibid., pp. 5–6.
[37] 'National Religion', pp. 61–2.

d. Underlying all that the disestablishers said and did (so Tulloch believed) was the assumption that religion is essentially a private, domestic matter – whereas in his opinion it was, and must be, inextricably bound up with the organised existence of the entire community. 'Religion', he affirmed, 'cannot be separated from the fibre of our national existence, and placed on one side of it as something essentially apart from it, without injury – it may prove fatal injury – to our old power and greatness'; and he recalled how the young Gladstone had once remarked that 'We may tremble at the very thought of the degradation that she [the State] would undergo, should she, in an evil hour, repudiate her ancient strength, *the principle of national religion.*'[38] Still more memorably, in a speech of almost Burkean eloquence delivered at the Assembly of 1883, Tulloch repudiated the idea of a National Church as being 'a mere aggregation of endowed churches':

> It is an organisation of the spiritual life of the nation – an institution created by the nation and existing for its sake, embodying the great thought that religion is not merely a private but a public concern – that the civil aspect of society is merely one aspect of our national life inextricably intertwined with the higher religious aspect, which deserves recognition, organisation, and support, no less than the other. This alone makes a National Church in the true sense, and is the idea which really lies at the root both of the Church of England and of the Church of Scotland.... Every truly national institution rests on an ideal and not a merely material basis. It is the embodiment of some higher thought which has established itself in our national history, because it has first dominated and inspired our national intelligence. In this sense alone are National Churches absolutely defensible.... Is our national life to be Christian or not? Is the State a moral and not merely a secular reality? These are the real questions that underlie Establishment or Disestablishment.[39]

Being the Church of the whole nation, as Tulloch contends, the Church of Scotland is clearly not the preserve of the wealthier classes; and to suggest that it is constitutes a serious distortion of the truth – particularly in the aftermath of the 1874 Patronage Act and its democratisation of the ministerial election process. Phrases like 'the Church exists for the people of Scotland' and

[38] Ibid., p. 57.
[39] Quoted in M. Oliphant, *Memoir of Tulloch*, p. 421.

'what we should think of is the good of the people of Scotland' occur and recur in Tulloch's utterances; and he seems to go out of his way – perhaps in recollection of the still-remembered Chalmers tradition, perhaps in deference to the growing social consciousness of the 1870s and 1880s – to emphasise the special concern of National Churches for the well-being of their poorer citizens.

> The Gospel, [he affirms in 1886] has been in this generation 'preached to the poor' within the national churches as nowhere else. While prosperous Dissent in our large towns has been gradually removing its centres of worship and of Christian work from the poor and crowded localities to be found in all these towns, these churches have stepped in and taken its place, and prosecuted Christian agencies in a manner which the merely voluntary churches have hardly anywhere attempted. We say this in no spirit of boasting. God knows the national churches of our country should have awakened far earlier than they did to this most urgent work, and done still more than they have done; while our dissenting churches have had a share in the labours of love, and care for the poor, which have happily inspired modern Christianity. But nowhere has the modern spirit of philanthropy – a bright foil to many spots of darkness in our social atmosphere – been realised more vividly or worked out with more intelligent and solid results, than within the two national churches.[40]

At this point we should perhaps observe that Tulloch's indictment of Voluntaryism is directed not only against its basic convictions but also against its animating spirit, which is (in his opinion) one of jealousy, bitterness, dogmatism and illiberality. The jealousy is no doubt a reaction to the increased prosperity of the Church of Scotland, now recovering after its post-Disruption years in the wilderness. The bitterness is manifest in the many exaggerations of the disestablishment campaign. The dogmatism and illiberality are detectable, *inter alia,* in Cairns's strictures on the alleged rationalism and ritualism of the Auld Kirk, and move Tulloch to agree with his old friend, Dean Stanley, that 'Establishment is a liberal thing, and Dissent is both narrow and narrowing.' And there is yet more to be said. The Voluntary movement is disturbingly clerical in its composition and management. Because of its connections with Edward Miall's Liberation Society it is open to the charge of being an English export. Worst of all,

---

[40] 'National Religion', pp. 52–3.

its appearance of devotion cannot cloak its essentially irreligious associations and consequences. As early as 1838, Gladstone had suggested that the campaign for English disestablishment was impelled not only by the force of Nonconformity but by 'all the enemies of law, both human and divine': in his darker moments, Tulloch suspects that an equally sinister alliance may be at work in the Scotland of the 1880s.

> The State [he writes] is regarded as entirely secular in its constitution and origin, and to be worked without any religious reference whatever. So prevalent is this idea that it has become a commonplace even with many religious people – a commonplace used for political ends, without any clear understanding of the essential principle which lies involved in it, and how far it cuts into the heart of national life. . . . 'Religion is too sacred for politics'; 'the school is to teach secular, and the churches religious instruction'; 'no public funds must go to the teaching of religion in any form'; 'theology, instead of being, as in the old times, the queen of the sciences, is, strictly speaking, not knowledge at all, but only a sort of shadow or imagination of knowledge' – are the sort of sayings one hears everywhere. They mark the rise of that current of Secularism which is inundating the civilised world. Still more significantly than in Mr Gladstone's youth, they come not only from the side of Nonconformity, but from those who are waging war against all religion whatever.[41]

And so to the heart of Tulloch's case for establishment. It is, quite simply, the old Reformed conviction – eloquently enunciated by John Calvin, adhered to by John Knox, battled for by the Covenanters and in no way denied by the settlement of 1690 – that an Established Church stands, as no 'sect' can, for the sovereignty of God and the headship of Christ over the nations. Chalmers held it 'when his manly intellect was in its prime'. So did Candlish, 'with all his subtlety'. So did M'Crie, 'the greatest among our older Dissenters.'[42] And Tulloch would stand with them. Of all his speeches on the subject of establishment and disestablishment, none seems to have been more impressive than that which he delivered at his last General Assembly, the Assembly of 1885. From it may be quoted some sentences whose message is essentially the same as was contained in many other, more low-key, utterances of previous years.

[41] Ibid., pp. 53–6.
[42] Speech delivered in Assembly of 1882, p. 14.

The Church of Scotland [so runs the passage which evoked the loudest cheers] is an Established Church. Because it is so, it is a witness for the great principle of a Christian State and of the maintenance of national religion; and it cannot forego that principle. It would forego its very existence if it did. . . . We must stand somewhere. We stand here. . . . Presbyterianism is dear to us, and all that is grand and heroic in its traditions . . . ; but it is not more valuable or more a principle of the historic Church of Scotland than that of national religion – that the Lord whom we serve is Head and King of nations as well as of Churches, and that a National Church is the only true expression of the homage which nations owe the Supreme Head, and of the manner in which Christianity should pervade all national life and society. . . . I would shut no door to Presbyterian union – nay, I would open the door as wide as possible. But there would be no use of doors at all, open or shut, if the citadel is surrendered; and to hope to strengthen Presbyterianism in Scotland by surrendering that which has been its central principle from the first – national religion – is to me a dream as wild, and a hope as impracticable of realisation, as ever entered into political imagination.[43]

In the final analysis, Tulloch's enthusiasm for a national Church was due not so much to the possibility it created of a whole nation subject to Christ as to what he saw as its implications for religious life at the local level. It is the parish church ideal which really fires his imagination; and though there is more than a touch of Victorian sentimentality – as well as anachronism and exaggeration – about the picture he paints, one cannot deny the affection which it expresses.

The very idea of the parish [he wrote in what was to be his final message to the Scottish people] is national. It is the product of State churches, unknown – save in a wholly different sense – in America and the colonies . . . If our national Churches had done nothing else for the country than plant into the national heart the idea of the parish, with all its sanctified and benign activities, they would have done for us something more than all dissenting churches together. And it may be questioned if any access of spiritual force, supposing such an access possibly to follow Disestablishment, would compensate for the breaking up of this idea and all its associations. Look upon the parish church as it is known by thousands in England and Scotland. . . . Think of the charities as well as benedictions which

---

[43] 'The Church of Scotland and its National Position' (1885), pp. 10–11.

radiate from it as a centre – blessing for the babe entering upon life, and for the sire closing it; the kindly visitation for the sick-bed, the help for the weak, the counsel for the strong; and all this from generation to generation linked each to each by natural piety. There never were sources of well-being – of Christian light and leading – comparable to the parish churches of our country. . . . And shall we sacrifice all this to the demands of an unfeasible religious equality. Shall we displace the parish minister, living in his own modest manse, and dispensing his modest bounties, temporal and spiritual, for the clamant hedge-preacher, or the Nonconformist zealot, living by the favour of some rich town congregation or patron, with a gospel of zeal rather than peace – of dogma rather than charity. Let us hope not. If we do, we shall never be able to replace the old picture. Our country parishes may not sink into spiritual darkness, but they will never be as they have been, the homes of an ancient piety, which has grown beautiful during years of quiet, and which is all the more fruitful and true because it does not cry, nor lift up its voice in the streets.[44]

Inspired by this philosophy, and conscious of the threat posed by the disestablishment campaign to all that he held most dear, Tulloch turned his back on the relatively peaceful seclusion of academic pursuits and gave himself up, during the last fifteen years or so of his life, to the agitations and demonstrations, the manoeuvring and lobbying associated with the world of politics. He proved to be a remarkably effective operator there, as even the briefest summary of his activities and achievements will reveal.

1. He realised, sooner than most, the dangerous situation created for the Auld Kirk by the Voluntaries' increasing bellicosity and their determination to capture the Liberal party and its leaders for their views. As early as 1868 he had a word of warning for the General Assembly apropos of Irish disestablishment (soon to be achieved).

It is all very well to say that there is no logical connection between the Church of Scotland or the Church of England and that of Ireland. There is no logical connection; but political movements do not move by logic. Unquestionably when you think of the principles that are moving many parties who strongly support Mr Gladstone, you cannot but apprehend grave results from them.[45]

[44] 'National Religion', pp. 69–71.
[45] *Scotsman* report, quoted in Oliphant, *Memoir*, p. 241.

And in July 1878 (some years before the Church Interests Committee came into being) he told his friend Robert Story that

> The impression made upon me by all I heard and learned in London . . . is very unfavourable to the prospects of the Church as an Establishment. Should the Liberals return to power, there is simply no doubt whatever of the Disestablishment question being raised. . . . I feel quite sure I do not exaggerate in the least, and unless something is done to enlighten public opinion in England about the Scotch Church, our days are numbered.[46]

Whoever else was surprised by Dick Peddie's disestablishment motions in 1882 and 1884, Tulloch certainly was not.

2. He did as much as anyone in Scotland to alert the church to these dangers, and to initiate counter-measures. It was a speech of his which persuaded the General Assembly of 1882 to set up the so-called Church Interests Committee 'to watch over, and take any steps they may think necessary and advisable in regard to any questions or measures which may be brought before the Legislature affecting the interests of the Church.'[47] And as its convener he presided until his death over that committee's imaginative and energetic activities in the cause of Church Defence: the production of pamphlets, the organisation of public meetings, the lobbying of MPs, the pressurising of candidates, and so on.

3. He strove – not altogether ineffectively – to persuade the politicians that it was not enough simply to secure a majority of Scottish MPs (still less, a majority of Scottish Liberal MPs) for disestablishment. As Gladstone himself once said (and was never allowed to forget it), the country as a whole must be consulted on the issue, plainly and openly.

> We are not willing [he told Glasgow Elders' Association in 1879] to have so grave a question as this, the existence of the old national Church of Scotland, treated as a side issue; it ought to be put fairly to the country. It is perfectly fair of any Liberal candidate . . . to say, 'I do not approve of the existence of the Established Church; that is my opinion, and my vote will be in accordance therewith.' Or again, it is fair to say, 'This question has not yet come within the sphere of practical politics; I have no opinion about it; but before I give a vote

46 Ibid., p. 326.
47 Speech in 1882 Assembly, pp. 1–2.

I will come back here to put the question to you, and the question will be put to the country.' All that is fair. But it is not fair for a man to come before a constituency and to evade this question, and then to go to Parliament and allow himself to be numbered by the head as a Church abolitionist and to vote according to the exigencies of party; he having been sent there, in the case, so far as I know, of every Liberal candidate, by hundreds of votes that would never have been given if he had taken up the attitude he in fairness should have done. . . . I have no fear of the verdict if the issue is put directly before the people.[48]

4. During the important elections of 1885, Tulloch argued that Liberals loyal to the Auld Kirk should put the Church issue before everything else, and even be prepared (as he himself was in East Fife) to see a Conservative candidate returned if the interests of Establishment could be served in no other way.

> You can only defend your rights [he told the Scottish people at that time] by making the Church a primary question in the forthcoming election. We do not ask you to vote for this or that candidate, or to prefer one political party to another. We do not meddle with general politics; but we ask you seriously not to vote for any candidate who is pledged to Disestablishment irrespective of a direct appeal to the wishes of the people.[49]

If Scottish Liberalism was eventually as split on the Establishment question as on Home Rule, much of the responsibility can be laid at the Principal's door.

5. Above all, Tulloch laboured – and laboured successfully – to provide the politicians with a different picture of the Scottish ecclesiastical scene from that which was given them by the Voluntaries, a picture which had at its centre the statistical facts. As he put it in the address 'To the People of Scotland',

> The Church of Scotland desires nothing more than 'a fair trial'. It might claim to rest on its prescriptive rights. It might appeal to the fact that the establishment of the Church of Scotland is declared in the Treaty of Union between England and Scotland to be 'a fundamental and essential condition of said Treaty or Union in all time coming'. But the Church is willing to be judged on its merits.

[48] Quoted in Oliphant, *Memoir*, pp. 346–7.
[49] 'Address to the People of Scotland', p. 8.

Among those merits, he believed, was its numerical superiority in membership over the Free Church and the United Presbyterians combined. 'Its communicants, which, according to a Parliamentary Return in 1874 . . . numbered 460,000, had increased four years later (1878), according to a similar Parliamentary Return, to 515,000; and there are now in full communion with the Church of Scotland 555,622 communicants, while with the Free Church there are only about 254,000, and with the United Presbyterian Church 178,042 – or in all 432,042.'[50] Even more impressive in this connection were two great demonstrations of the strength of the establishment which Tulloch masterminded in that crucial year, 1885. The first was a petition of over 500,000 Church of Scotland members, together with 150,000 adherents of other Churches, against the Disestablishment Bill, an extraordinary achievement in a mere three weeks' campaign. The second, equally remarkable in its own way, was a Declaration against Disestablishment signed by 64 per cent of all the electors in the parishes of Midlothian (Gladstone's own constituency), on the eve of the 1885 elections. Shown to the Liberal leader just before an important speech in the Free Church Assembly Hall on 11 November, this Declaration may well have tipped the scales against a promise which he was expected to make at that meeting in favour of disestablishment.[51]

There is much to be said for the view that the battle for disestablishment had been lost by the end of 1885 – and that in spite of the fact that the Grand Old Man finally declared in its favour in 1889, and that there were moments in the early 1890s when it seemed within an ace of success. Even before Tulloch's death in 1886, Gladstone had committed himself to Irish Home Rule: from that time onwards, Liberal unity (long a fragile thing) was shattered, and other matters than disestablishment in Scotland absorbed the time and attention of the politicians. The Conservatives were in office from 1895 to 1905; and when their antagonists eventually returned to power it was becoming clear that old ecclesiastical animosities had lost their potency and that Scottish Dissent was about to forsake disestablishment for Church Union as a remedy for their country's religious ills.

[50] Ibid., p. 3.
[51] The story, dramatically told, is in A. Gordon, *The Life of A. H. Charteris* (1912), pp. 400–2.

If 1885–6 was the turning-point of the disestablishment campaign, as seems more than probable, then Tulloch deserves much of the credit for the Auld Kirk's triumph over its enemies. But we have already seen that he was also a leading figure in the liberalisation of Scottish religious life and thought during the latter part of the nineteenth century. In the twin fields of Church Reform and Church Defence it is to be doubted whether any of his Victorian fellow-countrymen laboured as perceptively and indefatigably, or achieved as much, as he.

Chapter 8

John Caird (1820–98): Preacher, Professor, Principal

John Caird was not a towering figure on the world's stage. Even in the history of his own country and his own times he cannot, perhaps, be assigned a place in the front rank. But he made a valuable contribution to many eminently worthwhile causes, and for over half a century was never far from the centre of Scotland's ecclesiastical and academic life.

His adult years – he was born in Greenock in 1820 and died there in 1898 – spanned almost the entire Victorian age. During the earlier part of them, as minister in the parishes of Newton-on-Ayr (1845–7), Lady Yester's, Edinburgh (1847–9), Errol, Perthshire (1849–57), and finally the Park, Glasgow (1857–62), he acquired the reputation of being, if not the greatest preacher in any of the Scottish churches, at least the greatest within the Auld Kirk. He was, in consequence, one of the chief architects of the Church of Scotland's recovery of status and self-respect after the trauma of the Disruption. Preaching distinction – as the great Chalmers had proved not long before – opened many doors of opportunity in nineteenth-century society; and in Caird's case, where it was conjoined with theological and philosophical ability of no ordinary kind, it led him in 1862 to the University of Glasgow's Chair of Divinity and in 1873 to its Principalship, which he held until his death twenty-five years later.

Grandson of a blacksmith and son of a foundry-master who became partner in a well-known engineering works, Caird came to manhood at a time of rich opportunity. The theology, worship, social attitudes and behaviour patterns of the Scottish Churches were all more or less transformed in the years between the beginning of his life's work and its end; while Glasgow and its University were perhaps never so important as in the decades when, having returned to them from the East of Scotland, he connected his name almost indissociably with theirs. As Sidney Checkland recently reminded us in *The Upas Tree: Glasgow 1875–1975*, the period immediately after 1875 saw Glasgow emerge as 'the greatest of Britain's provincial cities, a regional metropolis, the second city of the British Empire, and on the European scale ... within the first six',[1] while one of Caird's biographers was hardly exaggerating when he described the quarter-century from 1873–98 as 'the most critical and eventful years in the history of the University [of Glasgow]'.[2] It was a time for greatness, and events were to show that John Caird did not lack the gifts which his age and situation required.

Only after his father's premature death did young John, who had already spent one year at the University on a kind of extended leave from the engineering works, finally abandon all thought of a career in industry. He decided to become a minister of the Church of Scotland, and returned to the Old College in the High Street to complete his studies in Arts and Divinity. This he did with distinction; then, having been licensed as a probationer of the post-Disruption Church of Scotland, he was presented to the West coast parish of Newton-on-Ayr. His time there was astonishingly brief (not much more than eighteen months altogether), and he does not seem to have made any lasting impression; but things became very different after his transference in 1847 – the year of Chalmers's death – to Lady Yester's in Edinburgh. Though the building which he was soon to pack with crowds of fascinated hearers had few, if any, outward attractions, it was located within the university quarter and by tradition a resort of students and their teachers. Caird seized his opportunity, and soon the Town Council began to realise that they had chosen no ordinary young man to occupy the well-paid living.

A celebrity almost overnight, he differed from the general run of popular preachers in combining eloquence with freshness of thought and fastidiousness of language; and even today his sermons read more pleasantly, and have less antiquated a flavour, than any of his contemporaries'. Upon the young he cast a particular spell, and tributes abound to his influence upon many who later became leaders in the Church. Dr Donald MacLeod,

---

[1] S. G. Checkland, *The Upas Tree: Glasgow 1875–1975* (1976), Preface.
[2] C. L. Warr, *Principal Caird* (1926), p. 193.

for example (brother and biographer of the great Norman), called his early preaching a 'sensation' and his very appearance 'fascinating'; Robert Story (in due course his successor as Principal of the University) opined that the Scottish pulpit could offer nothing higher; and Hugh McMillan from Greenock (who made his name as a writer on the relationship between science and religion) long remembered the loud sob which used to break from the congregation when one of Caird's 'marvellous' sermons drew to a close.[3]

Surprisingly enough, the ministry at Lady Yester's had hardly begun when it was brought to an abrupt end, in circumstances which recall what happened in Ayr only a year or two before. Presumably the pressures became too great for a young man who had not yet reached the age of thirty: at any rate, before the end of 1849 Caird migrated to the rural peace of Errol in the Carse of Gowrie (where, incidentally, his stipend was little more than half what it had been in the capital). There he had time, as never before, to read and to think; there he began to show his indebtedness to writers like Coleridge and Carlyle, and to acquaint himself with German theology and philosophy. But his effectiveness as a preacher was scarcely if at all diminished, and in 1855 he sprang to national fame when his sermon on 'Religion in Common Life' found favour at Balmoral. Published by royal command, and selling in tens of thousands throughout Britain and North America, it was acclaimed – rather excessively – by Dean Stanley as 'the greatest sermon in the language'.[4] There can be little doubt that it paved the way for Caird's return to a city pulpit: this time that of the newly created Park Chapel in Glasgow's West End.

Despite the change of setting, the old magic was immediately as evident as ever. The preacher was now at the height of his powers: mature, experienced, enriched by years of intense study and the stimulating company of his less orthodox brother Edward (later Professor of Moral Philosophy at Glasgow and Master of Balliol College, Oxford). Such crowds thronged to attend his opening service on the last Sunday of 1857 that admission had to

[3] Ibid., pp. 84–5.
[4] E. Caird, 'Memoir', in J. Caird, *The Fundamental Ideas of Christianity* (1899), vol. I, p. xxxii.

be by ticket only. For a detailed description of the kind of experience awaiting worshippers at the Park, recourse may be had to an article in *Fraser's Magazine* for August 1858 – the author being the gossipy but perceptive A. K. H. Boyd. Among other things, 'A.K.H.B.' had this to say: 'You feel that the preacher has in him the elements of a tragic actor who could rival Kean. . . . it is rather as though you were listening to the impulsive Italian speaking from head to foot, than to the cool and unexcitable Scot. . . . [and at the close] you think the sermon has been a short one: you consult your watch – it has lasted three-quarters of an hour.'[5] Such an account perhaps makes it easier to understand the rapt attention given to Caird's utterances by men like Disraeli, Charles Kingsley (who wanted to shout 'Bravo!' at the end of one of his addresses) and Joseph Chamberlain (who praised another as a 'complete masterpiece of eloquence').[6]

For the rest of his life Caird never ceased to preach, though a scrutiny of his later sermons and addresses, whether as Professor of Divinity or as Principal, suggests that his manner of delivery became more muted and less histrionic with the passage of time. A subtle change may also have taken place in the content of what he had to say – partly because of the academic nature of the audiences to which it was often addressed, partly because of the increasing influence upon him of Hegelian philosophy. One thing, however, is certain. From the outset of his public life to its close, discerning listeners were aware that his message differed in many important respects from that of his more traditional fellows in the ministry, and that his real significance lay much more in what he said than in the way that he said it. Put succinctly, he was one of the most powerful influences in that transformation of Scottish theology (already referred to) which took place during the second half of the nineteenth century; and his peculiar contribution to the thought of the time was made not only in such formal works of scholarship as his *Introduction to the Philosophy of Religion* (the Croall Lectures of 1878–9) and his posthumously published Gifford Lectures of 1892–3 and 1895–6, *The Fundamental Ideas of Christianity*, but also in the

[5] A. K. H. Boyd, 'Concerning a Great Scotch Preacher', in *Fraser's Magazine* (August 1858); also in Boyd, *The Commonplace Philosopher in Town and Country* (new edn, 1875).
[6] Warr, pp. 200, 275.

many sermons and devotional addresses which introduced a wider public to his views.

Before we look at that contribution, a couple of introductory remarks may be in order. To begin with, when dealing with someone as reticent about himself and his intellectual development as John Caird was, and particularly in the light of a remarkable dearth of letters and papers from his formative years, it would be foolish to enter on any confident assertions about how and when he came to adopt the distinctive attitudes with which we now associate him. One can only guess and surmise, inferring his inclinations and preferences as much from the things he did *not* say, the movements he did *not* join, as from anything more positive and explicit. It is worth remembering, however, that he had been a student at a time when theological and ecclesiastical conflict in Scotland reached heights that were never subsequently surpassed or even equalled. Resurgent Evangelicalism was at its most bellicose. The Ten Years' Conflict and the Non-Intrusion campaign brought Church and State into head-on collision, issuing (in 1843) in the catastrophe of the Disruption and the emergence of a self-confident and aggressive Free Church. Theological deviants were being ruthlessly punished, and a succession of alleged heretics – led by John McLeod Campbell, Edward Irving and A. J. Scott (of Greenock) – driven out of mainstream Presbyterianism by an alliance of Calvinist zealots and ultra-cautious ecclesiastics. We have no direct evidence of how Caird reacted to all this, but there are some fairly reliable clues. He showed not a sign in his own work of any indebtedness to the staunchly conservative Alexander Hill, who taught him Divinity at Glasgow – unless reaction itself betokens a debt. That he had little sympathy with the fervour of the Non-Intrusionists is more than suggested by his decision to remain within the shattered Establishment, while his subsequent popularity with students of the Dissenting Churches speaks for his indifference to denominational distinctions.

Again, it would be absurd to give the impression that Caird stood alone in his eirenic and catholic sympathies or in his endeavour to repel the many-sided threat to Christian faith presented in Victorian times by thinkers like Mill and Comte, Buckle, Darwin and Spencer. His exact contemporary, John Tulloch (Principal of St Mary's College, St Andrews, from 1854 to 1886), was similarly minded; and at a more popular level Norman MacLeod (minister of the Barony in Glasgow from 1851 to 1872) did much to create a less censorious and Puritanical mood in the Scotland of his day. Despite his undoubted competence, however, Tulloch was secluded in the country's smallest (and most vulnerable) university, and only became a national figure in his last years; while MacLeod, though a general favourite, lacked intellectual *wecht*. Caird, by contrast, possessed an unrivalled reputation as a preacher, great influence over many future ministers during his tenure of the Divinity Chair, and – after becoming Principal – a unique platform for the dissemination of his views throughout the University, the city, the Church and even the nation. If not a solitary figure, he was a peculiarly important one.

In any summary of Caird's characteristic beliefs and attitudes the following would seem to be particularly worthy of inclusion:

1. Confidence that the times were favourable for the construction of a viable theological system

The lecture Caird delivered at the opening of the University's new buildings on Gilmorehill in 1870 bore the revealing title, 'A Plea for a Scientific Theology'. It contained phrases such as these:

> We have means and appliances at our disposal ... which no earlier age of inquirers has possessed. Philological and historical criticism has in our day made great advances. Inquiries into the authenticity and structure of ancient documents, the limit of their authority, and the principles of their interpretation, are now conducted in a far more thorough, sifting, and at the same time more liberal, tolerant, and truly scientific spirit than in former times. Physical science has in many directions made vast strides since the latest of our Creeds and Confessions were constructed, and so enabled us to remodel our views of the conditions of inspiration, and the limits of Scriptural teaching outside of the province of moral and religious truth ... ; and surely we may hold, without presumption, that the logic and philosophy of our day are in advance of that contentless scholastic logic and barren nominalism which cumbered the earth when most of our traditional creeds and systems were being built up. May we not, then, enter on our labours with no unhopeful spirit?[7]

---

[7] Caird, 'Memoir', pp. lxxxi–lxxxii.

A quarter of a century later, the same – perhaps typically Victorian – confidence underlay Caird's Gifford Lectures, which were nothing less than a bold attempt to refashion every article of Christian doctrine in the light of the new learning and its insights.

2. *Assurance that Christian faith is essentially reasonable*

Like many theologians around 1860, Caird was strongly opposed to Professor H. L. Mansel's rejection (in *The Limits of Religious Knowledge Examined*) of metaphysics and metaphysical theology on the ground that what lies outside human experience cannot be humanly described, and that there can be no knowledge of God apart from his exclusive self-revelation in Christ. Caird considered such an attempt to secure the Faith by denying men's ability to criticise it as (in his brother Edward's words) 'calling in the devil to protect the sanctuary'.[8] A key passage in his 1863 Inaugural lecture, therefore, ran as follows: 'It is well to study and learn the limits of human knowledge, but it is not well or wise to prescribe ignorance as the remedy for presumption.... Hopeless and universal indeed would be our ignorance, if that can never claim to be knowledge which is not perfect knowledge.' Then – quoting 1 John 5:20: 'He hath given us an understanding to know Him that is true' – the new professor concluded: 'It is to this knowledge, insofar as it admits of a systematic or scientific development, that I have been called, however unworthily, to act as your guide.'[9] Just over ten years later, in a lecture entitled 'The Universal Religion', Caird affirmed that the authority of the Gospel was 'that which is the most majestic and irresistible – the authority of reason and righteousness'.[10] And towards the very end of his life he told an acquaintance that 'Christianity and Christian ideas are not contrary to reason, but rather in deepest accordance with the intellectual and the moral needs of man.'[11] In an age when agnosticism was becoming as common as atheism is today, Caird's robust advocacy of a reasoned and reasonable faith had a strong

---

[8] Ibid., p. liii.
[9] Ibid., pp. lvi–lviii.
[10] J. Caird, 'The Universal Religion: A Lecture delivered in Westminster Abbey on the Day of Intercession for Missions, November 30 1874' (1874), p. 11; quoted in A. P. F. Sell, *Defending and Declaring the Faith: Some Scottish Examples 1860–1920* (1987), p. 81.
[11] Caird, 'Memoir', p. cxxxi.

appeal for thinking Church folk. It helps to explain his sway over an entire generation of divinity students and ministers.

3. *Concentration on the Person of Jesus Christ*

During his ministry at Lady Yester's, and while already suspect of 'unsoundness' on the essentials, Caird once remarked: 'I am never weary of recurring to the thought of the personal nearness, the mysterious yet most familiar sympathy, the profound and unerring wisdom, the mingled majesty and tenderness of that divine yet gentlest of Consolers.'[12] In 'Religion in Common Life' he struck the same note: 'To know Christ as my Saviour – this is the beginning of true religion.'[13] It sounds once again in one of his later University sermons: 'Yes! it is here and nowhere else that the essence of religion lies: – not ecclesiastical order, not theological soundness, not even morality and purity of life, but love and loyalty to Christ.'[14] Even in the Gifford Lectures – where, as so many would judge, the native hue of Christian conviction is sicklied o'er with the pale cast of Hegelian thought – we come upon passages such as this:

> It is not merely theoretically, as a matter of speculation, that we can conceive of the absolute union of the human and the divine. It is the very central fact of our Christian faith that once for all it has been realised, and that in the person and life of Christ we can recognise . . . a mind that was the pure medium of Infinite Intelligence, a heart that throbbed in perfect unison with the Infinite Love, a will that never vibrated by one faintest aberration from the Infinite Will, a human consciousness possessed and suffused by the very spirit and life of the living God.[15]

One suspects that this kind of Christocentric religion was not entirely compatible with loyalty to the cut-and-dried propositions of Westminster Calvinism. Caird, at any rate (like quite a number of late-Victorian Broad Church men), never expressed the slightest enthusiasm for the theology of Confession and Catechisms. His heart was elsewhere.

[12] Warr, p. 107.
[13] J. Caird, 'Religion in Common Life', in *Aspects of Life: Twelve Sermons* (n.d.), pp. 298–9.
[14] J. Caird, *University Sermons: Preached before the University of Glasgow 1873–1898* (1899), pp. 23–4.
[15] J. Caird, *The Fundamental Ideas of Christianity* (1899), vol. II, p. 171.

4. *Elevation of life over doctrine*

One of Caird's sermons, originally delivered in Errol, bears the title, 'The Comparative Influence of Character and Doctrine', and contains this admonition: 'We should have respect to the sequence of the apostle's counsels in the text, "Take heed unto *thyself and unto the doctrine*".'[16] The same idea recurs in 'The Reformation and its Lessons', a kind of sermonic essay published in Norman MacLeod's periodical, *Good Words*, which maintained that 'there may be the utmost intellectual accuracy where there is little or no piety, and the purest and most fervent piety where there is little intellectual accuracy'.[17] And it appears yet again in 'What is Religion?', one of the University sermons.

> The essence of religion [declares the preacher] is something more catholic than its creeds.... In modern times, could dogmatic differences be wider than those which separate Newman from Arnold, or the author of *The Christian Year* from Frederick Robertson, or all of these from Chalmers and M'Cheyne; yet, can we hesitate to think that there is a something profounder than ecclesiastical and dogmatic differences, in which as religious, as Christian men, these good men were really at one? And could we get at that something – call it spiritual life, godliness, holiness, self-abnegation, surrender of the soul to God, or, better still, love and loyalty to Christ as the one only Redeemer and Lord of the spirit – would not the essence of religion live in that, and not in the superficial distinctions which kept these men apart?[18]

Such all-embracing comprehensiveness was liable to elicit very diverse reactions; but at least it served as a partial antidote to the acrimony which, even in Caird's time, marred the religious scene.

5. *Summons to tolerance and charity*

Caird seems to have been more aware than most of his contemporaries that complete agreement on theological matters was exceedingly unlikely. As he said in the sermon on 'What is Religion?':

[16] J. Caird, 'The Comparative Influence of Character and Doctrine', in *Aspects of Life*, p. 254.

[17] J. Caird, 'The Reformation and its Lesson', in Caird, *Essays for Sunday Reading* (1906), p. 242.

[18] J. Caird, 'What is Religion?' in *University Sermons*, pp. 22–3.

Truth, indeed, is one; and there might be hope of unanimity if each man could see the truth with a mind perfectly developed and free from all external bias or conditions foreign to its own pure light. But men do not so see it. They see it with minds of different temperaments and degrees of intelligence; some contemplative, some practical, some ratiocinative, some sentimental; some with the temperament of the mystic, others of the logician; some with weak, confused, illogical minds, others with minds of different measures of breadth and culture; and it is impossible that the aspect which truth assumes to each and all of these should be precisely the same. Moreover, the principles according to which men think, the mould into which their opinions are cast, depend greatly on their early and hereditary associations, on the age and country they live in, on the intellectual atmosphere in which they have been accustomed to breathe.[19]

Caird also believed that where men like Carlyle, Sterling, Clough and F. W. Newman were concerned – men totally devoid of what he called 'the offensive levity or ribald flippancy of a former time' – it was impossible to dismiss their views with a simple anathema.[20] Like his Broad Church contemporary, John Tulloch, he contended that modern believers had a duty, both individual and corporate, to show charity and tolerance towards those who differed from them. And he even hinted that an 'iron ration' creed, of the kind sometimes suggested by Free and United Presbyterian churchmen in the confessional debates of the seventies, eighties and nineties, might be the best way forward. As he put it in 'The Reformation and its Lessons',

> The ideal of a church platform which commends itself to all but bigots is ... that which under a creed or confession of the simplest form – enunciating but those grand facts and verities of God, of Christ, of sin, of salvation, on which the great mass of Christians are agreed – can comprehend the largest range of opinions in the sympathies of a common faith and love.[21]

6. Faith in Progress

No other item in the list of Caird's characteristic beliefs and attitudes makes him more obviously a creature of his time than this. As early as 1846, Dickens ended his *Pictures from Italy*

---

[19] Ibid., pp. 21–2.
[20] J. Caird, 'Is Unbelief a Sin?' in *University Sermons*, p. 234.
[21] 'Reformation and its Lessons', pp. 244–5.

with a robust assertion of 'the lesson that the Wheel of Time is rolling for an end, and that the world is, in all great essentials, better, gentler, more forbearing, and more hopeful, as it rolls!'[22] Caird seems to have agreed with him.

> In all history [he once declared] there is discernible not only a plan, but that plan one which involves progress, a sure and gradual movement or march onwards to a glorious consummation. In knowledge, in purity, in happiness, the world has a splendid destiny before it, to which each successive event and epoch in history is helping us on. The life of the race ... is ever through successive stages – infancy, childhood, youth, manhood – advancing to maturity; with this difference, that whilst the life of the individual in this world reaches its zenith ... and then declines into the second childhood of old age, the life of the race is one ever-growing, never in the long run retrograding, and its glorious maturity is a point yet to be reached, from which it will still ever advance into new developments of knowledge and goodness and blessedness.[23]

That was in the 1860s when the tide of Victorian optimism was at the full. Had the writer lived, not until 1898 but for another twenty years to 1918, he might have wished to moderate his confidence.

Any really comprehensive survey of Caird's thought would have to examine such other facets of it as his Hegelian opposition to the making of hard-and-fast distinctions between philosophy and theology, the Church and the world, the moral and the religious life, faith and reason. But perhaps enough has been said to convey the flavour – and the force – of his thinking on the supreme issues of human nature and destiny.

Caird can hardly be called a churchman in the fullest sense: he was too indifferent to ecclesiastical courts and their pronouncements for that. But even outside the realm of theology, strictly interpreted, his influence on church life and policy was by no means insignificant, as a glance at two matters that greatly concerned late nineteenth-century Scotland should reveal.

The first was the movement for liturgical renewal. Scottish worship since Covenanting times had been notable for its austerity, its eschewing of all inessential adornments and its concentration

---

[22] C. Dickens, *American Notes and Pictures from Italy*, Oxford Illustrated Dickens (1987), p. 433.
[23] 'Reformation and its Lessons', pp. 231–2.

on the intellectual and the didactic. A reaction became evident in the decades after the Disruption – a reaction to which both Evangelicals and Moderates contributed. Improvements in travel familiarised worshippers with other traditions than their own. Historical research led to the republication of early Reformed service books, and so to the discovery that extreme Puritanism had not always reigned in Scotland. The waning of scholastic Calvinism, and the pervasive influence of the Romantic Revival, pointed in the same direction. By the 1860s, the so-called 'Renascence of Worship' was well under way.

No one with a taste as sensitive as Caird's could be indifferent to such changes. Quite early in his ministry at Lady Yester's he was suspected of introducing prayers drawn from ancient liturgies into his 'extempore' devotions. At Errol he set up a permanent Communion table, covered (so report had it) by a pall of crimson velvet; he also paid particular attention to the training of the choir. Although the Park Church did not acquire an organ while he was there, we are told that he infused 'a new note of reverence, good taste, and culture' into the services.[24] Above all, he lent his prestigious support to the work of the Church Service Society, one of the prime motive forces in the liturgical 'revival', and served from 1865 (the year of its foundation) as Vice-President.

At the same time, he was always a rather cautious patron of the Society. His considered verdict on the whole subject of worship appears in an address on 'The Simplicity of Christian Ritual', which he included in the 1858 volume of *Sermons*. Though recognising that spoken language can be 'inferior in force and intelligibleness to the unuttered language of symbol or sign',[25] and that ritual observances in his own time were marked by their 'scantiness, unobtrusiveness, and seeming poverty',[26] he was careful to emphasise that 'our gracious Lord, in His loving wisdom, hath prescribed no one form of speech or song, no one inflexible language of worship, for His church on earth'.[27] He also pointed out that 'the simplicity of the Christian rites serves

[24] Warr, p. 239.
[25] J. Caird, 'The Simplicity of Christian Ritual', in *Aspects of Life*, p. 227.
[26] Ibid., p. 230.
[27] Ibid., pp. 242–3.

as a safeguard against those dangers which are incident to all ritual worship'.[28] His considered verdict, therefore, is contained in the following *dicta*:

> Banish from the service of God all coarseness and rudeness – all that would distract by offending the taste of the worshipper, just as much as all that would disturb by subjecting him to bodily discomfort, and you leave the spirit free for its own pure and glorious exercise. But too studiously adorn the sanctuary and its services; obtrude an artificial beauty on the eye and sense of the worshipper, and you will surely lead to formalism and self-deception. . . . Better that the world should stay away than join Christ's ranks on false pretences; better that the hearts of men should remain utterly cold than that, warmed by spurious feeling, they should deem themselves inspired by a pure and holy flame.[29]

Alongside the reform of worship, Caird was also much concerned for the reform of secular society. The half-century before his birth, and the half-century after it, saw the breakdown of a unified Scottish community under the impact of industrialisation and its concomitants. At the same time the Church, in thrall to contemporary economic theory, ceased to offer a distinctively Christian critique of the social order, and more or less ignored the part played by what we would now call 'environmental factors' in social distress. State intervention in economic matters was deplored, political democracy distrusted, trade unionism regarded with suspicion or even outright hostility. Almost every pulpit proclaimed a strongly individualistic and 'spiritualised' gospel. Around 1850, however, thoughtful and sensitive churchmen began to feel their way to a rather different attitude. There was a sharper awareness of the gravity of Scotland's social problems, and – particularly in the last two or three decades of the century – increasing clarity about what must be done to deal with them. Nowhere was the change more evident than in the Glasgow presbytery of the Auld Kirk – partly, no doubt, because the situation was graver within its bounds than anywhere else, but partly also because of the lead given by a group of exceptionally able and determined ministers, Marshall Lang, Donald MacLeod and David Watson in particular. Gradually the conviction emerged

---

[28] Ibid., p. 243.
[29] Ibid., p. 249.

that the physical circumstances in which people lived, as well as their own sinfulness, were responsible for much of the prevailing misery and immorality, and that evangelisation would stand a greater chance of success if environmental evils were removed.

To this change of heart Caird made a significant contribution. Perhaps his days in the engineering works at Greenock had alerted him to the magnitude and urgency of Scotland's social problems. Perhaps his parochial experience at Lady Yester's, in the slums of Edinburgh, had intensified his awareness. In any case, the older he became the more evident were the signs of his concern. At Errol, he set up an 'industrial school' for the girls of the parish, as a means of introducing what he called 'some approach to neatness, taste and comfort among our sordid, degraded Scottish poor'.[30] His efforts – and his choice of words! – did not always win him his parishioners' appreciation; but what he achieved (a teacher and an assistant, six boarders, and something like one hundred day-pupils by 1856) was impressive, and not unworthy of comparison with Chalmers' trail-blazing example at St John's, Glasgow, between 1819 and 1823. While at the Park, in response to a cry for help from Norman MacLeod, he recruited workers for mission on what one of his biographers calls 'sane and practical lines' in a poverty-stricken area of the Barony parish.[31] Above all, the this-worldly emphasis of his mature theology, so discernible in the celebrated 'Religion in Common Life' sermon of 1855 (an emphasis fiercely attacked in periodicals like the Evangelical *Record* and the *Free Church Monthly Record*) had obvious implications for social theory and action.

An article which Caird published in the *Christian Treasury* in 1875 drew attention to the *preventible* causes of destitution and vice, summoned Christian philanthropists to 'investigate the physical causes and conditions of living among the poorer classes, their employment, food, house accommodation, and the ways these can be improved', recommended the alliance of religion with political and social wisdom, and asked whether there was not a need for what he called 'a deeper conception of the rights and duties of property' and a 'modification of the conditions that

---

[30] Caird, 'Memoir', p. xxvi.
[31] Warr, p. 172.

affect the distribution of wealth and the relations of capital and labour'.[32] His sympathy with the underdog appears in his expostulation at the City Council's refusal to open the East End Palace to working people on Sundays: 'Could they not offer them *this* brief refuge from the wretchedness of their narrow and crowded and noisy and too often fireless hearths? Oh! the prejudice and bigotry of men!'[33] And towards the end of his life he chose his native town of Greenock as the setting for a remarkable tribute to trade unions, together with an appeal for the improvement of women's working conditions. On the plight of union-less women workers, he declared his belief that they had to endure 'more of the worst kind of sweating, paid cruelty and oppression, and all kinds of injustice than ever were attempted with men'. As for the unions, they had 'gained for working men a degree of independence and unity that could not have been otherwise gained', procured them 'better bargains in the struggles of trade' and 'done a great deal to educate and discipline men for the great political work now thrown on them by the institutions of the country'.[34]

The impression left by Caird the preacher and the thinker is of a man who, while never self-important or unnecessarily contentious, possibly did as much as any of his clerical contemporaries to advance the causes of theological, liturgical and social reform. What, finally, of Caird the academic?

The regard which the old Glasgow College felt for her future Principal was made clear as early as 1860, when she conferred on him the DD degree. Two years later he was called to the Divinity Chair. The appointment, which he received with a mixture of satisfaction and alarm, caused grave disquiet among traditionalists in the Church, and he once had occasion to refer to 'the censorship to which, in common with every man who speaks one word out of the routine jargon that stands for faith, I

---

[32] *Christian Treasury* (Feb. 1875), p. 79; quoted in D. C. Smith, *Passive Obedience and Prophetic Protest: Social Criticism in the Scottish Church 1830–1945* (1987), p. 250.

[33] H. Jones, 'Principal Caird: An Address, Delivered to the Students of the Moral Philosophy Class on the opening day of the Session 1898–99' (1898), p. 12.

[34] *Scottish Pulpit* (4 Nov. 1891) p. 115; quoted in Smith, *Passive Obedience and Prophetic Protest*, p. 308.

am subjected'.[35] The content and implications of his teaching have been examined above, but something requires to be said of his behaviour and effectiveness as a professor. He brought zeal, tinged with perfectionism, to his task. At least in the early days he was at his desk by 6 a.m.; and if one student's manuscript notes of his lectures (taken over a two-year period and still extant) are anything to go by, they could have been published, with little alteration, as a remarkably comprehensive survey of Christian doctrine, replete with historical references and careful discussion of the great controversial issues.[36] His hearers learned to expect interpretative principles from him, rather than an irresistible system, to cultivate openness of mind, to discard their in-built antagonisms to science and philosophy and to seek the verification of dogma in experience. Unlike the more Olympian figures in the professoriate, he treated them with respect and a kind of shy courtesy; and they appreciated (most of the time!) the fact that – again somewhat unusually – he prescribed no textbooks, subjected them to a daily oral examination and supplemented the lectures with a weekly essay. 'Attendance at Dr Caird's class', an admiring disciple tells us, 'marked an epoch in the life of every one of his students. To many of them it meant a complete revolution in their way of looking at things.' But – 'No novelty of thought . . . touched us so much as the man himself. We regarded him with what I believe to have been an altogether unique combination of reverence, affection and confidence.'[37]

During his tenure of the Chair, Caird helped to make a number of important policy decisions. In the mid-sixties he successfully supported a proposal (long under consideration) to revive the BD degree; and thereafter assisted in opening the BD examinations to Arts graduates who had studied in one or other of the 'Dissenting' seminaries rather than in the Faculty of Divinity. This ecumenically-minded gesture greatly broadened the degree's appeal, and it has been estimated that between 1866 (when the new arrangement came into operation) and 1896 nearly as many extra- as intra-mural candidates obtained it.[38] Less successful was his attempt to make the awarding of the DD degree dependent

---

[35] Warr, p. 175.
[36] Now in Glasgow University Library.
[37] Caird, 'Memoir', pp. lxix–lxxi.
[38] Ibid., pp. xcii–xciii.

either on the passing of an advanced examination or the submission of a thesis. The motive, of course, was to raise academic standards; but for a variety of reasons the scheme was eventually abandoned.[39] More importantly, in 1868 Caird persuaded the University to confer an honorary DD on John McLeod Campbell, the first great questioner of Westminster Calvinism from within the Church of Scotland.[40] Campbell is now often considered to be Scotland's most eminent theologian, but he had been deposed as heretic by the General Assembly of 1831; and this belated distinction reveals just how far opinion had moved in the intervening years – thanks, in no small measure, to Caird's own influence. After the College's transportation to Gilmorehill, he was also a moving spirit in the revival of religious services within the University. (In the days before the move, seats were reserved for staff and students in St Paul's Church.) Both as Professor and, later, as Principal, he made himself responsible for the chapel arrangements, conducted worship regularly, preached frequently, and improved inter-Church relations by inviting clergymen from other bodies than the Auld Kirk to take part.[41]

Despite the administrative gifts which he undoubtedly possessed, Caird was not by inclination a great committee man. During his time as a professor he did not, in general, involve himself very prominently in Senate debates. But hardly had he joined the university staff than plans began to mature for migration from down-town Glasgow to the heights of Gilmorehill, and in the planning and execution of that great venture he played his full part. Above all, the persuasive power of his eloquence seems to have ensured the generous financial support of a number of wealthy citizens.[42] Then, in 1873, Principal Barclay died, and Caird's country-wide reputation as a speaker, his intellectual stature and his great personal charm – together, perhaps, with his fund-raising successes – induced the Senate to make him their unanimous nominee for the vacant post. For the next quarter of a century he presided over the University's affairs, as well as representing it at innumerable solemn or celebratory occasions

---

[39] Ibid., pp. xciii–xciv.
[40] Ibid., pp. lxxxviii–xc.
[41] Ibid., pp. xcv–xcvii.
[42] Warr, pp. 192–3.

in the city and far beyond it. They were years of rapid and continuous change. When he came to the Divinity Chair the University was still absorbing the effects of the 1858 Act of Parliament. But in 1876, not long after his elevation to the Principalship, yet another Universities Commission was called into being; and in 1889 an equally portentous set of enactments found its way on to the Statute Book. Old privileges were being eroded, new standards of efficiency introduced; and battle raged between the upholders of ancient native traditions and those who (like Edward Caird and, perhaps less whole-heartedly, his brother John) favoured the introduction of new, allegedly 'Anglicising' ways. The Senate was obliged to surrender many of its powers to the Court, and to accept a greater measure of outside control. The Arts degree was reshaped. The Faculty of Law was expanded, the Faculty of Medicine reorganised, a Faculty of Science created. Boards of Studies were instituted, the Students' Representative Council called into being, the Students' Union built. Women were admitted to study and graduation – with the Principal's enthusiastic support. Several new Chairs and many new lectureships were founded, and of course a number of important professorial appointments made. These last were of particular concern to Caird, and his brother assures us that 'where the subject of the Chair was one on the qualifications for which he felt himself able to form a clear and definite opinion he was immovable in his resolution to carry the man he approved, and threw all his energy and influence into the scale'.[43] Though notable scholars like John Nichol of English Literature, John Veitch of Logic and the great Lord Kelvin himself were already in post when Caird came to the Principalship, we may assume that he was very much involved in the choice of Richard Jebb and then of Gilbert Murray for the Greek Chair, Andrew Bradley for English, Robert Story for Ecclesiastical History, Henry Jones for Moral Philosophy, and that stormy petrel, William Hastie, for Divinity.

He must have been as tough, in his own way, as any fitter in the Greenock yards, for he was into his seventies when he delivered his first course of Gifford Lectures in 1890–1, and did not finally decide to retire until, after serious illness, he had passed the age of seventy-seven. Only then (to use his own words) did he hear

---

[43] Caird, 'Memoir', p. cxxxiii.

'the ringing-in bell'.[44] He died in his native town on 30 July 1898, just one day before his resignation was due to take effect.

One of the most fitting tributes paid to the much-lamented Principal (though it overlooked his eminence as a preacher) came from Sir Henry Jones, who spoke of 'his attainments as a scholar and reflective thinker', 'his simple devotion to the retired interests of a studious life' and 'above all, . . . the humility of his spirit and the exceeding beauty of his character'.[45] A generation after Caird's death, another distinguished Scottish theologian and academic, John Baillie, told a conference of American college teachers that 'The greatest chapters in the history of education are those that tell of individual magnetic personalities, of men whose power lay as much in the inherent transmissive quality of their own consecration as in any counsels they gave'.[46] He might have been speaking of John Caird.

SELECT BIBLIOGRAPHY OF WORKS BY JOHN CAIRD

University Addresses (1898).

University Sermons (1899).

The Fundamental Ideas of Christianity (with a Memoir by Edward Caird, Master of Balliol), 2 vols. (1899).

Introduction to the Philosophy of Religion: being the Croall Lectures for 1878–9 (new edition, 1901).

---

[44] Ibid., p. cxxxiii.
[45] H. Jones and J. H. Muirhead, *The Life and Philosophy of Edward Caird* (1921), p. 8.
[46] J. Baillie, 'The Fundamental Task of the Theological Seminary', in *Reformed Church Review*, no. 3 (July 1922), p. 281.

Chapter 9

The Religious World of
Henry Drummond (1851–97)

Henry Drummond has never been an easy person to categorise; but it is helpful to remember that – whatever else may be said about him – he was undeniably a Scottish churchman of the late-Victorian period, evincing many of its distinctive characteristics and bound up in many of its peculiar controversies. His entire life, like that of his near-contemporary, Robert Louis Stevenson, fell within the second half of the nineteenth century, while his tragically short adult career spanned almost exactly its closing quarter – to be precise, the twenty-five years between his arrival in New College, Edinburgh, as a student of theology in the autumn of 1870 and his illness-enforced departure from the Free Church College in Glasgow (where he had taught for the best part of two decades) in the spring of 1895.

During that brief but tumultuous period, Scottish Presbyterianism's theological complexion changed more rapidly and profoundly than at perhaps any other time between the Reformation and our own day. The Free Church, in particular, in which Drummond had been brought up, and whose servant he became, quite suddenly surrendered its cherished early reputation as one of the most staunchly conservative and traditionalist bodies in Christendom – deeply committed to the scholastic Calvinism of the Westminster Confession of Faith, ardently proclaiming its belief in Holy Scripture as 'the *unerring* standard of the Word of God', strongly Sabbatarian, wary alike of liturgical, homiletic and social innovations, and proud of its universally acknowledged position within the mainstream of Evangelical faith and life. Instead, it joined its sister churches in Scotland in an extensive and fundamental refashioning of religion as it had been known to John Knox and his associates, to the Covenanters, and even to a high proportion of church folk in the generations between William Carstares and Thomas Chalmers.

Drummond himself was by no means an initiator of the changes just mentioned. In most of them he was not even a prominent figure. But such was his almost uncanny sensitivity to the intellectual and spiritual currents of the day that his attitudes and utterances frequently mirrored the central concerns and convictions that were reshaping belief and conduct in the years when Gladstone dominated the political scene, when Huxley and Spencer carried the banner of Darwinian science, and when Protestants north of the Anglo-Scottish Border looked for leadership to such magisterial figures as Robert Rainy (in the Free Church), John Cairns (in the United Presbyterian Church), and the redoubtable Auld Kirk triumvirate of John Tulloch in St Andrews, John Caird in Glasgow and Archibald Hamilton Charteris in Edinburgh.

A more questioning, less serenely satisfied, attitude to credal and confessional statements in general, and to the Westminster Confession in particular, was one aspect of Victorian Scotland's religious revolution which found a voice in Henry Drummond.

As late as 1865, Principal Robert Candlish of New College may well have spoken for most Scottish Presbyterians when he referred to the Westminster 'Standards' (the Confession and the Catechisms) as 'the only safe anchorage in any and every storm';[1] and certainly all ministers, whether Free, United Presbyterian or Established, were still required at ordination to profess their unreserved adherence to the faith as formulated in the 1640s. But in the very year of Candlish's pronouncement Principal Tulloch of St Andrews sounded a very different note. Rejecting what he called 'the popular ecclesiastical notion of creeds and confessions as *credenda* to be accepted very much as we accept the statements of Scripture itself', he went on to assert that 'Those creeds and confessions are neither more nor less than the intellectual labours of great and good men assembled for the most part in synods and councils, all of which, as our Confession itself declares, "may err, and many have erred". They are stamped with the infirmities no less than the nobleness of the men who

[1] R. S. Candlish, *The Fatherhood of God* (2nd edn, 1865), p. 289.

made them.'² By Drummond's time, the views of Tulloch and others similarly minded had gained the upper hand in all three Presbyterian bodies in Scotland. In 1879, the United Presbyterian Church redefined its relationship to the Confession, its 'principal subordinate standard', allowing ministers and office-bearers some freedom in their interpretation of it. In 1892, the Free Church followed suit with another Declaratory Act; and the Church of Scotland behaved similarly at the first available opportunity (in 1910). The old exclusiveness – and possibly the old precision and consistency – of Reformed theology was relegated to the past; suspicion of 'dogmatism' and the elevation of life over doctrine were in the ascendant.

Drummond's whole-hearted sympathy with the new mood cannot be doubted. 'There is', he once observed, 'no more unfortunate word in our Church's vocabulary than "Standard". A Standard is a thing that stands. Theology is a thing that moves.'³ Of traditional Reformed doctrine he remarked: 'We too can still preach it, but to some of us it has a hollow sound. If we could confess the honest truth, our words for it are rather those of respect than of enthusiasm; we read it, hear it, study it and preach it, but can hardly say it kindles or moves us.'⁴ Going even further, he accused it of offering the world an un-Christianised God whose outstanding characteristics were anger and vengeance, of laying all the emphasis on the believer's status rather than his character, and of giving the impression that salvation was 'a thing that came into force at death' instead of being 'a thing for life'.⁵ (There are echoes in this of famous sermons by Caird on 'The Comparative Influence of Character and Doctrine' and by Tulloch on 'Religion and Theology'.)

The threatened decline of vital religion in British society was, Drummond believed, at least partly due to the propositional theology of the outgoing age, 'tied up in neat parcels, systematised and arranged in logical order', whereas for him biblical truth was 'a fountain'. Above all, he desired – in the spirit of Horace Bushnell (and perhaps George Macdonald) – to have

---

² J. Tulloch, 'Theological Controversy' (1865), pp. 26–7.
³ H. Drummond, *The New Evangelism and other Papers* (2nd edn, 1899), p. 7.
⁴ Ibid., pp. 10–11.
⁵ Ibid., p. 18.

preachers appeal not so much to the reason as to the imagination. 'God's truth', he contended, 'will not go into a word. You must put it in an image.' Indeed, the new evangelism of his dreams

> will never say that it sees quite clearly. It may remain ignorant, but it will never presume to say there is no darkness, no mystery, no unknown. . . . It is not all clear as the old theology; it has the dimness of an older theology which sees through a glass darkly, which knows in part, and which, because it knows in part, knows the more certainly that it shall know hereafter.[6]

(One might add that for Drummond religious truth was in the final analysis communicated not through propositions but through *persons* – a conviction which he made good in innumerable instances by the almost numinous quality of his own deeply impressive character.)

Another aspect of Victorian Scotland's religious revolution may be seen in the application to biblical study of the principles and methods of literary and historical criticism. Effected by the same influences which had helped to erode the impregnability of Westminster Calvinism, this momentous development was pioneered – or at least made respectable – in Drummond's part of the world by his Old Testament teacher at New College, the ever-memorable Andrew Bruce Davidson. As a result of Davidson's labours (which were, of course, anticipated or paralleled or carried further by numerous other scholars in Britain, Europe and North America), students of Holy Writ learned to read it with the aid of historical rather than dogmatic spectacles, to pay as much attention to the original context of its pronouncements as to their later significance and to recognise that even the most sublime topics had been handled by human – and therefore fallible – intermediaries. They were also encouraged as exegetes to follow the good example of those sixteenth-century reformers who had deferred less to ecclesiastical tradition and time-honoured dogmatic formularies than to what in their considered opinion the text of Scripture actually said.

The implications for the ordinary believer of this cataclysmic change have been described by one particularly discerning commentator as follows:

[6] Ibid., pp. 23-33.

It was . . . as if the piety of the Church had habitually been meeting with its Divine Friend in confidence and comfort within the same familiar house; but one day found the place invaded by architects and builders who were partly demolishing it, wholly rearranging it and making it seem new and strange in every room. Even though they asserted that these changes were merely external and that the One formerly met with was still there, still the whole *genius loci* seemed affected by the new conditions.[7]

What the same writer described as 'a panic of consternation and a storm of controversy' naturally accompanied the critical movement: it reached its climax in 1881 with the deposition of Davidson's star pupil, William Robertson Smith, from his Old Testament Chair at Aberdeen for what was described as 'a singular and culpable lack of sympathy with the reasonable anxieties of the Church as to the bearing of critical speculations on the integrity and authority of Scripture'.[8]

Drummond, however, seems to have had very little difficulty in adapting to the new situation. Though I have come across no record of the impression made upon him by Davidson's lectures, it is difficult to think of his being unmoved by their combination of meticulously careful scholarship, spiritual and psychological insight and restrained if sometimes almost shattering eloquence. We know for a fact that he was among those who deplored Professor Smith's deposition, and that he was a life-long friend and admirer of Marcus Dods, to whose congregation in Glasgow he belonged and whose controversial candidature for the New Testament Chair at Edinburgh he warmly supported. He was also – and this can hardly have been without effect – a teaching colleague in the Free Church College at Glasgow of Smith's faithful defender, Professor J. S. Candlish, of the *avant garde* Professor A. B. Bruce (subject, with Dods, of a heresy trial in 1890) and, during the mid-nineties, of his own future biographer, Professor George Adam Smith, who was himself to be accused of heresy in the early years of the present century.

We therefore find him (in, for example, an article on 'The Contribution of Science to Christianity' which appeared in the *Expositor* in 1885) speaking of the 'Bible in two forms' that

[7] P. C. Simpson, *The Life of Principal Rainy* (1909), vol. I, pp. 312–13.
[8] J. S. Black and G. Chrystal, *The Life of William Robertson Smith* (1912), p. 425.

confronted modern man. 'The one is the Bible as it was presented to our forefathers; the other is the Bible of modern theology.' His preference, clearly, was for the latter; and although he made no secret of his indebtedness to what he called 'the development theory' of evolutionary science, it is also clear that he had absorbed the teaching of biblical scholars like Davidson, Robertson Smith and Dods.

> The Bible [he averred] is not a book which has been made; . . . it has grown. . . . it is not an even plane of proof text without proportion or emphasis, or light and shade; but a revelation varied as nature, with the Divine in its hidden parts, in its spirit, its tendencies, its obscurities, and its omissions. . . . It is a record of inspired deeds as well as of inspired words, an ascending series of inspired facts in a matrix of human history.

Again, he was anxious to point out that the revolution in biblical studies had not been destructive, nor was the transformed book 'a mutilated Bible': the main warrant for what had taken place was to be found in Holy Scripture itself. And he summed up his attitude – very characteristically – as follows:

> Instead . . . of reading all our theology into Genesis, we see only the alphabet there. In the later books we see primers – first, second and third: the truths stated provisionally as for children, but gaining volume and clearness as the world gets older. Centuries and centuries pass, and the mind of the disciplined race is at last deemed ripe enough to receive New Testament truth, and the revelation culminates in the person of Christ.[9]

Various other aspects of late-Victorian thought and life found either a moving spirit or an exemplar in Henry Drummond; but no study, however cursory, can avoid mentioning two movements in which he was deeply involved and from which his fame was in large measure derived. These were, of course, the Darwinian revolution in science and the Evangelical revivalism associated with the names of Moody and Sankey.

Darwin's epoch-making treatises were both published in the years immediately before Drummond entered on his life's work: *The Origin of Species* in 1859 and *The Descent of Man* in 1871.

---

[9] Drummond, *New Evangelism*, pp. 177–83.

Together, they raised profound questions for Christian theology – not least its doctrines of man, of creation, of providence and of Scripture – and created divisions within the Christian camp which the passage of time has only partially overcome. According to one modern authority, at least three distinct responses were made by the churches to the Darwinian challenge: the traditionalist, which preserved classical doctrines with little modification; the modernist, which sought to reformulate the faith in the light of the new knowledge; and the liberal (a mean, as it were, between more extreme positions), which agreed with modernism in welcoming the scientific evidence for evolution but held that too great a departure had been made from traditional views of God and man.[10] If we must use such terminology, it is clear that Drummond stood among the 'modernists', whose entire understanding of things was dominated by the concept of evolution – though we should remember that in his case the dominance of evolution was combined with deep devotion to the person of Jesus Christ.

The two volumes which publicised Drummond's views in Britain, on the Continent of Europe and in North America – *Natural Law in the Spiritual World* (1883) and *The Ascent of Man* (1894) – were bestsellers in their day; but they have not worn very well. Even at the time, percipient critics like the young theologian James Denney drew attention to basic flaws in the earlier work, describing it as 'a book which no lover of men will call religious, and no student of theology scientific'; while the fullest recent history of the period – Drummond and Bulloch's *The Church in Late Victorian Scotland* – remarks, devastatingly, that Drummond was 'essentially an amateur and a dilettante, of no importance as scientist or theologian. His academic qualifications were of the slightest, and his great gifts lay in communication.'[11] It is true, of course, that distinguished scientists like Professor Balfour Stewart and Professor P. G. Tait (authors of *The Unseen Universe* of 1875, to which Drummond was greatly indebted) and Professor Archibald Geikie, the pioneer geologist,

[10] I. G. Barbour, *Issues in Science and Religion* (1968 edn), p. 365 and elsewhere.
[11] J. Moffat (ed.), *Letters of Principal James Denney to his Family and Friends* (n.d.), p. 11; A. L. Drummond and J. Bulloch, *The Church in Late Victorian Scotland 1874–1900* (1978), p. 26.

were much more favourable; but it can be objected that they were all personal friends. In our time, too, the eminent historian of science, Dr Joseph Needham, declared in his *Time the Refreshing River* (1943) that '*Natural Law in the Spiritual World* is a naive work, but it has the naiveté of something fundamentally true', and even gave it as his verdict that 'when all criticisms have been made *Natural Law in the Spirtual World* remains a great book'.[12] As a Marxist, however (though also an Anglo-Catholic!) Needham might perhaps be expected to welcome Drummond's identification of spiritual and natural laws; and in any case the general weight of scholarly opinion seems to point in another direction. Without anticipating the final judgment of history, it must be admitted that most present-day authorities are unimpressed by what they see as Drummond's regrettable subservience to the 'social Darwinism' of Herbert Spencer, find his application of biological concepts to the spiritual realm generally unconvincing, and look with disfavour on what Dr J. R. Moore has discerningly described as 'the naturalisation of the spiritual world'.[13]

What verdict then are we to pass on this facet of Drummond's career? Without straying into fields of continuing controversy, three comments would seem to be in order. Firstly, whatever our view of Drummond's principal thesis, at least we may credit him with homing in upon topics of primary importance and appealing to the often unspoken interests and questionings of a large section – untrained but nevertheless concerned – of the general public. As Professor Owen Chadwick pointed out in his Gifford Lectures on *The Secularisation of the European Mind in the Nineteenth Century,*

> Perhaps a popular book upon a theme among the most profound and difficult known to man is rather a symbol, the focus of the inarticulate longings of a decade, than an instructress like a book of elementary physics, and if so, its influence might be seen in its focussing and not in its instruction; articulating an attitude towards life which some people wanted to articulate and could not articulate for themselves or did not like to articulate for themselves.[14]

[12] J. Needham, *Time the Refreshing River* (1943), p. 29.
[13] J. R. Moore, 'Evangelicals and Evolution', *Scottish Journal of Theology*, vol. 38 (1985), pp. 383–417.
[14] O. Chadwick, *The Secularisation of the European Mind in the Nineteenth Century* (1975), p. 172.

In other words, *Natural Law in the Spiritual World* and *The Ascent of Man* are important chiefly because their author knew what chiefly mattered to numerous thinking people in the 1880s and 1890s, what they wanted to think about even more than what they thought. Like a highly sensitive anemometer, Drummond helps us to measure the intellectual wind pressure of his day.

Secondly, we should be able to welcome the positive attitude to natural science which Drummond adopted at a time when many Christian believers found antagonism only too easy. There is, for example, something disarmingly attractive about assertions such as this (from his article on 'The Contribution of Science to Christianity'):

> Religion is probably only learning for the first time how to approach science. Their former intercourse, from faults on both sides, and these mainly due to juvenility, is not a thing to remember. After the first quarrel – for they began the centuries hand in hand – the question of religion to science was simply, 'how dare you speak at all?' Then as science held to its right to speak just a little, the question became, 'What new menace to our creed does your latest discovery portray?' But we do not speak now of the right to be heard, or of menaces to our faith, or even of compromises. Our question is a much maturer one – we ask what *contribution* science has to bestow, what good gift the wise men are bringing now to lay at the feet of our Christ.[15]

Thirdly, even Drummond's denigrators are prepared to concede that – wrong-headed though he may have been in many particulars – he nevertheless did something to lessen the estrangement between science and religion in the age of Huxley and Tyndall. Professor Colin Russell of the Open University speaks for quite a number of conservative Evangelicals when he contends that 'Drummond could elevate evolution to a cosmic principle (which he then Christianised) precisely because he sat so lightly to the Biblical doctrines which, in other men, restrained and modified their allegiance to any principle of universal progress.' But at the same time he allows that those who, like Drummond, attempted a synthesis between biblical and evolutionary thought deserve credit for (in Russell's phrase) 'bridging these troubled waters' and diminishing the baneful tumult between science and

---

15 Drummond, *New Evangelism*, p. 155.

religion.[16] It is an important concession and one which we may believe Drummond himself would have appreciated.

Despite all that has been said so far, it was almost certainly as a missionary preacher that Drummond did his best work. The nineteenth century was very much a century of 'revivals': from the activities of the Haldanes at its beginning, through William Burns and Robert Murray M'Cheyne in the pre-Disruption years to the great (predominantly layman-led) movement of 1859 and the mass evangelism of a host of transatlantic missionaries in its final quarter. It was in the company of two of the latter – Dwight L. Moody and Ira D. Sankey – that Drummond really found his vocation; but in his hands evangelism and revivalism became rather different from anything that had previously been known in Scotland. The essential content of his preaching may have been the same as that of all his predecessors (though he struck a new note, as we have seen, in what he had to say about both Scripture and the Confession), but the methods by which he communicated his message displayed an unprecedented sensitivity to the individual needs of his hearers. while the message itself was altogether kindlier, less minatory and more exclusively concerned with Jesus Christ as the embodiment of the saving love of God than that which had long distinguished revivalistic preaching in Scotland.

Galvanised into action during Moody's first and most effective Scottish campaign between 1873 and 1875, and proving himself equally at home with large crowds and with individuals in the inquiry room, Drummond displayed from the outset a unique command of oratory and counselling skills. Working men in the Possilpark district of Glasgow, gentry and nobility at Grosvenor House (the Duke of Westminster's residence) in London, the lads of the newly created Boys' Brigade, young men of the YMCA and – above all – student gatherings in Britain, North America, Australia and the Continent of Europe, all acknowledged his well-nigh mesmeric persuasiveness and charm.

Nowhere was he more effective than in Edinburgh's Oddfellows Hall, where for the last ten years or so of his life every winter weekend found him addressing hundreds of students (medical

---

[16] C. Russell, *Cross-currents: Interactions Between Science and Faith* (1985), pp. 165 and 162.

men in particular) on central topics of the Faith, under the bene-volent patronage of eminent academics from various university departments. The cost to Drummond was considerable, but the admiring account given by his biographer, George Adam Smith, suggests that the results were more than commensurate with the time and energy expended.

> He shut himself off [writes Smith] from the pulpits of his Church, denied his friends, turned from the public, banished reports, and endured infinite misrepresentation, if only he might make sure of the students. . . . And measured by results, almost everything [else] he did seems less; for the field was one on which other ministers of religion had many failures, and he conspicuously succeeded. Hundreds of men who never went to church were won for Christ at his meetings. He invented methods that are now employed wherever students join for religious service. He preached the Gospel of Christ with a fullness and with a pertinacity of personal application which he never excelled on any other platform. And so he influenced thousands of lives, which are now [1898] at work among many nations, in all those professions of governing and teaching to which the University is a necessary introduction.[17]

All, it seems, was unpretentious and straightforward, with an avoidance of clerical or theological catch-phrases, ponderously literary forms of expression, and high-pressure religious sales talk. To quote Smith's biography again: 'There is no sensation in the addresses, nor any imposition of authority; no artificiality or false mysticism; but the style is as simple as the thinking; it is one sensible man talking to others of his own generation.'[18] And of course the central, over-arching theme (as in most liberal-Evangelical preaching at that time) was not the Church, nor the fallenness of humanity, nor even the biblical 'scheme of salvation', but Jesus Christ. According to his biographer's testimony, 'He [Jesus Christ] was for him the source of all life and light; the assurance of the forgiveness of sins; the daily nourishment of the soul; the one power sufficient for a noble life; the solution of all problems; the motive and example of all service.'[19] It is surely no coincidence that out of all Drummond's many addresses the one which has worn best and best represents the heart of his message

[17] G. A. Smith, *The Life of Henry Drummond* (1899), pp. 294–5.
[18] Ibid., p. 326.
[19] Ibid.

is that model sermon on 1 Corinthians 13: 'The Greatest Thing in the World'.

Needless to say, there were criticisms, as when he was accused of preaching a lamentably one-sided gospel and (in particular) of playing down the centrality of the Atonement in the proclamation of Christian truth. Part of his answer appears in what he wrote to an anxious relative on the subject. 'Of course,' he replied, 'you may think I make an error of judgment in my reading of the popular pulse, and in not writing books about the fundamentals. But there seem to me many more books on those aspects of Christ's work than the others, and I must give the message that, *in addition,* seems to me to be needed.'[20] His most effective retort, however, is to be found in a brief exchange of letters with his old associate, Sankey, as late as 1892. The American quoted some phrases, attributed to Drummond, which ran as follows:

> The power to set the heart right, to renew the springs of action, comes from Christ. The sense of the infinite worth of the single soul, and the recoverableness of a man at his worst, are the gifts of Christ. The freedom from guilt, the forgiveness of sins, come from Christ's cross; the hope of immortality springs from Christ's grave. Personal conversion means for life a personal religion, a personal trust in God, a personal debt to Christ, a personal dedication to His cause.

Were these, Sankey asked, indeed Drummond's words? Did he stand by them still? Back came the unequivocal reply: 'These *are* my words, and there has never been an hour when the thoughts which they represent were not among my deepest convictions.'[21] If there was anything new in Drummond's message, it consisted partly in a shift of emphasis and partly in the impact of his own remarkable character and personality.

That personality was his supreme gift to the Christian cause. He had his detractors, naturally; but quite a few who began by being suspicious of him were eventually conquered – or almost conquered – by one whom today's world would no doubt describe as 'charismatic'. In 1886, the great panjandrum of religious journalism, William Robertson Nicoll, said about him: 'I cannot believe that all that evangelising, banqueting, reconciling and

[20] Ibid., p. 411.
[21] Ibid., pp. 7–8, 412–13.

philandering can ever be the material of a sincere and healthy life.'[22] Two years later, though referring rather off-takingly to Drummond's well-known sartorial elegance – 'He has a Sapphire Blue Velvet waistcoat like the Body of Heaven in its clearness' – Nicoll had begun to surrender: 'What he said was excellent, and his manner was even better than his matter – both manly and modest – just the right thing.'[23] And by 1897 we find him expressing penitence for earlier criticisms.

> Of course [he wrote] I was sensible of the peculiar spell Henry Drummond always had, a spell that fascinated some, and in others excited an unaccountable feeling, not in the least of repulsion, but of resentment. . . . One felt as if an advantage were being taken of his mind by a power not of the nature of reason, and was irritated by it. . . . I am sorry now when I think of it, for Drummond was the most generous and gentle of men, and it must have been to him inexplicably and gratuitously rude.[24]

Theological conservatives never abandoned their suspicion (unless they were as generous as Moody); but it was not Drummond the man but his ideas that they found distasteful. In personal encounter, he captivated most people. 'One did not realise', wrote John Watson (the popular novelist, 'Ian Maclaren'), 'how commonplace and colourless other men were till they stood side by side with Drummond. . . . [He was] the most vital man I ever saw, who never loitered, never wearied, never was conventional, pedantic, formal, who simply revelled in the fullness of life.'[25] Professor Geikie, whose favourite pupil Drummond was, averred that he had 'never met with a man in whom transparent integrity, high moral purpose, sweetness of disposition, and exuberant helpfulness were more happily combined with wide culture, poetic imagination, and scientific sympathies than they were in Henry Drummond'.[26] Equal admiration was shown by Professor Carnegie Simpson in his biography of Principal Rainy,

---

[22] T. H. Darlow, *William Robertson Nicoll: Life and Letters* (1925), p. 70.

[23] Ibid., p. 87.

[24] Ibid., p. 155.

[25] H. Drummond, *The Ideal Life and other unpublished Addresses* with Memorial Sketches by W. Robertson Nicoll and Ian Maclaren (3rd edn, 1899), pp. 26 and 28.

[26] Smith, *Drummond*, pp. 9–10.

where he remarked that although Drummond passed through two of the severest ordeals that can befall anyone – immense popularity and intense pain – neither succeeded in changing him from 'the natural and unselfish and pure soul he had always been'; and George Adam Smith (who made the same point at the beginning of his study) quotes the striking if characteristic testimonial of D. L. Moody that 'Some men take an occasional journey into the 13th of First Corinthians, but Henry Drummond was a man who lived there constantly, appropriating its blessings and exemplifying its teachings.'[27]

More than half a century after Drummond's tragically early death, Principal David Cairns of Aberdeen paid him one of the most memorable tributes of all – a tribute which perhaps brings out more clearly than any other both the personal charm and the theological importance of Henry Drummond.

> I am sure [wrote Cairns] that *for his audiences* Drummond's methods were much better [than Moody's]. He understood us, for he had singular intuitive gifts, and knew that many of us students were honestly groping our way, in a very troubled period of thought, to further light. . . . Not that he was either a theologian or a philosopher. He was neither to any considerable extent. But there is an inner region, in religious as in moral matters, in which faith and ideals have their birth. Theologies and philosophies formulate and attack or defend these. But they cannot create them. The pure or penitent in heart see God, and then they think about Him, and theologies and philosophies are the result. In the inner sphere Drummond had a good deal to say to us. . . . When he died . . . still in his prime, I felt as if I had lost a dear friend. I still remember the day, with its whirling snow! . . . I am certainly thankful to have had him as one of my leaders in spiritual things, for he helped me greatly in a transition time at once to hold fast to what was permanent in the old tradition and at the same time to go on into the new world of thought with a new freedom.[28]

---

[27] Simpson, *Rainy*, vol. II, p. 170; Smith, *Drummond*, p. 8.
[28] *David Cairns: An Autobiography* (1950), pp. 113–17.

Chapter 10

John and Donald Baillie: A Biographical Introduction

During the penultimate decade of the nineteenth century three sons were born to the Reverend John Baillie, Free Church minister of Gairloch, Ross-shire, and Annie Macpherson, his wife. All eventually entered the full-time service of the Church. Peter, the youngest, trained as a medical missionary, but soon after his arrival in India died in a drowning accident at the age of twenty-five. The other two – John, born in 1886, and Donald Macpherson, born in 1887 – followed their father into the Christian ministry; and by the middle decades of the twentieth century they were among the most influential and highly regarded theologians of the English-speaking world.

After her husband's death, Mrs Baillie took the family first (in 1890) to Inverness, and then (in 1905) to Edinburgh; and throughout the years down to the end of the First World War the careers of John and Donald followed almost identical paths. From Inverness Royal Academy both went to the University of Edinburgh, where they gained distinguished Firsts in Philosophy – John in 1908 and Donald in 1909. Both held temporary assistantships in the Philosophy Department under their old teacher, Professor Pringle-Pattison. Both then spent another four years in training for the ministry at New College, Edinburgh, the premier theological seminary of the United Free Church of Scotland. Both undertook summer vacation study in Germany, John at Jena and Marburg, Donald at Heidelberg and Marburg. Both became assistant ministers in Edinburgh congregations, John at Broughton Place church, Donald at North Morningside. After the outbreak of war, both saw service with the YMCA in France, John for the duration, Donald quite briefly before returning to Scotland to take temporary charge of a vacant congregation in the Borders (St Boswells, near Melrose). Only with the coming of peace did their ways really diverge.

In 1919 John married Florence Jewel, a remote descendant of the celebrated Elizabethan bishop. From then until 1927 he held the Chair of Christian Theology at Auburn Seminary, New York; from 1927 to 1930 the Chair of Systematic Theology at Emmanuel College, Toronto; and from 1930 to 1934 the Roosevelt Chair of Systematic Theology at Union Seminary, New York. While in North America he published, *inter alia*, *The Roots of Religion in the Human Soul* (1926), *The Interpretation of Religion* (1929), *The Place of Jesus Christ in Modern Christianity* (1929), and *And the Life Everlasting* (1933) – works which gave evidence of his mastery of both philosophical and dogmatic theology.

Meanwhile, Donald remained in Scotland and in the pastoral ministry. In 1919 he was called to the little United Free congregation at Inverbervie in Kincardineshire, where he remained until 1923. Thereafter, he held the charges of St John's, Cupar (from 1923 to 1930, by which time the congregation had entered the re-united Church of Scotland) and of St Columba's, Kilmacolm (from 1930 to 1934); and in 1927 he published his first and for long his only book, *Faith in God and its Christian Consummation*.

Not until 1934 did the brothers' careers at last come together again. In that year Donald's increasing reputation as a scholar secured his appointment to the Chair of Systematic Theology at St Mary's College, St Andrews, the Divinity Faculty of the University. There he taught until his death in October 1954 – by which time he had achieved international recognition as the author of *God Was in Christ: An Essay on Incarnation and Atonement* (1948) and as one of the leading figures on the Faith and Order Commission of the World Council of Churches. Three collections of his writings appeared posthumously, further enhancing his reputation: *The Theology of the Sacraments and Other Papers* (1957), and two volumes of sermons, *To Whom Shall We Go?* (1955) and *Out of Nazareth* (1958).

The year which took Donald to St Andrews also brought John back to Scotland as W. P. Paterson's successor in the Chair of Divinity at Edinburgh. There at New College he remained until his retirement in 1956 – though there was a break for war service (again with the YMCA) in 1940. Between 1940 and 1945 he presided over the deliberations of the Church of Scotland's impressive 'Commission for the Interpretation of God's Will in the Present Crisis'. In 1943 he was called to the Moderatorship of the General Assembly, and in 1950 he became Principal of New College and Dean of the Faculty of Divinity at Edinburgh. He was named one of the six presidents of the World Council of Churches at Evanston, USA in 1954, was appointed a Companion of Honour by the Queen in 1957, and served on the joint committee of Anglicans and Presbyterians which produced the controversial 'Bishops Report' in 1957. His many publications during those productive years included *A Diary of Private Prayer* (1936), *Our Knowledge of God* (1939), *Invitation to Pilgrimage* (1942), *What is Christian Civilisation?* (1945), *The Belief in Progress* (1950), *Natural Science and the Spiritual Life* (1951) and *The Idea of Revelation in Recent Thought* (1956). After his death in Edinburgh in September 1960 three further volumes made their appearance: his undelivered Gifford Lectures, published under the title, *The Sense of the Presence of God* (1962), *Christian Devotion* (1962) and *A Reasoned Faith* (1963).

In what follows an attempt will be made to assess the Baillies' theological achievement, first, by examining their intellectual and spiritual inheritance and how they dealt with it, and second, by describing their distinctive contribution to the religious life and thought of their time.

Their inheritance

a. Highland Theology and Piety

John Baillie's first substantial publication after returning to Scotland in 1934, *Our Knowledge of God*, contains the following autobiographical sentence: 'I was born into a Christian home, and God's earliest disclosure of His reality to my infant soul was mediated to me by the words and deeds of my Christian parents.'[1] The home referred to was, of course, the Free Church manse at Gairloch in Wester Ross; and it is not without significance that the writer's father and mother were Christians of a very special kind. Like nearly all their West Highland contemporaries outside Arisaig and Moidart and the southernmost islands of the Outer Hebrides, they were not only Celts by race but Calvinists by

---

[1] J. Baillie, *Our Knowledge of God* (1939), p. 5.

conviction; and these two influences – the Celtic and the Calvinist – were clearly evident not only in their lives but also in the lives of their children.

When John retired from the Divinity Chair at Edinburgh in 1956, his fellow-Invernessian, John A. Mackay (one-time President of Princeton Theological Seminary), contributed a 'Lyrical Appraisal' to the *Scottish Journal of Theology* which referred, in passing and half humorously, to 'somewhat of a paradox': that the first Scottish President of the World Council of Churches should have come from a region which the ancient Romans did not consider to be in any way part of the *oikoumene*, or civilised world.[2] Despite Rome's contrary belief, of course, there was (and still is) a rich and distinctive Celtic culture; and Mackay was surely right when he suggested that the Celtic strain in the Baillies' make-up was at least partly responsible not only for the quite exceptional clarity and grace of all that they wrote but also for their lifelong commitment to the essential unity of piety and learning. 'The fact', he observed, 'that to a greater extent than any [other] professional theologian of our time John Baillie's work [and we should include Donald's name here too] combined the finest scholarship with a deep devotional spirit harks back to Highland religion at its best.'[3] According to the same writer, John's *Diary of Private Prayer* – and, we may add, the early *Daybook of Prayer* for which Donald was largely responsible – had its roots deep in West Highland soil; and one suspects that this may also be said of both brothers' interest in religious experience.

But if the Celtic influence is clearly perceptible in various aspects of the Baillies' life and thought, it was the Calvinistic orthodoxy and Evangelical fervour of the late-Victorian Free Church that played the most prominent part in their religious upbringing. The father of the family, who arrived in Gairloch from a charge at Moy and Tomatin (Inverness-shire) in 1875 and married Annie Macpherson ten years later, was once described by his eldest son as 'a Calvinist divine of strong character and courtly bearing'. The mother, though perhaps less severe and more flexible in outlook, shared her husband's religious loyalties to the full, and

---

[2] J. A. Mackay, 'John Baillie: A Lyrical Appraisal', *Scottish Journal of Theology*, vol. 9 (1956), p. 227.
[3] Ibid.

was 'not only conversant' with the intricacies of the Westminster Standards but also 'well able to answer any objections that might be brought against them'.[4] The atmosphere these two created and the teaching they gave made an indelible impression on their sons. One early tribute to their influence may be found in the article entitled 'Confessions of a Transplanted Scot' which John contributed in 1933 to an American compilation, *Contemporary American Theology: Theological Autobiographies*, whose editor was Vergilius Ferm of Wooster College, Ohio. Drawing attention, with characteristic lucidity and stylishness, to what we might call the devotional ingredients in Highland Calvinism, Baillie declares: 'I have never, since these days, had the good fortune to live in a community that was, generally speaking, so well acquainted with the contents of the Bible or so well able to explain and defend what it professed to believe.' And he adds that 'Not many systems of thought have been devised which (once certain initial premises are granted) hang together in so coherent a whole, or in which the vulnerable Achilles heel is so hard to find.'[5]

Interestingly enough, a complementary passage in *And the Life Everlasting*, published the next year (1934), fills out these remarks in a slightly bantering but nevertheless fundamentally serious way.

> Among the very earliest pictures my memory provides [so John tells us] is one which, though I see it but dimly, has come back to me again and again during the preparation of the following pages. I am sitting on my father's knee in the day-nursery of a manse in the Scottish Highlands, contentedly gazing into the fire which burns brightly on the hearth. My father asks me what is the chief end of man and I reply, with perfect readiness, that man's chief end is to glorify God and enjoy him forever. This is, of course, the first question and answer of the Shorter Catechism which, having been agreed upon by a notable body of divines assembled at Westminster, was prescribed by the General Assembly of the Kirk of Scotland at its meeting in Edinburgh in July 1648, as a 'Directory for catechising such as are of weaker capacity'. My own infant capacity must have

---

[4] J. Baillie, 'Donald: A Brother's Impression', in D. M. Baillie, *The Theology of the Sacraments and Other Papers* (1957), pp. 13–14.
[5] J. Baillie, 'Confessions of a Transplanted Scot', in V. Ferm (ed.), *Contemporary American Theology: Theological Autobiographies*, Second Series (1933), p. 33.

been very weak indeed, for 'chiefend' was to me a single word, and a word whose precise meaning was beyond my imagining. But I did grasp, I think, even then, something of the general teaching that was meant to be conveyed, and I grew up understanding and believing that only in the everlasting enjoyment of God's presence could my life ever reach its proper and divinely appointed fulfilment.[6]

On what might be called the devotional (rather than strictly doctrinal) side of Christian orthodoxy, John's 'Confessions' waxes even more eloquent. Alongside adherence to the official symbols, he maintains, should be set 'as deep and sincere a development of personal religion as could, perhaps, anywhere be pointed to in the Christian world'. And he continues, in one or two paragraphs which call for extended quotation:

The practice of prayer, private, domestic and public, was given a primary place in the daily and weekly round and was a deep reality for men's thoughts. There was a strong evangelical note, so that one's mind was constantly being turned upon the necessity of regeneration, and yet any kind of sensational or over-emotional 'evangelistic' movement was looked at askance. For never in any type of religion was there a greater sense of solemnity than in this one. Nowhere else, however imposing and fitting may have been the ritual, have I ever been so aware of the *mysterium tremendum* as in these rare celebrations of the Lord's Supper. Here, if ever, *das Numinose*, 'the sense of the holy', was found prevailing, the comparative rarity of the occasion giving to the sacramental feast that very same acuteness of emphasis which in another tradition (that which I have since learned to prefer) is fostered rather by the opposite rule of frequency.

In recent days and in certain other parts of the world to which Scottish influence has penetrated, Presbyterianism has on occasion become a markedly unsacramental religion, the 'coming to the Lord's table' being sometimes regarded as not very much more than a pleasant piece of old-fashioned sentiment and therefore an optional addition to one's central religious duties. Nothing, however, could be a greater departure from *original Scottish religion* as I knew it in my youth.

The whole year's religion then seemed to me to revolve round the two half-yearly celebrations, together with their attendant special services stretching from the 'Fast Day' on Thursday until the following Monday evening. The Scottish sacramental doctrine is a very 'high'

---

[6] J. Baillie, *And the Life Everlasting* (1934), p. 3.

one, though not in the sense of conformity to the too crude theory that developed within the Latin countries.[7]

Out of this rich soil flowered the subtle theology of *Our Knowledge of God* and *God Was in Christ*, the restrained but profound piety of the *Diary of Private Prayer* and Donald's lectures on the Sacraments. It has often been argued that Scottish religion during the last two centuries or so has ever and again been revitalised by blood transfusions from the Gaelic-speaking North-West. Advocates of such a view could hardly find a better example of the vivifying power at work in the Highland religious tradition than the contribution made to twentieth-century life and thought by those sons of a Ross-shire manse, John and Donald Macpherson Baillie.

b. Humanist culture

Alongside the influence exerted by Highland theology and piety there existed in the minds of the youthful Baillies the very different, and at times frankly inimical, inheritance of humanist culture.

A glimpse of the encounter between these contrasting views of human nature and human destiny is provided by John in the biographical sketch of his brother which he published in 1957 as an introduction to Donald's *The Theology of the Sacraments*. After referring to the sharpening of mind that resulted from the family's 'home training in theological dialectic', he continues: 'The sharpening, however, would have been much less had it not been for our growing doubts about some of the premises on which the [Calvinist] system rested. These, as I can now see, were first generated in our minds by the considerably different climate of thought to which we were introduced by what we learned at school.'[8]

The school in question was Inverness Royal Academy, then passing through one of the best periods in its long and distinguished history; and the intellectual climate alluded to has been increasingly dominant in the Western world since the Renaissance.

Our minds [the elderly professor recalled] were awakened and our imaginations stirred by what we heard there, and we were given the

---

[7] 'Confessions', pp. 33–4.
[8] 'Donald: A Brother's Impression', p. 14.

keys of what to us, brought up as we had been, was something of a new intellectual kingdom – even if our own independent reading and our eager discussions with some of our fellow-scholars had as much to do with the actual unlocking of the doors as what our masters (some of whom were very remarkable men) had to tell us.

It was an exciting time. 'Together we explored the riches of European literature. Together also we served our own apprenticeship in the literary art, especially in the making of what we thought was poetry.'[9]

But along with the enrichment and the exhilaration came problems and perplexities, for it was exceedingly difficult – indeed, well-nigh impossible – to reconcile the Calvinist *Weltanschauung* with that to which they had now been admitted. Just how difficult is made plain by one of the more arresting paragraphs in John's reminiscences of those days.

> I have often reflected [he observes] that parents who dutifully bring up their children in a traditional orthodoxy which has never subjected itself to the challenge of Renaissance and Aufklarung, and who then send them to a school whose whole ethos is of humanist inspiration, seldom realise the extent of the spiritual stress and strain to which they are then subjecting them. Our minds, for example, were soon set afire by the reading of Shakespeare, but there was no room at all for Shakespeare within the Puritanism of our early upbringing; no room for theatre of any kind; but no room especially for Shakespeare's large and generous and delicately discriminating appreciation of the human scene. Again, we were trained at school to develop a fastidious sense for the weighing of historical evidence, and for distinguishing fact from legend; but our training at home did not allow us to practise this skill on the Bible stories. Or once more, we were abruptly introduced to the world-view of modern science, and we could not make it square with the up-and-down, three-storey, geo-centric universe of the Biblical writers and our Catechisms, or with their assumptions about the natural history of the human race.[10]

There is considerable room for debate about the details – perhaps even the desirability – of the reconciliation which the Baillies later sought to effect between humanistic culture and traditional theology. What cannot be disputed, however, is that

[9] Ibid.
[10] Ibid., pp. 14–15.

neither John nor Donald was in any doubt as to the need for such a reconciliation; and that if they eventually attained an eminent place among the Christian thinkers of their time they were also, without any equivocation, men of the modern world. Their understanding of the Faith was deeply affected by the intellectual revolution we associate with the Renaissance, the Age of Reason and the scientific advances of the nineteenth century. And it is significant that when the Baillie family migrated to Edinburgh in 1905 they chose to attend, not the local Free church (as apparently they had done in Inverness, even after the schism of 1900) but South Morningside United Free church – and that when John and Donald embarked a few years later upon theological study it was to New College (by then a seminary of the liberal United Free Church) and not the inflexibly Calvinistic Free Church College next door to it that they gravitated. A great divide had been crossed.

No change quite so basic as that which has just been noted took place in the brothers' overall outlook during their sojourn in Edinburgh as students of philosophy. The tensions already referred to were, however, by no means entirely resolved. Indeed, it was in the years between 1905 and 1910, approximately, that John and Donald were forced as never before to come to grips with the most negative aspects of modern thought so far as Christian faith was concerned: the exuberant belief in evolutionary progress; the continuing influence of the Comtian system of atheistic humanism; the mechanistic materialism which at the beginning of this century seemed to be carrying all before it. Looking back on the pre-war period from the vantage point of the 1930s, John opined that

> he must indeed have been a bold man, and must have risked the sneers of all the emancipated and knowing ones, who dared to speak a word against the principle of universal causation or the invariability of natural laws or the conservation of energy or the conservation of matter or the non-inheritance of acquired characteristics or the point-for-point correspondence of mind with brain.[11]

Yet in all their struggles with the difficulties created for traditional orthodoxy by recent developments in European thought the Baillies never allowed themselves to draw a sharply divisive

[11] 'Confessions', p. 39.

line between faith and culture. What they did, rather, was to counter unbelieving humanism with the weapons of the mainstream humanist tradition of the West. In that battle three distinct influences above all seem to have enabled them to keep their footing: the remarkably healthy atmosphere (as they saw it) of church life in Edwardian Edinburgh, the steadying effect of their new-found delight in literature and the arts and their continuing sensitivity to the beauties of the natural world, and the middle-of-the-road attitude in matters philosophical of their honoured mentor, Professor Pringle-Pattison.

Describing the prevalent temper of Edinburgh's religious life in the last decade before the war, John remembered how

> Robert Rainy and Marcus Dods [New College's most prominent representatives of liberal Evangelicalism] were then well-known and venerable figures in its streets. Alexander Whyte and John Kelman [preachers of roughly similar outlook to these academics] were at the height of their powers. During several winters I was a keenly interested member of Dr. Whyte's famous Bible class.... And who that ever heard or saw John Kelman can forget the fine manliness of his spirituality or the breeze of fresh air that he carried with him wherever he went?

And he continued:

> Moreover, one was of an age to become deeply interested in the various arts, and to entertain dreams of travel such as might give these interests greater opportunity of development. And one's exploration of general literature was as eager as ever, and one's own scribblings as frequent. Thus there was not likely to be any entirely sharp cleft between one's general spiritual life and the philosophical conclusions that were gradually taking shape in one's mind.[12]

Of particular importance, what John called his 'progress towards a more secure mental outlook' was greatly aided, not only by 'the two great philosophers of ancient and modern times respectively, Plato and Kant', but also by the teaching of Professor Pringle-Pattison, that stalwart opponent of the extreme Hegelian Idealism then represented in Britain by F. H. Bradley and Bernard Bosanquet.

[12] Ibid., pp. 38–9.

I was more and more becoming convinced [he tells us] of the essential wisdom of my honoured teacher (and later my very dear friend), Pringle-Pattison. These were the days of high (and now almost historic) debate between Pringle-Pattison and Bosanquet. I wonder if there are many who now doubt that the former, whether or not his own position be ultimately acceptable, at least carried off the honours.

According to his admiring pupil, Pringle-Pattison contended that 'our experience does not reveal itself all on one plane, but on a variety of planes', and that 'it is the business of a comprehensive philosophy to assign to each level of experience its true place and measure of importance, according to the degree of value and ultimacy which it finds it to possess'.[13] In agreement with this view, the Baillies took to their theological studies at New College three basic principles or convictions which (John suggests) they never really abandoned. These were: (1) 'interpretation by the highest', (2) regard for religious faith as 'a way of knowledge which is at least equal to any other in point of reliability and which leads us into the presence of a Reality that is not discoverable by any other means', and (3) rediscovery of the 'organic connection between faith and morals'.[14]

Before entering upon the study of Divinity, the brothers had travelled quite a fair distance along the road to a reconciliation of the two principal elements in their spiritual and intellectual inheritance, Highland religion and humanist culture.

c. Liberal Evangelicalism

John and Donald Baillie entered New College in immediately successive years, John in 1908 and Donald in 1909. All the evidence we have indicates that their religious views and attitudes differed in no important respect from those of their thinking contemporaries in the United Free Church generally and of their theological teachers in particular. Between 1860 and 1910 (roughly speaking) a revolution had taken place in Scottish religion. Its effect had been to give a predominantly liberal tone and temper to what until then had been a very conservative form of Presbyterianism; and by the Baillies' time all New College's

[13] Ibid., p. 40.
[14] Ibid., pp. 41, 51 and 54.

best-known teachers – men like Alexander Whyte (the Principal), H. A. A. Kennedy (the Professor of New Testament), H. R. Mackintosh (the Professor of Systematic Theology) and Alexander Martin (the Professor of Apologetics and Pastoral Theology) – were both inheritors and proponents of that revolution. The new orthodoxy which these men represented, and to which John and Donald gave their carefully considered allegiance, was marked by three outstanding characteristics: commitment to the use of historical and literary criticism in the study of the Bible; wariness of what seemed to be undue emphasis on credal and confessional statements; and respect for the methods of natural science.

Apropos the first, in his 'Confessions' of 1933 John tells us that 'the historical study of the New Testament' was one of the new worlds that opened up to him at New College. He then goes on:

> During my first year as a student of theology a small group of us – most of whom were 'philosophers' – made a habit of meeting together once a week for the study of the Greek text of Mark. The following year we received much stimulus from the lectures of the very distinguished scholar who then occupied the Chair of New Testament in our college. And in the summers I listened to the lectures of two equally distinguished New Testament scholars in Germany. I have never since lost my interest in these studies.[15]

What the Baillies found at New College and in Germany was a fairly general consensus on the 'assured results' of the literary and historical criticism of the Bible, Old and New Testaments alike. Theories concerning the non-Mosaic authorship of the Pentateuch, the non-Davidic authorship of many of the Psalms, and the non-apostolic authorship of the Gospels – theories soon to be canonised in Peake's famous *Commentary* which first appeared in 1919 – were widely accepted. It seems probable that an evolutionary interpretation of Israel's religion had become the rule rather than the exception. Many biblical narratives ceased to be understood literally, and the existence of diverse attitudes among the New Testament writers was either tacitly assumed or openly asserted in most scholarly circles.

Extremer versions of the new approach aroused little enthusiasm at New College; but there were relatively few

---

[15] Ibid., pp. 44–5.

dissenters when Marcus Dods, whose brief Principalship ended in the year when Donald Baillie became a divinity student, declared in his inaugural lecture as a professor (1889) that the doctrine of verbal inspiration was a theory 'which has made the Bible an offence to many honest men, which is dishonouring to God, and which has turned inquirers into sceptics by the thousand – a theory which should be branded as heretical in every Christian Church'.[16] Dods eventually became an honoured figure in his own communion and beyond, earning praise from Alexander Whyte for his 'noble catholicity of mind and heart'.[17] And of course Whyte himself (Principal of New College during the greater part of the Baillies' sojourn there) had said at Dods's professorial induction that

> The historical, exegetical and theological problems connected with New Testament study in our day are not the ephemeral heresies of restless and irreverent minds; they are the providential result of that great awakening of serious thought, and of scholarly and devout inquiry, which began at the Reformation and has been in steady progress in the best schools of Christendom ever since.[18]

It was not without significance for the Baillies' general development that men of such markedly liberal views should set the tone of New College in the last decades before the War. Indeed, the convictions they then formed remained with them to the end of their days.

As late as 1956, for example, John wrote as follows in *The Idea of Revelation in Recent Thought*:

> The intelligent reading of the Bible – 'in the Spirit, but with the mind also' – and the reading of it so as to understand how it *Christum treibt*, depends entirely on an ability to distinguish what is central from what is peripheral; to distinguish its unchanging truth from its clothing in the particular cultural and cosmological preconceptions of the time and places in which it was written; to distinguish also between its essential message and its numerous imperfections – historical inaccuracies, inaccurate or conflicting reports, misquotations or misapplied quotations from the Old Testament in the New, and such like; and withal to distinguish the successive levels of

---

[16] M. Dods, 'Recent Progress in Theology' (1889), p. 30.
[17] A. Whyte, *Former Principals of New College* (1909), p. 50.
[18] G. F. Barbour, *The Life of Alexander Whyte* (1924 edn), p. 259.

understanding both within the Old Testament and in the transition from that to the New. We must be as frank in our acknowledgement of this as is, for example, Dr. [C. H.] Dodd, when, having quoted some passages from Isaiah, he goes on: 'Any theory of the Bible which suggests that we should recognise such utterances as authoritative for us stands self-condemned. They are relative to their age. But I think we should say more. They are false and they are wrong. If they were inevitable in that age – and this is a theory which can neither be proved nor disproved – then in so far that age was astray from God. In any case the men who spoke so were imperfectly harmonised with the will of God'.[19]

In perhaps the very last autobiographical statement which we have from him – 'Some Reflections on the Changing Theological Scene', which appeared in the *Union Seminary Quarterly Review* in 1957 – John recalled how in the battle of the 1920s between fundamentalists and modernists he had been very ill at ease with the latter, who seemed to him 'to be using their new-found freedom to read their own very nineteenth-century predilections and philosophy of life into the Biblical teaching, and thus to be corrupting the true and original Christian message'. Yet he had 'scant enough sympathy' with the fundamentalists. They, he reckoned,

> thought of themselves as defending the tradition of their Puritan forefathers, and so in a sense they were, but their defence was inevitably tempered very differently from the original formation of that tradition. The Puritans might be said to have been naive fundamentalists, because up to that time the plenary inspiration of Holy Scripture and the reliability of Biblical history had never been challenged. But in endeavouring to occupy the self-same position the fundamentalists of 1919 were belligerently repudiating the whole development of modern documentary criticism and scientific historiography which had grown up in the intervening period, and I had no doubt at all in my mind that in doing this they were defending a lost cause.[20]

The second distinguishing mark of pre-war Liberal Evangelicalism – a wariness of undue emphasis on credal and confessional statements – had brought about the great Declaratory

[19] J. Baillie, *The Idea of Revelation in Recent Thought* (1956), p. 120.
[20] J. Baillie, 'Some Reflections on the Changing Theological Scene', *Union Seminary Quarterly Review*, vol. XII, no. 2 (Jan. 1957), pp. 3–4.

Acts of 1879 (in the United Presbyterian Church) and 1892 (in the Free Church), as well as the Church of Scotland's Act on the Formula of Subscription in 1910, all of which weakened the hold of the Westminster Standards on the thinking of ministers and other office-bearers in Scottish Presbyterianism. In 1903, Professor W. A. Curtis's inaugural lecture from the Chair of Systematic Theology at Aberdeen asserted that the doctrinal details of the Westminster Confession could 'no longer be claimed to represent the spontaneous beliefs of the great majority of our preachers and teachers'.[21] Four years later, Curtis's view found support in an important compilation entitled, *Creed Revision in Scotland: Its Necessity and Scope*, whose authors included such fine scholars as John Herkless, James Moffatt, E. F. Scott and R. H. Strachan. Though no teacher at New College was among them, J. H. Leckie later became one of Donald Baillie's close friends, and neither of the brothers would have quarrelled with *his* analysis of the situation in the year before John began the study of theology.

> The fact of dominant force today [observed Leckie in his contribution] is that the professed creed of the Church does not any longer, *as a system,* have any particular relation to its religious life. The Westminster Confession is not expounded in our theological colleges. You may search the libraries of many divines and find no copy of it there. It was read by many official Presbyterians when the decision of the House of Lords in the Church case [1904] gave it a new and painful interest. No man writes his sermons with conscious regard to its venerable propositions, nor does any theological professor compose his books in the light of its authority. The central thoughts, also, of the Confession are no longer the central thoughts of living faith. The doctrine of Predestination, which is the keystone of the Westminster arch, holds no vital place in the belief of modern man; while, on the other hand, the idea of the Divine Fatherhood, though it is the centre of real faith today, finds no adequate expression whatever in the ancient creed of the Presbyterian Church.[22]

Leckie may have been an exceptionally forthright expositor of the view then prevailing, yet even the briefest scrutiny of John Baillie's earlier works suggests that he was in general sympathy

---

[21] Quoted in J. K. Mozley, *Some Tendencies in British Theology* (1951), p. 146.
[22] *Creed Revision in Scotland* (1907), p. 54.

with it. *The Roots of Religion* (1926) contains a reference to 'the many who have lost their way in [Christianity's] maze of doctrines and of sects', and goes on to declare: 'We must make re-discovery, and help others to make re-discovery, of the true centre of gravity in this accumulated mass of tradition.'[23] And in *The Place of Jesus Christ in Modern Christianity* (1929), while affirming that 'the Christian epic' – Santayana's phrase – 'reflects and embodies the most profoundly important truth that has ever presented itself to the mind of man', Baillie also opines that 'to a large number of men and women of our day this great drama reads, not like a history, nor yet like a philosophy, but . . . like a chapter from the world's mythology'. He then adds:

> And you and I understand these feelings of theirs well enough, and even share them ourselves in no small measure. The fault, we feel, is at least not all on one side. We cannot think that all this modern estrangement from the traditional epic of salvation [the epic to which Westminster bore witness] is *wholly* due to spiritual obtuseness and corruption of heart on the part of our eagerly-seeking contemporaries. We are ready to acknowledge that in part at least it is due to some serious defect in the epic itself.[24]

The Baillies' later writings undoubtedly show them both reverting to a much more central position on the theological spectrum than is discernible in these early pronouncements. 'I am convinced, and have long been convinced', said Donald in a lecture to his fellow-ministers which eventually found its way into *The Theology of the Sacraments*, 'that we ought to be preaching Christian doctrine much more than we are.'[25] But his own published sermons, while unashamedly doctrinal, are marked by a simplicity – and a catholicity – which devotees of the Westminster tradition, and old-fashioned dogmatists in general, could hardly have found congenial. As for John, though his last publication, *A Reasoned Faith*, contains a whole series of addresses on 'The Substance of the Faith' which proclaim the Christian gospel in unequivocal fullness,[26] there is no evidence that he wished to return to the

---

[23] J. Baillie, *The Roots of Religion in the Human Soul* (1926), p. 40.
[24] J. Baillie, *The Place of Jesus Christ in Modern Christianity* (1929), pp. 11–12.
[25] D. M. Baillie, *Theology of the Sacraments*, p. 141.
[26] J. Baillie, *A Reasoned Faith* (1963), p. iii, passim.

iron-clad Calvinism of his Presbyterian forbears. Even in such a mature work as *Our Knowledge of God*, he was concerned to point out that the members of the Westminster Assembly were 'too intellectualistic in their interpretation of Christian faith, too much in love with credal orthodoxy, too ready to understand revelation as consisting in communicated information'.[27] In so saying, he gave evidence of his continuing indebtedness to the mood that had been so powerfully active in the Scottish churches during his student days.

Liberal Evangelicalism's deference to the methods and findings of natural science (the third strand we have detected in its pre-war outlook) must not be understood as meaning that Scottish theologians in the Edwardian period were disposed to make extreme claims for science or to ignore the dangers attendant upon exclusive absorption in its pursuits. 'Science', averred H. R. Mackintosh, New College's renowned professor of Systematic Theology from 1904 to 1936, 'is irrelevant to the convictions by which the religious man lives and could make nothing of them one way or the other. There is no scientific way of discovering or proving the love of God, the redeeming power of Christ, the forgiveness of sins, the hope of immortality. In short, there are more kinds of knowledge than one.'[28] At the same time, apologists for the Faith in early twentieth-century Scotland frequently affirmed their belief that the discoveries of biology, chemistry and physics, if properly understood, could only reinforce the Christian interpretation of the universe; and few if any of them were inclined to repudiate the main principles of evolutionary theory. New College even had a Chair of Natural Science. The Baillies shared the prevailing attitude, though in their maturity they perhaps expressed it with greater caution than their predecessors had done.

After devoting a good deal of attention in the early fifties to the relations between science and religion (witness, for example, his 'Philosophical Discourse' on *Natural Science and the Spiritual Life*, delivered in 1951 before the British Association for the Advancement of Science), John proclaimed the inestimable value

[27] J. Baillie, *Our Knowledge of God*, p. 72.
[28] H. R. Mackintosh, *The Christian Apprehension of God* (1929), pp. 40–1.

of science to the human race, not least in the religious sphere – though of course it could be dangerously misused. In his estimation, it had a three-fold service to render to 'the things that matter absolutely'. First, it exposed the manner of nature's operations, and so enabled humanity to harness these operations for the attainment of ends which were spiritually discerned to be worth seeking. Second, it revealed the instrumentality by which God works out His purposes. Third, it helped to provide 'that element of otherness and conflict which is so necessary as part of our spiritual discipline'.[29]

In the article just quoted, John then went on to affirm that

It is to our Christian advantage to pursue our scientific researches with unabated vigour. No good will ever come of setting any limit to the advance of scientific knowledge. The relations of science and faith are not such that faith comes in where science stops, or comes in to fill up the gaps and supply the missing links. God is not a stop-gap. He is not to be discerned through the cracks of our experience but as giving meaning to the whole. Or, to put it more abstractly, purpose is not to be called in where mechanism fails, or primary causes where no secondary causes are to be discovered. Rather is mechanism everywhere, and is everywhere the servant of purpose. The two conceptions are not alternatives but complementary.

At the same time, he warned against an even more fatal error than 'curtailing scientific enquiry to make room for faith': namely, 'to allow our faith to be stifled by our science'. And so to what we may take as his concluding observation on the subject:

When the two kinds of knowledge appear to conflict, or when we have most difficulty in seeing how they dovetail into each other, it is quite unreasonable, and in the end it is as unscientific as it is faithless, to cut the Gordian knot by abandoning either in order to abide by the other, by abating either to give the other greater room, or by whittling down both so that they may be more easily mortised. What we must rather do is to accept this strain as inherent in our human situation, resolutely resisting the temptation to resolve it in a premature way, living with it humbly as befits us, and profiting by the discipline it imposes, until such time as a maturer wisdom brings its own better solution.[30]

[29] J. Baillie, 'Relating Science to Faith', in J. Baillie, R. Boyd, D. Mackay and D. Spanner, *Science and Faith Today* (1953), pp. 57–8.
[30] Ibid., pp. 59–60.

Shaped by their inheritance of Highland theology and piety, humanist culture and the Liberal Evangelicalism then dominant among thinking Scottish Presbyterians, John and Donald Baillie were by 1912–13 ready to embark upon the careers for which they had long been preparing. One further influence, however, was about to take a hand in their development – an influence whose impact can only be described as cataclysmic. The war which broke out in August 1914 did more than postpone the brothers' entry into settled employment: it helped to deepen many of their most firmly held convictions (as well, no doubt, as shattering some comfortable illusions), and gave an added urgency and passion to the ministry which they were henceforth to exercise.

For nearly all who took part in it, or came in contact with it, the Great War constituted the most memorable episode of their lives. Even for intellectuals, who tend to march to a different drum from other people, it was profoundly important – and the Baillies were no exception to the general rule. John, in particular, found his whole way of life transformed and his range of experiences immeasurably widened. 'The years – much less than four – which I spent in France during the War', he reported nearly two decades later in his 'Confessions of a Transplanted Scot',

> were fallow years for me, as for so many others. I hardly read a page either of divinity or of metaphysics, and I had little time or opportunity for consecutive thinking. Yet the period brought with it a very great broadening of experience and, above all, such an understanding of the mind and temper, the spiritual needs and capacities, of average (perhaps I should rather say of *normal*) humanity as I at least had not before possessed.

Referring to a character in E. M. Forster's *The Longest Journey* who was 'only used to Cambridge, and to a very small corner of that . . . more skilled than [his companions] were in the principles of human existence, but . . . not so indecently familiar with the examples', Baillie added this revealing sentence: 'When I turned again to my old pursuits after the War was over, the khaki figures still seemed to keep their place in the background of my mind, and in much of what I have written since these days a clairvoyant reader may find them haunting the margins of the page.'[31]

---

[31] 'Confessions', p. 56.

His wartime experiences clearly strengthened John's already very considerable desire not only to grasp but also to communicate what is *real* in religion. *The Roots of Religion*, his first book, bears ample testimony to this. At its outset, he examines 'the main features of the situation that is at present confronting the Christian Church' and calls to his help the numerous books and articles which were written during, or immediately after, the Great War about the religion of the men who were engaged in it. His researches lead to a two-fold conclusion. First, the soldier was deeply concerned for *reality*, not least in matters of faith.

> Not only ... was the army's religion the religion of the nation's prime manhood, but it was the religion of that manhood when face to face with the most searching and testing experience that had come to it for long centuries. In their own vernacular, these men were 'up against it' as they had never been before. They were thrown back upon the roots of their being, and there was in consequence among them – as one can testify not only from the literature but from one's own long experience among them – a most remarkable and hardly-to-be-exaggerated sense for reality and for the difference between reality and sham. No word indeed appears more commonly in the literature of which I am speaking than just this word *reality*.[32]

Second, however, and most disturbingly, Baillie had to report the general impression that the churches had failed to satisfy this passion for reality. 'If we put all the evidence together,' he told his readers, 'one main charge stands out in the very boldest relief, and that is that there is a lack of reality about the religion of the Christian Church, and a conspicuous unrelatedness to the real problems of human life.'[33]

The Roots of Religion was a preliminary attempt to uncover the reality of the Christian faith and to demonstrate its relevance to the problems of life – but it might be said, without overmuch exaggeration, that the whole course of John's career, and Donald's also, was devoted to the same endeavour.

Their Distinctive Contribution

Neither of the Baillies founded a theological school, though many of the most important teaching posts in the English-speaking world

---

[32] J. Baillie, *Roots of Religion*, p. 4.
[33] Ibid., pp. 11–12.

were, from the 1940s onward, occupied by scholars who had studied under them. They had no desire to turn out little replicas of themselves, and they did not do so; but their teaching by no means lacked distinctiveness. Attention has often been drawn to the strongly church-centred character of all their activity, as well as to their interest (much greater than has perhaps been customary among Scottish theologians since the days of Thomas Chalmers) in social questions. Here, however, there is space only for a very selective consideration of three aspects of the brothers' work which marked them off from quite a number of their contemporaries, and for which Christians still have reason to be grateful.

a. Apologetic Concern

The Reasonableness of the Christian Faith, the title of a little book published by Professor David S. Cairns of Aberdeen in 1918, might serve as a kind of motto for much if not all of what John and Donald Baillie stood for and strove to demonstrate in the years between 1926 (when *The Roots of Religion* made its appearance) and 1963 (when *A Reasoned Faith*, a posthumous collection of John's addresses and sermons, closed the long list of their publications). Whatever else may be said about them, the brothers were pre-eminently apologists for the Faith, and their life's work was dominated from beginning to end by an apologetic concern. In our consideration of this theme, valuable help is to be found in an address given at New College, Edinburgh, in 1983 by John Baillie's successor in the Divinity Chair, Professor John McIntyre.

Among Professor McIntyre's observations may be noted the following:

1. He suggests that it was what he calls 'theology's compresence in the University with other disciplines'[34] which challenged John Baillie – whose entire career was spent either in a university or in theological colleges closely associated with their university neighbours – to explore the relationship of theology to other branches of learning.

---

[34] J. McIntyre, 'Theology and University: John Baillie', *New College Bulletin*, no. 14 (Sept. 1983), p. 20.

2. He highlights one of the key phrases in *Our Knowledge of God* – 'a mediated immediacy' – as being especially characteristic of Baillie's understanding of that relationship. According to McIntyre, the concept implies 'a rejection of the idea that we know God directly and intuitively, by means of some sixth sense, which some have and some do not have. It is awareness of God which occurs, as he [Baillie] sometimes said, borrowing Lutheran language, "in, with, and under" other entities, such as other selves, the world, human history.' And he continues: 'The university setting is not irrelevant; for God is thought to be known in those fields in which other disciplines operate. In fact, a religious awareness is often presented as an alternative interpretation of phenomena already within the range of those other disciplines.'[35] It is not difficult to see how such an understanding enabled John Baillie to relate sympathetically to the world of culture around him and to pursue the task of persuading his colleagues in Arts and Science that the theological quest was less alien from them than they had been inclined to think.

3. He argues, most interestingly, that while the apologetic enterprise spanned the whole of John Baillie's career its underlying presuppositions changed quite markedly in course of time.

In the earlier years, he had worked on the assumption that any apologetic that is to be relevant and effective today has to be directed at people who are thought of as sharing the Christian heritage, and whose awareness of other traditions is only second-hand. That assumption informed his *Invitation to Pilgrimage* which though published in 1942 summed up his attitude for some time previously. My impression is that by the time of his writing *The Sense of the Presence of God* [published posthumously in 1962] he had widened the target of his apologetic thrust, directing it as much at those who actively rejected the Christian Tradition, or had never at any time stood within it, as at those who lived on its dividends without declaring their capital.[36]

---

[35] Ibid.
[36] Ibid., p. 19.

4. He draws attention to the fact that 'One special feature of the kind of apologetic which John Baillie practised was that he not only endeavoured strenuously to understand those who objected to the Christian faith or one aspect of it, but set himself to state the faith or aspects of it as lucidly as he could.' Observing that 'Faithful statement is worth more than many refutations,' McIntyre continues:

A good example of this purpose is to be seen in the way in which he dealt with variant forms of the interpretation of history across the centuries in his *The Belief in Progress*. He did so in a manner which dealt with the problem in hand, which also however anticipated the intense discussion of the nature of hope which was to come some twenty years after that book was written.[37]

All this, in Professor McIntyre's estimation, made John Baillie 'one of the most distinguished practitioners of the discipline of theology as it occurs in and is affected by the situation within a university'.[38] The same could equally be said about his brother Donald – as anyone will agree who has read the tributes paid to him at his death by Principal Knox of St Andrews and Principal Taylor of Aberdeen University, together with Professor Rudolf Bultmann of Marburg's assessment of *God Was in Christ* as 'A model of versatile and understanding dialogue with other theological and religious outlooks.'[39]

The Baillies' dedication to the apologetic task was almost inevitably bound up with a concern for the maintenance or improvement of standards in religious education. It was at least in part through its theological seminaries that the Church confronted the intellectual world: one of John's most interesting pronouncements, therefore, was a lecture entitled 'The Fundamental Task of the Theological Seminary', which he delivered at the Conference of Theological Seminaries of the United States and Canada held in Toronto in June 1922. He was then in his earliest professorial appointment (at Auburn, New York), and at the very outset of his long teaching career; but it would seem that the convictions he then expressed were never departed from, and indeed continued to motivate him throughout the remainder of his life.

37 Ibid.
38 Ibid., p. 18.
39 J. Baillie, 'Donald: A Brother's Impression', pp. 34–6.

At the heart of the lecture lies a careful consideration of the ever-recurrent question, What kind of training do our ministers require, vocational and practical or scholarly and intellectual? Baillie's answer begins with an assertion that the modern theological school had its origin in two very diverse but confluent sources: Jesus' teaching of the twelve, and the education provided in the philosophical schools of Athens. Historians like Harnack may have believed that the fusion of rational criticism (derived from Greece) with the allegedly simple Galilean gospel was a retrograde step, but the young professor does not agree. 'One of the things that mark off Christianity from all other religions', he avers,

> is precisely this – that though having its rise, like nearly every other great religious force, in an entirely popular movement among a primitive and backward people in a half-forgotten corner of the world, it yet has had the spiritual vitality to graft into itself the best fruits of the most advanced culture that the race has known, and to develop in the process into being the greatest spiritual force in the modern world.

In the light of this fact of history, Baillie is moved to remark that the question with which he began is really a superficial one. 'Priests or scholars? Of course, if we must choose, we will say priests. But if history has taught us anything, it has taught us that within Western civilisation the priest is not likely to be effective if he is not a scholar too. And is not contemporary experience teaching us the same thing?'[40]

But there is still more to be said. Observing that 'the great problem facing the Christian Church at the present moment is the defection or alienation, to a very serious extent, of two classes in the community – the intellectual class and the masses', Baillie believes that this is in large measure a problem of the Church's making.

> It seems to me clear that *one* reason why the intellectuals in our midst sit on the whole so very loosely to the Church is that the Church itself is not, as it once was, at the forefront of intellectual attainment, nor are its ministers, as they lately were, the intellectual leaders of their communities. I can testify with personal experience

[40] J. Baillie, 'The Fundamental Task of the Theological Seminary', *Reformed Church Review*, vol. I (1922), pp. 266–7.

to cases in which it is very generally assumed by even the leading business and professional men of a city that the ministers who represent the Church in their city are second-rate men with second-rate minds. And I know also that an even more extreme view is constantly taken by students and teachers of other subjects of the student body of certain theological seminaries.

As for the average person, reports brought back from the Western Front of religious attitudes incline Baillie to suspect that '*at last* the mass of men have begun to do their own thinking, instead of letting the priest think for them', and that 'a far greater proportion of the disloyalty of the masses than is commonly allowed is due to intellectual dissent or doubt or puzzlement'.[41]

'What we have to explain', the professor adds, 'is why so many ... were and are entirely sceptical as to the ability of the accredited representatives of the Christian Church to help them, and so ready to assume that the chaplain's philosophy was a ready-made affair, or, in their own vernacular, a "put-up job".' And his conclusion is that

> there has never been an age in which it is more necessary than it is now for the Christian minister to be alert mentally and well-equipped intellectually. The minister who fulfils the priestly function only, and is neither prophet nor thinker, may succeed in ministering effectually to the small circle in his community who are already completely loyal to the Church; and one cannot help remarking a certain tendency among us to rest content with that as the main part of the minister's work. Surely, however, the minister's effectiveness can be measured in one way only – by his success in meeting the religious needs of the whole community. In a modern community he can have no such success unless he be able, among other things, to inspire general confidence in himself as a keen-minded, fearless and well-equipped seeker of the truth about God and Man and Life and Destiny.[42]

The general thrust of Baillie's argument is therefore clear. It is the seminary's task to equip men who can provide the leadership he has described.

> Here is something which we teachers of divinity *can* do – we can (according to the measure of our native ability and theirs) teach the young men to *think* – to think fairly, to think deeply, to think boldly,

[41] Ibid., pp. 267–70.
[42] Ibid., p. 270.

to think humbly. I believe that there are no questions that should be more in our minds about the students we graduate each year than these: Do they clearly know exactly what they are recommending when they recommend Christianity? And do they clearly know, and profoundly feel, why it is more worthy to be recommended than any other solution of the great riddle of life?

So he concludes:

> The problem of Christianity in the coming years will not be solved by turning out men who (in addition to being devoted servants of their race, for that must go without saying) are good speakers, experts in homiletic form and illustration, able organisers and administrators, diligent pastors, and the like. It can be resolved only if it is represented in our communities by men who can answer, in such a way as to inspire trust, the often very independent questionings of the modern mind. I believe that what the men of today are looking to the Church to provide is above all things *guidance* – not comfort, not good fellowship, not even religious exaltation and inspiration, and certainly not either oratorical thrills or social evenings, but light on the great puzzle of life. And I believe that if the Church will but realise in a really enterprising way her role as teacher, she has a magnificent future before her in our generation.[43]

Imbued with convictions such as these, and calling upon his contemporaries to 'reflect . . . whether it is likely that Christianity can continue her influence undiminished if our ministers cease to be looked up to as leaders of thought as well as of worship',[44] John Baillie strove as few of his generation did to present a clear and cogent case for Christian faith, to strengthen the ties which by tradition have bound Church and University together, and to raise the standards of theological education not only in his homeland but throughout the English-speaking world.

b. Sensitivity in the treatment of doubt and unbelief

There are some arresting sentences in John Baillie's *Invitation to Pilgrimage* where he advises the Christian apologist always to bear in mind that 'the debate between belief and unbelief is by no means a debate between himself who believes and another who disbelieves. It is also in large part a debate within himself, who

[43] Ibid., p. 272.
[44] Ibid., p. 272.

both believes and disbelieves, and who must ever continue to pray humbly, "Lord, I believe; help Thou mine unbelief".' And he continues:

> When we who are within the visible Church of Christ reason with those who are without, we are never in the position of feeling that there is in our interlocutors no disposition to believe, and in ourselves no disposition to doubt. . . . We still do not find faith easy, and hence our *apologia* is always in some sort addressed to ourselves as well as to our neighbours. . . . The most moving and persuasive arguments are always those in which the arguer is felt to be holding high debate with himself. . . . When one looks back over the road oneself has travelled, anything like dogmatism appears very much out of place; anything also like a fencing method or a parade of dialectical skill or the desire to score merely a plausible victory over the opponent.[45]

Elsewhere in the same volume the writer is even prepared to say of believers and unbelievers that

> in our outlook on *everything*, in our response to *all* life's alarms, there is something that we have in common and again something that divides us. And I am sure that the bit of the road that most requires to be illuminated is the point where it forks. If we could only discover why it is that, when a certain stage is reached, we take different turnings and begin to walk apart, we should perhaps be doing all that we can humanly do. The rest is not in our hands, but in the hands of Something or Someone not ourselves; for faith is not an achievement but a gift.[46]

Behind such candour and sensitivity there lay, in the case of both brothers, a history of personally experienced scepticism and anguish. In the course of an address before the British Association in 1951, Donald referred to the difficulties which 'sincere and honest souls' have with belief, and commented: 'Far be it from me to speak of these difficulties with anything but respect and sympathy.'[47] There is evidence that from an early age he was haunted by doubts which his brother subsequently diagnosed as due to the conflict then raging in his mind between traditional

---

[45] J. Baillie, *Invitation to Pilgrimage* (1942), pp. 18–19.
[46] Ibid., pp. 8–9.
[47] D. M. Baillie, sermon delivered before the British Association for the Advancement of Science, 12 Aug. 1951, in D. M. Baillie, *To Whom Shall We Go?* (1958), p. 171.

orthodoxy and the humanist ethos. Even during his schooldays they caused him considerable distress; at university their impact was still greater. As John comments in the biographical essay which introduces *The Theology of the Sacraments*,

> Donald was afterwards to be a valiant defender of the faith ... but he had to pass through a long struggle from which only slowly was he able to emerge. It brought with it nervous strain of an acute kind. He could not coerce himself to the methodical reading of the texts required for the approaching examinations, but would rather concentrate his thought for hours at a stretch on a single page, or even sentence, in one of them which seemed to promise some possible relief of his problem. And how often did I see him sit for a whole evening, staring at a book but not seeing it, while his mind kept reverting in spite of himself to a spiritual predicament concerning which the book had no real enlightenment to offer![48]

By the time he got to New College, Donald's struggle for faith had 'measurably eased'. But it was by no means altogether a thing of the past, and John's memoir of him suggests that perhaps the shadow never entirely dissipated.

> Even in his latest years [we are told] he had periods of depression, in which life seemed to be emptied of its divine meaning. He was in the poorest possible health then, a martyr to a long-standing asthmatic condition, and the depression was physical as well as mental. He would put to himself and to me the question as to whether the extreme bodily lassitude was the cause or the result, or merely the accompaniment, of the darkness of the soul. But one thing was always clear to him – that without God and Christ human life was without significance of any kind, devoid of all interest. He would say, 'When the darkness is on me, I walk down the street, and see the people walking aimlessly about, and shops and cars and a few dogs, and it all seems to mean nothing, and to matter not at all!' It was Pascal's *misère de l'homme sans Dieu*.[49]

Nor was John altogether exempt from such *Anfechtungen*. In *The Idea of Revelation* he recalls a conversation he once had with a lawyer in the United States whose expression of elemental doubt brought back the memory of his own youthful agonisings.

---

[48] J. Baillie, 'Donald', in D. M. Baillie, *Theology of the Sacraments*, p. 20.
[49] Ibid., pp. 21–2.

'You speak', he said, 'of trusting God, of praying to Him and doing His will. *But it's all so one-sided.* We speak to God, we bow down before Him and lift up our hearts to Him. But He never speaks to us. He makes no sign. It's all so one-sided.' Nor was it without real understanding and fellow-feeling that I heard him speak thus, for there had been a time when I used to say the same things to myself... I can remember, during my student days in Edinburgh, walking home one frosty midnight from a philosophical discussion on the existence of God, and stopping in my walk to gaze up into the starry sky. Into those deep immensities of space I hurled my despairing question, but it seemed to hit nothing, and no answer came back ... the stars that night did not seem to say to me, 'The hand that made us is divine.'[50]

Against the background of experiences like these, the brothers spent a great deal of time and energy in tackling the religious difficulties of their contemporaries and in suggesting how – despite such difficulties – a return to faith might be made. An illuminating (and very typical) passage from Donald's first book, *Faith in God and its Christian Consummation*, published in 1927, well illustrates their approach, and merits quotation *in extenso*. 'What counsel', he asks, 'would the wise counsellor give to a man in the modern world who professed himself perplexed by universal doubt regarding the truth of religion?' His answer runs as follows:

Instead of simply arguing with the doubter and endeavouring to prove religion, or telling him to make up his mind to believe, by an effort of will, or even advising 'religious practice' [references, these, to notions first publicised by William James at the end of the nine-teenth century] *the wise counsellor would probably say something like this.* 'Underneath your doubt, don't you feel at least a basal kind of certainty about the meaning of your life in the universe? You may feel uncertain about all the dogmas of religion as you have been accustomed to conceive them. But, to go down to something much more simple and elemental, can't you find in the bottom of your heart an ineradicable conviction that the universe is not without a purpose of good, which makes it worthwhile for you even to face your doubts and play the man; that all is not blind chance, but that there is a meaning and principle of good at the heart of things?'[51]

Commenting on this suggested answer, Donald adds:

[50] J. Baillie, *Idea of Revelation*, pp. 137–8.
[51] D. M. Baillie, *Faith in God*, p. 155.

You are appealing to a conviction which you think he has even underneath his doubts. And if you are successful, and he confesses to such a conviction, you will tell him that he is not so entirely devoid of belief as he had miserably supposed; that this is already the beginning of faith, though it looks so different from the dogmas he had been doubting; and that this faith is enough to begin with, enough to live on for the time, until, through faithfulness to it, he gradually finds it growing into something more explicit. It may be no more than what R. L. Stevenson calls

> The half of a broken hope for a pillow at night
> That somehow the right is the right
> And the smooth shall bloom from the rough.

Stevenson cries out, 'Lord, if that were enough?', and again, 'God, if this were faith?' Well, you would tell your doubter that it *is* enough to begin with; it *is* faith, though he does not realise it. And it is to this deep, fundamental, unrealised faith ... that you make your appeal.[52]

There is a not dissimilar passage in John's first book, *The Roots of Religion*, published just a year previously. Addressing 'the needs of those who have difficulty about the acceptance of religious belief',[53] he writes:

I may be in the direst uncertainty about the nature of this 'scheme of things entire', about its constitution and construction, about its origin and destined end; but I *know* that love is better than hate, that courage is better than cowardice and honour than treachery, and that it is right to help one's fellow-traveller out of the ditch and to pour oil and wine into his wounds. There may be little to know, and little assurance in the knowing of it, but there is always plenty to do, and for the man who looks it straight in the face, plenty of assurance that it is worth doing.[54]

And so the argument moves, by way of quotation from Carlyle ('Do the duty which lies nearest to thee') and the Baillies' early favourite, F. W. Robertson ('It must be right to do right') to this conclusion: our method of dealing with doubt

should consist simply in the attempt to bring to clear consciousness, and to express in precise language, the nature of the compulsion

[52] Ibid., p. 156.
[53] J. Baillie, *Roots of Religion*, p. 205.
[54] Ibid., pp. 212–13.

which in every age has led earnest seekers after righteousness to trust in an Eternal Righteousness, and has inspired devoted workers to believe that they are working for a more-than-human Cause. . . . It is agreed that there is nothing of which I am more certain than that an absolute obligation is laid upon me to do the right and eschew the wrong. But what is it that thus obliges me, if it be not some larger order of things to which I stand related? How can values like truthfulness and unselfishness and courage have any claim upon me, if they are not grounded in the all-enclosing System to which I belong? How can the Ultimate Reality demand Righteousness in me, if Itself be not righteous?[55]

How such argumentation translated into the language of the pulpit may be seen in a sermon broadcast by Donald more than a quarter of a century later, on Low Sunday 1954. Offering 'some simple bits of encouragement and counsel for those times when [like the prophet Elijah in 1 Kings 19:4] you are under the shadow of the juniper tree', the preacher summarised his message in the following 'heads': '(1) Remember that *this is part of the common experience of the Christian life*. . . . (2) Remember that *what really matters in the Christian life is not our feelings, our emotions, our moods, but how we live*, with dedicated wills, in faith and love. . . . (3) In your bad hours, remember *the fellowship of your fellow-Christians*, and lean upon it' – this last point being driven home by a beautifully apposite quotation from Bunyan's *Pilgrim's Progress*.[56]

Before leaving this subject, notice should be taken of some interesting comments that John had to make on the subject of creditable and discreditable doubt and the origins of the former.

Part of the reason why I could not find God [he writes in *Our Knowledge of God*] was that there is that in God which I did not wish to find. Part of the reason why I could not (or thought I could not) hear Him speak was that He was saying some things that I did not wish to hear. There was a side of the divine reality which was unwelcome to me, and some divine commandments the obligatoriness of which I was most loath to acknowledge. And the reason why I was loath to acknowledge them was that I found them too disquieting, involving for their proper obedience a degree of courage and self-denial and a resolute reorientation of outlook and revision of

[55] Ibid., pp. 233–4.
[56] D. M. Baillie, *To Whom Shall We Go?*, pp. 152–5.

programme such as I was not altogether prepared to face. . . . For some of what God would say to me I had a very ready ear, and I was therefore greatly disquieted by my doubts as to whether He was really addressing me at all. But because there were other of his words to which I turned a deaf ear, my deafness seemed to extend even to that for which I was most eagerly listening.

He then comments:

It seems to me that this is very commonly the case. . . . We seek God 'carefully with tears'. But because we are so loath to find Him as He is, sometimes we cannot find Him at all. We have conceived our own idea of God, but it is an idea in the formation of which our sloth and selfishness have played a part; and because there is no God corresponding to our idea, and because we are looking for none other, we fail to find the God who is really there. . . . We cannot be assured of His care if we reject His claim. Before religion can be known as a sweet communion, it must first be known as an answered summons.[57]

There is, however, another side of the matter, and a few lines further on the writer seeks to deal with it. 'But is *all* our doubt of God', he asks, 'to be explained in this way? Or is part of it of quite another kind? Are we sometimes led to doubt God's reality by thinking which, however mistaken, is nevertheless quite honest, and which, though crooked intellectually, is straightforward enough morally?' The reply is unhesitating. 'Plato would answer this latter question in the affirmative. . . . Doubt may sometimes spring, not from the corruption of sin, but from the limitation of finitude'[58] – and if there is no recognition of this in Paul we must simply realise that while 'honest doubt' may have been absent from the society in which the apostle lived it is undeniably present in ours, as it was in ancient Athens.

We come therefore to the final query in this connection, and to Baillie's response.

How then are we to account for such honest doubt and denial of God's reality? The answer is perhaps twofold. First, there is the circumstance that our conviction of God first forms itself in our minds in close association with a wide context of other beliefs. In

[57] J. Baillie, *Our Knowledge of God*, pp. 55–7.
[58] Ibid., pp. 57–8.

the course of our later intellectual development, however, many of those other beliefs are seen by us to be false and are quite rightly surrendered. The effort of dissociation that is then required to separate our deep-seated belief in God from that part of its original context which we have now been forced to reject, is an effort to which our mental powers are not always equal, so that we are faced with the difficult alternative of keeping our belief in God and keeping with it certain other beliefs the falsity of which seems quite obvious to us, or else surrendering these false beliefs and surrendering with them our belief in God also.[59]

Baillie continues:

Secondly, however, we must consider the appeal of arguments that are directed, not against the original context of our belief in God, but against that belief itself. In ancient Greece, and again in Western Europe since the Renaissance, but especially in the nineteenth century, there have been current a number of philosophical outlooks which found their starting-point elsewhere than in belief in God – that is to say either in external nature or in man.... Not having set out from the reality of God, not only have they (as indeed we should have expected) failed to arrive at any conviction of His reality, but they have conducted us towards a conception of universal being from which God seems to be definitely excluded. Many men of our time are therefore in the position that, while they do (as I should contend) believe in God in the bottom of their hearts, they cannot think how to answer the arguments which certain prevailing philosophies direct against His reality, and are thus led to doubt Him 'with the top of their minds'.[60]

Not everything that the Baillies had to say about doubt and unbelief will strike the present-day reader as convincing. Their reliance on Kant is probably greater than ours would be; their indebtedness to Carlyle and F. W. Robertson (and Ritschl?) does not impress us as it did our fathers; their assumptions about the continuing existence of a lively Christian culture seem strangely optimistic in the 1990s. Yet their candour, their genuine if unassertive piety, and their refusal, in the spirit of Isaiah's Servant, to 'break a bruised reed' or 'quench the smoking flax' can still evoke our admiration.

[59] Ibid., pp. 59–60.
[60] Ibid., pp. 60–1.

c. Resistance to the Barthian onslaught

As the 1920s gave place to the 1930s and the storm clouds of another World War began to gather, new influences from Europe gradually transformed the theological scene. In particular, churchmen became acquainted with the names of Karl Barth, Emil Brunner and their associates, and with what has at different times been called 'the Theology of Crisis', 'the Dialectical Theology' and 'the Theology of the Word of God'. They were thereby introduced to a temper and attitude very far removed from that which had prevailed among them for something like half a century. Dogmatic rather than apologetic, it started not from humanity – its predicament, its virtues, its self-consciousness – but from God and the divine Word of judgment and salvation. It proclaimed a complete discontinuity between the Christian revelation and human life even at its best. Supernaturalistic, authoritarian, strongly Church-centred, it was given to paradox and contemptuous of the unredeemed intellect, stressed the transcendence rather than the immanence of God and fiercely opposed a number of modern 'isms', including psychologism, historicism and subjectivism. In short, it was bent upon questioning, if not reversing, the dominant tendencies of Christian thought as they had developed in the West throughout the nineteenth century.

Scotland, like other predominantly Protestant countries, was very deeply divided in its response to the new movement. As I have suggested elsewhere, its theologians fell, roughly speaking, into four main groups: the first, those who were only superficially influenced and in consequence continued the 'Liberal-Evangelical' tradition without much change; the second, those whose entire outlook was affected but who in the end withheld their entire approval; the third, those who may be described as real but cautious admirers; the fourth, those in whom we can discern the unqualified zeal of out-and-out converts. To the first group may be assigned David S. Cairns of Aberdeen; to the third, H. R. Mackintosh; and to the fourth (at least in his early days), George S. Hendry, later of Princeton. The Baillies belong fairly clearly in the second group, and both of them – John in particular – had much to say in their maturer writings about Barth and Barthianism.[61]

---

[61] A. C. Cheyne, *The Transforming of the Kirk* (1983), pp. 207–17.

Though he responded with considerable enthusiasm to the ebullient pre-war liberalism of New College, John always had his reservations about it. On going to the Chair of Systematic Theology at Auburn Seminary, New York, therefore, he seems to have decided to act as a kind of mediator between two extremes, what one contemporary called 'a conservative biblicism which is suspicious of all modern scientific conclusions' and 'a liberal modernism which is equally eager to assimilate every new scientific suggestion as the messianic deliverer of religion from its bondage to custom and tradition'.[62] The consequence was that he appeared while in America to be a conservative among liberals, and in Scotland a few years later a liberal among conservatives.

Yet the general movement of his thought – at least after the publication of his first three volumes, *The Roots of Religion*, *The Interpretation of Religion* and *The Place of Jesus Christ in Modern Christianity* – was fairly steadily towards a greater traditionalism. Of the years around 1930 he wrote later:

> I remember being vaguely haunted by the feeling that, exhilarating as the thought of this [liberal] period had been, it was now approaching something like a dead end. It seemed as if there were nowhere much further to go along the paths we were then pursuing. As things fell out, however, we had not long to wait before we found ourselves being headed off in a totally different direction. . . . The turning-point is most conveniently marked by the publication of Karl Barth's *Epistle to the Romans* in 1918.[63]

By 1931, influenced by Barth and such other thinkers as Kierkegaard, Buber, Brunner and Tillich, Baillie could publish an article with the revealing title, 'The Predicament of Humanism'.[64]

Despite all this, however, it is clear that John never gave his complete allegiance to the new Swiss and German fashions – as one of his students at Union Seminary, Dietrich Bonhoeffer, noted with regret.[65] In 1933, he remarked in his 'Confessions of a Transplanted Scot' that

[62] D. S. Klinefelter, 'The Theology of John Baillie: A Biographical Introduction', *Scottish Journal of Theology*, vol. 22, no. 4 (Dec. 1969), p. 427.
[63] Quoted, ibid., p. 428.
[64] Referred to, ibid., p. 429.
[65] D. Bonhoeffer, *No Rusty Swords* (1970), pp. 85–6.

the so-called Theology of Crisis seems to me, as regards one side of its teaching, to have grown out of precisely those aspects of Ritschlianism which I found myself from the first rejecting [he means, particularly, its 'narrow Lutheran Christocentrism', its 'inhospitable attitude toward whatever religious insight stands outside of the Christian tradition' and its 'extreme opposition to mysticism'] and this in spite of the fact that the Ritschlian system is in other respects the object of its direct and very bitter attack.

He also notes, parenthetically, that 'Professor Barth listened to Herrman's lectures at Marburg very nearly at the same time as I was listening to them, but we must have been attracted and repelled by very different sides of our teacher's thought.'[66]

In that same article, Baillie spelled out in some detail his agreements and disagreements with the new theology. On the positive side:

Its protests against our over-weening humanism, our cheap evolutionism, our smug immanentism and our childish utopianism have been most challenging, and in what it has to say about our human insignificance as over against God and about our utter dependence on Him for our salvation it is difficult to do anything but rejoice. In debate with my theological friends in this country [the USA] I have, more often than otherwise, found myself defending the Barthian positions against the very opposite principles which are professed by perhaps the majority of them.

On the negative side:

Yet even here I am unwilling to follow Professor Barth all the way. There are indeed many things which he might have been the first to teach me, and in which I might be ready to follow him more unsuspectingly, had I not learned them first from von Hugel – and learned at the same time to beware against understanding them in too one-sided a fashion. Barth and von Hugel have very much the same medicine to administer to our erring modernism, but only von Hugel is careful to provide also a suitable antidote against an overdose.[67]

So – bearing in mind Justin Martyr's assertion that 'whatever things have been rightly said by anyone belong to us Christians', as well as von Hugel's aphorism that '"In my flesh abideth no

---

[66] 'Confessions', p. 52.
[67] Ibid., p. 53.

good thing" will somehow have to be integrated with "the spirit indeed is willing but the flesh is weak"',[68] Baillie kept his balance even in the headiest days of the Barthian challenge; and although practically all his references to Barth in *And the Life Everlasting* (1934) were favourable, this was no longer the case in what may be his most important work, *Our Knowledge of God* (1939).

Nor did the further passage of time remove his misgivings. In the years immediately after the Second World War he began (as one commentator put it) 'to move beyond his earlier neo-orthodoxy, on the basis of a renewed confidence in reason'.[69] The closing pages of the posthumously published Gifford Lectures, *The Sense of the Presence of God*, therefore, contain not only the last but also perhaps the strongest expression of his resistance to Barthian teaching. 'That it provides a much-needed correction to certain errors into which we have lately been inclined to fall', he writes, 'I cannot doubt; but it administers this medicine in so brusque and defiant a way, and in such merciless overdoses, that in the end I find myself not only refusing to swallow it but at the same time suspecting that something is wrong with the prescription.'[70] He quotes from Gustav Wingren's 'cogent and indeed merciless refutation of Dr. Barth', in which the Swedish theologian had remarked that 'Barth has the ability to a very large degree of being able to employ the language of Scripture in a system that is totally foreign to the Bible', and comments: 'I should probably not myself have been so outspoken as Dr. Wingren, but I am in full agreement with him none the less.'[71]

Despite his considerable indebtedness to the great Swiss master, John was never really an adherent of the Barthian school, and his most memorable utterances seem always to have been of a mediating kind. 'I believe', he declared in the late fifties,

any effective and significant post-Barthian movement must go *through* Barthianism, not repudiating the remarkable contribution it has made to all our thinking but entering fully into its heritage, while at the same time correcting its deficiencies and also recovering for us much

---

[68] Ibid., pp. 53–4.
[69] Klinefelter, 'John Baillie', p. 433.
[70] J. Baillie, *The Sense of the Presence of God* (1962), p. 182.
[71] Ibid., pp. 255–6.

that was of value in those early ways of thought that were too brashly jettisoned.[72]

There is reason to believe that Donald shared his brother's views. Though *God Was in Christ* exhibits considerable indebtedness to the movement, approval is mixed with criticism. At one point, the author comments on its 'curious combination of theological dogmatism with historical scepticism'; at another, he 'almost ventures to say that it does not take the Incarnation quite seriously'; and in the end the impression he gives is of rather cautious detachment.[73]

Now that the Barthian tide has receded, arousing less enthusiasm – and less revulsion – than in former days, it is possible to regard the Baillies' open but critical attitude to it as not the least of their many services to the Christian thinking of our time.

This brief and very impressionistic introduction to the life's work of the Baillie brothers must not close without mentioning what in the end of the day was perhaps their greatest strength. Quite unconsciously, John drew attention to it in his early lecture on 'The Fundamental Task of the Theological Seminary'.

> The ideal required for our theological schools [he affirmed] is that we, the teachers, should be the kind of men who, without knowing how, and whatever be the subject of our discourse, inspire and awaken and change men. The greatest chapters in the history of education are those that tell of individual magnetic personalities, of men whose power lay as much in the inherent transmissive quality of their own consecration as in any counsels they gave.[74]

Many who were their students either in North America during the 1920s and early 1930s, or in Scotland at St Mary's College, St Andrews, and New College, Edinburgh, in the late thirties, the forties and the fifties, would testify that in so saying the young professor foretold with remarkable accuracy what would be the final verdict on the teaching careers of John and Donald Macpherson Baillie.

[72] Quoted in Klinefelter, p. 433.
[73] D. M. Baillie, *God was in Christ: An Essay on Incarnation and Atonement* (1948), pp. 37 and 53.
[74] 'Fundamental Task', p. 281.

Chapter 11

John and Donald Baillie:
Their Churchmanship

It was within the Christian Church and for its sake that John and Donald Baillie lived their lives and did their thinking. Even their earliest work manifests a concern for what might be called 'realised Christianity'. At the climax of his argument in *The Roots of Religion* (1926), John reminds the reader that

> To be a Christian . . . is not merely to think this and the other, nor is it merely to do this and leave the other undone; it is rather to have living and personal experience of the fellowship of Christian love. . . . It is to know, with all the saints of all the ages, something of the breadth and length and depth and height of the love that was in the heart of Christ and, illumined and strengthened by that knowledge, to place all our reliance upon the love of God and be filled with His fullness.[1]

And the final paragraph of Donald's *Faith in God and its Christian Consummation* (1927), after a reference to the paradox which seems to be inherent in all our speech about God and His purposes, concludes with these words: 'Yet it is not altogether by thinking the matter out, but rather by living it out in daily Christian faith and love, that we shall arrive at a deeper insight . . . And a book about faith cannot better end than upon this note of hope and expectation.'[2]

The ecclesiastical implications of this emphasis on Christian *praxis* receive fuller and more explicit treatment in two of the brothers' later writings. The epilogue to Donald's *God Was in Christ* (1948) is significantly entitled 'The Body of Christ', and (in the author's own words) views the landscape thus far traversed

---

[1] J. Baillie, *The Roots of Religion in the Human Soul* (1926), pp. 203–4.
[2] D. M. Baillie, *Faith in God and its Christian Consummation* (2nd edn, 1964), p. 301.

'from the vantage-point of the Church of Christ, since it is the Church that has to tell the story'. Indeed, the closing pages of the book are something akin to a rhapsody on the theme of the Church, which is variously described as 'the new People of God, the new Israel, the Ecclesia, the Body of Christ . . . the nucleus of the new humanity . . . God's instrument of reconciliation through the age'.[3] Still more eloquent is the chapter on this same topic with which John concludes his *Invitation to Pilgrimage* (1942). Arguing that 'It is only in Christ that we can enjoy full communion with one another, and . . . only in our togetherness with one another that we can enjoy full communion with Christ,' he offers the following thoughts on Christian community:

> God has apparently done everything He possibly could, short of exercising actual compulsion upon our wills, to prevent us from making our religion a private luxury. . . . For what more could He have done than so to order things that men can find salvation only by betaking themselves to one place, where they are bound to meet one another – to the hill called Calvary; by encountering there a single historical figure – the figure of Jesus; by listening to the selfsame story; by reading in the same book; by praying the same prayers in the same Name; by being baptised into the same fellowship and partaking of the same sacred meal – 'all made to drink into one Spirit'; by drawing in fact their whole spiritual sustenance from the same unbroken tradition handed down from age to age? . . . You and I owe all the knowledge of God that we have to our upbringing in the one tradition and our reception into the one fellowship of the Church of Christ, and the only way that is open to us whereby we should bring to others the blessings of that knowledge is by initiating them into the same tradition and receiving them into the same Church.[4]

Against the forceful appeal of totalitarianism, therefore, or what could be represented as the exclusive individualism of the humanist ideal, the Baillies contended (to continue with John's argument) that 'our only hope lies in finding another and nobler form of community which will unite us in a stronger solidarity,

---

[3] D. M. Baillie, *God Was in Christ: An Essay on Incarnation and Atonement* (1948), pp. 203, 208–9.

[4] J. Baillie, *Invitation to Pilgrimage* (1942), pp. 122–3. This thought occurs repeatedly in Baillie's writings: cf. his *A Reasoned Faith* (1963), pp. 18 and 165–6.

and call forth a more deep-seated and passionate devotion than even our [wartime] foes can claim to possess'.[5] And so the ardent apologetic of *Invitation to Pilgrimage* closes by taking us, as it were, to the very door of the Christian Church:

> I hope, then, that I have provided sufficient reason why we should all seek the fellowship of the Christian Church, there to rekindle our ideals and rehabilitate them in a solidarity that is stronger than all the solidarities of earth. There may be many that have lately been saying of themselves, with Coleridge's Ancient Mariner,

> > . . . this soul hath been
> > Alone on a wide, wide sea,
> > So lonely 'twas that God Himself
> > Scarce seemed there to be.

> But I hope I have given good reason why they should now decide, again with the Mariner,

> > To walk together to the kirk
> > With a goodly company.

> > To walk together to the kirk
> > And all together pray,
> > While each to his great Father bends,
> > Old men, and babes, and loving friends,
> > And youths, and maidens gay.[6]

Some idea of the kind of churchmanship to which such warmly expressed convictions gave rise may be obtained by considering three aspects of the Baillies' distinctive contribution to Christian faith and life during the 1920s, thirties, forties and fifties: their style of preaching, their approach to social questions, and the ways in which, as increasingly enthusiastic supporters of the Ecumenical Movement, they sought to do justice to both Catholic and Protestant elements in the Christian tradition as a whole.

a. Preaching

Since the Reformation, the sermon has invariably occupied a central place in Scottish religion. It is hardly surprising, therefore, that some of the Kirk's ablest theologians have also been among

---

5 Ibid., pp. 127–8.
6 Ibid., pp. 130–1.

its most effective preachers – or that the Baillie brothers should deserve inclusion in the latter as well as the former category.

Donald's reputation as a prince of the pulpit has perhaps stood higher in recent years than John's. That this is so may be attributed at least in part to the very deep impression made by *To Whom Shall We Go?* and *Out of Nazareth*, two volumes of sermons by the younger brother which were posthumously published in the 1950s. Each of them won glowing opinions for its author's skill in handling the profoundest and most difficult topics without subjecting his audience to overly demanding dogmatic disquisitions or exegetical exercises. (In this connection, special notice may be taken of the sermon on 'The Glory of the Cross' in the earlier volume, and that on 'The Mystery of the Trinity' in its sequel.)

There is always something indefinable and incommunicable about preaching power, but two aspects of Donald's unusual effectiveness spring immediately to mind. The first is the beautiful simplicity of structure and language which characterises all his work. In this regard, the Memoir by Professor John Dow which forms the prefix to *To Whom Shall We Go?* contains an interesting reminiscence of Donald's early years.

> Donald [we are told] knew from the beginning what a sermon should be. I can recall his first student 'outline'. We wondered what this brilliant philosophy student would produce. A magnificently articulated structure with four heads and many subsections like a class essay? No, we saw on the blackboard a model outline of attractive simplicity and directness. And so his sermons continued all along.[7]

One or two examples from the published sermons should illustrate what John Dow meant. The sermon for Palm Sunday on Matthew's citation of Zechariah 9:9 ('Thy King cometh unto thee, meek, and sitting upon an ass') subdivides as follows: '(1) What did it mean for the man who first wrote it? (2) What did it mean to the people who thought of it that day, hundreds of years later, as Jesus rode into Jerusalem? (3) What did it mean to Jesus? (4) What does it mean for us, after 1900 years?'[8] The sermon on

---

[7] J. Dow, Memoir, in D. M. Baillie, *To Whom Shall We Go?* (1955), p. 19.

[8] *To Whom Shall We Go?*, pp. 137–43.

Election from Matthew 4:18–20 (the call of Simon and Andrew) makes four points: '(1) God always chooses us before we choose Him. (2) God does not choose us because we deserve it. (3) God does not choose us to be His favourites, but to be His servants. (4) When God chooses and calls us, we also have to make our choice.'[9] The New Year sermon on Jeremiah 9:23–4 takes each clause of its text in turn: '(1) Let not the wise man glory in his wisdom. (2) Let not the mighty man glory in his might. (3) Let not the rich man glory in his riches. (4) But he that glorieth, let him glory in this, that he understandeth and knoweth Me, saith the Lord.'[10] And that on 'Thy Father which is in secret' (Matthew 6:6 expounds what are called 'three simple truths about the spiritual life': '(1) Every man's soul is his own secret. (2) There is One who knows all our secrets. (3) There is One who can lead us into the secret of God.'[11]

Alongside the simplicity, bordering on elegance, of the structure and language of Donald's sermons, mention should also be made of their other peculiar strength: the striking appropriateness and practicality of the illustrative material used to drive the message home. Perhaps the most memorable instance of this – though too long for quotation here – occurs in the title sermon of *Out of Nazareth*. But two others may be cited. The first comes from what was probably a Whitsunday sermon on Joel 2:28: 'Your sons and your daughters shall be prophets.' Towards its close the preacher remarks:

> That [the story of Pentecost] is a very old story. Can we translate it into the language and interests of our modern world? Let us try, with the aid of a little imagination. (1) You take your seat in a railway compartment. In the opposite corner sits a labouring man, reading his newspaper. You look at him, and try to picture the life he leads. A rough, bare life, you think; hard work all day, a quiet pipe in the evening, a football match to watch on a Saturday afternoon; and, if he is a particularly decent man, he goes to church once in a while on a Sunday morning. So you sum up his life. Is that all? I wonder. When the man puts down his paper and leans back and shuts his eyes, what is he thinking of? Perhaps he is thinking of GOD. Perhaps

---

[9] Ibid., pp. 180–5.
[10] D. M. Baillie, *Out Of Nazareth: A Selection of Sermons and Lectures* (1958), pp. 92–6.
[11] Ibid., pp. 17–24.

he is bringing the light of his faith to bear upon the great issues he
has been reading about in his newspaper – labour troubles, party
politics, war and peace among the nations. Perhaps he is connecting
all these things with the God he believes in. Why not? He is a working
man. So was Jesus. And you don't know what depths of Christian
faith there may be in the heart and life of that man. (2) Or you go
into a shop in the city. A girl at the counter serves you. What does
she care for, except to get on as well as she can in her own line, and
meanwhile get as much fun as she can out of her wages when working
hours are over, a round of rather selfish and empty pleasures filling
up her evenings and weekends? And that is all. Is it? It may be. But it
may also be that that girl has visions and dreams that would go
straight to the heart of Christ Himself. It may be that behind the
scenes of what seems a very common-place existence there is a brave
unselfish life of burden-bearing for other people, sustained perhaps
by the fellowship of the Church of Christ and by a living faith in
God.[12]

The second example of felicitously down-to-earth sermon
illustration and application comes from a Communion address
on 'Christ washing the disciples' feet'. It runs as follows:

Through many of the days of our lives, we Christian men and women
are pretty unaspiring. We haven't much of the heavenly vision, we
let it fall away and come to be content with a very mediocre Christian
life. The world has its claims, and we become preoccupied with them;
and our neighbours may be difficult, and we become loveless towards
them; and our devotions sometimes seem a waste of time, and we
become slack about them. And so the days run on, and we are living
on a pretty commonplace level, though perhaps we hardly know it,
with only half our hearts in the service of Christ. And suddenly
perhaps (it sometimes happens at a communion season) we get a
glimpse of the poor lives we are living, and we also get a glimpse of
the beauty of holiness, the glory of a real genuine whole-hearted
Christian life. Yes, and lest we should be discouraged, we at the
same time get a glimpse of the wonderful, infinite love of God in
Jesus Christ, and His power to help us, and His high purpose for us,
that we should be perfect as He is perfect. Then we are fired with
holy enthusiasm and aspiration. We resolve in our hearts that
henceforth we will not go back nor turn from God at all. Our hearts
leap out in faith to God, cast themselves upon His grace, consecrate
themselves to His will, dedicate themselves to His service. Our whole

[12] *To Whom Shall We Go?*, pp. 35–6.

hearts go out to Christ our Master. They were indeed His already, but we remember it now in a fresh moment of dedication: 'Lord, not my feet only, but also my hands and my head.'[13]

Although John's sermons are not quite so readily accessible as his brother's, a few of them appear in the little collection edited by Professor John McIntyre and published in 1962 under the title, *Christian Devotion*, while others are to be found in the Baillie Papers at New College, Edinburgh. In their own way they are as impressive as Donald's: more academic in expression, certainly, but equally thought-provoking and perhaps more unusual. This is particularly true of a sermon on 'the conversion of the mind' which was preached at Great St Mary's, Cambridge, in November 1944. The text – 'bringing every thought into captivity to Christ' (2 Corinthians 10:5) – gave rise to a meditation on all those thoughts, little ones and great ones, fleeting fancies and ruling ideas, which according to the apostle must be subjected to his Lord. In the course of it, the preacher had much to say that was both psychologically wise and spiritually discerning, including this on our 'little thoughts':

> If anybody were to ask you what you have been thinking about today, only one or two things would at first occur to you. They would be what I should call your officially acknowledged thoughts: they would no doubt concern matters of public or professional or family importance, and though not always very weighty they would at least be eminently respectable. These are the thoughts that pass what the psychologists call the 'Censor'. But we know that our minds are also at all times giving hospitality to all sorts of unofficial contents. What was in my mind as I waited for the bus at the corner? What visions did I see in the clouds of my tobacco smoke, as I leaned back in my chair to enjoy my after-dinner pipe? What were my thoughts as I lay awake in bed last night? What were my dreams when at last I went to sleep? And what my day-dreams during my idlest waking hours? – If the soul is really dyed the colour of its leisure thoughts [the reference is to an aphorism of Marcus Aurelius] then it is clear that a man is not really converted until his leisure thoughts are converted. . . . He [Christ] is . . . as interested in my idle moments as my busy ones, as much in my reveries as my resolutions, as much in my castles in the air as in the more solid edifices of my public and professional life. No man is really Christ's until his day-dreams are

Christ's – aye, and his night-dreams too, if they are anywise subject to his control.[14]

Two other sermons from the years immediately after the Second World War take us very near to the heart of Baillie the believing academic. In 1949 (the year before he became Principal of New College) John preached in Belfast on the occasion of Queen's University's centenary celebrations. Taking as his text the words from Luke 12:48, 'For unto whomsoever much is given, of him shall much be required', he offered his hearers a meditation on university life under three heads: its responsibilities, its temptations and its limitations. What he had to say on the first of these sounds a note which we can recognise as distinctively his own.

> The special responsibilities [he observed] all presuppose, and do not in the least degree replace or mitigate the one fundamental responsibility which we share before God with every member of the human race. You and I are men and women first, and students only afterwards, and therefore in the first instance it is exactly the same demands that God makes on us all. Surely our Puritan fathers were right when they said that on the Day of Judgment we shall stand before God, stripped not only of our earthly possessions and dignities, but stripped also of our accumulated learning. They were right, because that is how we stand before God *now*. There is one demand God makes on us all. And we all know what it is. It is to do justly and to love mercy and to walk humbly before Him all the days of our life. It is to give our souls without reserve to His keeping. It is to put our whole trust in the merits of His blessed Son. Nothing else matters until that has been settled. All our high culture, all our specialist knowledge, is so much useless lumber and rubble, except as it is built upon that foundation and used for its further upbuilding.

A little further on, there occur these typically Baillian phrases: 'the grim truth is that we have all of us more knowledge than we are willing to use or to use for the right ends. There may be much that we do not know, but we all know enough to be better than we are, and to make our society an altogether better thing than it now is.' And the conclusion is as follows:

[14] J. Baillie, Sermon preached in Great St Mary's, Cambridge, 1944 (in New College Library, Edinburgh, ref. A.b.a.12).

I believe that we shall stand firm only if, in cultivating our intellects, we take heed not to lose our souls; only if, while becoming ever more complex in knowledge, we remain simple at heart; only if, as sinful men and women, whose lives stand naked in His sight, we first put ourselves right with God, and then bring every thought, all our knowledge and all our learning, into captivity to the obedience of His Christ.[15]

Three years earlier, in the Great Hall of Birmingham University, Baillie preached a sermon on Martha and Mary with the title, 'Only one thing is necessary'. It ended with some phrases which sum up his message not only on that occasion but also on many others:

The one thing needful, then, is not money or power or fame or a successful career. And . . . I hope I may assume that it is not what we call culture – a cultivated mind. . . . We should be fully prepared for the discovery that the one thing needful is *the same for everybody* – the same for peasant and plutocrat, the same for household drudge and high-born student, and (incidentally) the same also for students and professors. Further, we should be prepared to learn that it is something of an entirely non-competitive character, and in no sense a limited commodity of which somebody else must have less because I have more. What is it then? What is this pearl of great price? What is the one thing needful, the good part which Mary chose? The story puts it quite simply: 'she sat at Jesus' feet and heard His Word.' And that is what it is.[16]

No doubt the Baillies will be longest remembered for their theological work. But at least from the mid-thirties, by which time John had begun teaching in Edinburgh and Donald in St Andrews, they were widely regarded as being among the most distinguished preachers of their generation. Churches and university chapels across the English-speaking world vied with each other for their services; and in the light of the sermons just looked at, as well as many others equally worthy of consideration, which are still available in printed or manuscript form, it is not hard to understand why.

[15] J. Baillie, Sermon preached before the Queen's University of Belfast, 1949 (in New College Library, Edinburgh, ref. A.b.a.12).
[16] J. Baillie, Sermon preached in Great Hall of Birmingham University, 1946 (in New College Library, Edinburgh, ref. A.b.a.12).

b. Social attitudes

'A concern for social justice lay very near to the core of his understanding of Christian faith.' With these words (to be found in the biographical essay which he prefixed to Donald's post-humously published *The Theology of the Sacraments*) John introduced the most explicit account anywhere available of his brother's attitude to social questions. He continued as follows:

> He was zealous not only for religious but for political and especially *economic* freedom; zealous also for equality, not in a doctrinaire understanding of it, but in the sense of the removal of the many unjustified inequalities with which he felt our society to have traditionally been burdened. He was thus inclined rather strongly to the left in his political convictions, about which he was always outspoken, though refusing to sell out to any single system of economic doctrine and hesitating to attach any label to his views. He would say, 'I don't know whether I'm a socialist or not, but I do certainly think, etc.'[17]

As will presently be seen, there is little doubt that the writer of the above shared the views he was describing. For both brothers were very much the heirs of a revolution in social attitudes which had taken place in the Scottish churches during the closing decades of the nineteenth century and the opening decades of the twentieth – the very period in which John and Donald Baillie came to maturity and did a great deal of their most strenuous thinking. In the words of one recent historian, Scotland in the years before the First World War witnessed

> the first significant break from traditional Christian social concern based on an acceptance of the existing order, and which expressed itself in charitable and reclamation work, and a new Christian social concern based on a suspicion or rejection of the existing order and which expressed itself in social criticism and in more dynamic and radical forms of social action.[18]

The process of deepening social concern and intensifying social criticism which had marked the late-Victorian and Edwardian

[17] J. Baillie, 'Donald: A Brother's Impression', D. M. Baillie, *The Theology of the Sacraments and Other Papers With a Biographical Essay by John Baillie* (1957), p. 32.

[18] D. C. Smith, *Passive Obedience and Prophetic Protest: Social Criticism in the Scottish Church, 1830–1945* (1987), p. 356.

periods looked for a time as if it would be carried even further by the impact of the 1914–18 War, that shatterer of nineteenth-century complacency. As everyone knows, of course, end-of-war hopes soon ran into the sand, and were succeeded, as the 1920s gave way to the 1930s, by a reactionary mood of disillusionment, cynicism and opportunistic self-interest. Yet the setback proved to be only temporary. The onset of the Second World War precipitated another tremendous surge of questioning and heart-searching, not least in the Churches; and among the advocates of extensive reconstruction (along with his contemporary William Temple, Archbishop of Canterbury from 1942 to 1944 and author of an immensely influential paperback, *Christianity and the Social Order*) was John Baillie. A relatively recent home-comer to Scotland (in 1935), he soon acquired a considerable reputation as thinker, teacher and administrator – a reputation which in May 1940, that month of supreme crisis, led to his appointment as convener of the General Assembly's special 'Commission for the Interpretation of God's Will in the Present Crisis'. That body's formidable task was defined as 'to seek reverently to guide the Church in the interpretation of the Holy Will and Purpose of God in present-day events, and to examine how the testimony of the Church to the Gospel may become more effective in our own land, overseas and in the international order'.[19] During the succeeding quinquennium it produced a series of searching and wide-ranging reports which served as a kind of high-water mark in the social thought of twentieth-century Scottish Christianity.

The 'Baillie Commission' (as it was often called) had to handle a vast array of complicated and controversial topics; and sub-committees were set up to deal with Church Life and Organisation, Social and Industrial Life, Marriage and the Family, and Education. But in every case their handiwork was discussed and licked into shape by the parent body, while plenary sessions considered the more fundamental theological problems that arose along the way, together with matters bearing upon the future task of International Reconstruction. Five annual reports were

[19] *God's Will for Church and Nation. Reprinted from the Reports of the Commission for the Interpretation of God's Will in the Present Crisis as Presented to the General Assembly of the Church of Scotland During the War Years* (1946), p. 7.

made to the General Assemblies of 1941 to 1945 inclusive – three of these being made available for a wider public by the SCM Press under the titles *God's Will in our Time*, *The Church Faces the Future* and *Home, Community and Church*. In 1946, after the Commission's discharge, a composite volume, containing whatever seemed likeliest to be of permanent interest in its findings, came out under the title *God's Will for Church and Nation*. Excluded from this compilation was a good deal of material relating to the internal life and organisation of the Church of Scotland, as well as sectional reports on such topics as 'the Feeding of Europe, the Treatment of the Vanquished Nations, our Duty to the Jewish People, Religious Freedom, and so on' which (in the convener's words) had been .'left behind by the march of events'. But what remained – the real legacy of the Commission's work – amounted to an astonishingly comprehensive epitome of responsible and forward-looking thought in the Kirk.

John Baillie's personal responsibility for the conclusions reached by his committee cannot, needless to say, be established in any detail. But those who were familiar with his confidence in the force of reasoned argument, his ability to combine the overall view with regard for particularities, his coolly balanced way of presenting a case and his lucid, rather 'literary' style – as well as his somewhat imperious manner, which allowed little scope to obstructionism or ill-considered dissent – readily gave him much of the credit for both the form and the content of the reports. All the more interesting is it, therefore, to discern the general direction in which their analysis of society pointed.

After distinguishing between 'ultimate spiritual principles' and 'secondary and more specialised principles which exhibit the relevance of the ruling principles to the particular field of action in which guidance is needed', the 1942 Report laid down the following 'relevant middle axiom' for the proper conduct of socio-economic affairs: 'Economic power must be made objectively responsible to the community as a whole. The possessors of economic power must be answerable for the use of that power, not only to their own consciences, but to appropriate social organs.'[20] Such a position no doubt appeared startling enough to conservative-minded churchmen like Dr John White, minister of

[20] Ibid., p. 62.

the Barony church in Glasgow; but greater surprises were to come. Building on the 1942 axiom, the Commission asserted two years later that 'the common interest demands a far greater measure of public control of capital resources and means of production than our tradition has in the past envisaged'. And it then went on to sketch an understanding of things whose 'left-wing' or 'socialist' tendencies are sufficiently conveyed in four quite radical sub-headings: 'The Tyranny of Private Interests', 'The Necessity of a Greater Measure of Communal Control for the Rehabilitation of our Social and Industrial Life', 'The Necessity of Communal Control for the Conscientious Discharge of our World Responsibilities' and 'The Necessity of Communal Control for the Revitalisation of our Democracy'.[21]

Of course, Baillie and his associates were careful not to suggest that the implementation of their proposals would inevitably bring about a kind of heaven on earth. 'Even democracy built round the idea of common control has no inherent certainty of curing our disease,' they conceded.

It is sometimes claimed by the secular theorist that such a construction would, by the mere planning of production for use, lead to the guarantee of employment for all, to the removal of the fear of bankruptcy, to the disappearance of the anxiety and bitterness associated with competition, to the limitation of production to socially valuable commodities, and to the equal sharing both of necessary suffering and of the achievements of social development. The Christian will make no such claim, and will indeed doubt whether so Utopian an ideal is ever likely to be realised on earth.

Yet they immediately went on to assert that

this deeper insight does not release the Christian from the obligation to put forward such claims as *can* be substantiated, viz., that failing a greater measure of public control, and its resolute development as a soil not inimical to the nurture of Christian faith and life, economic chaos must inevitably issue in an end of such limited democracy as our nation has already enjoyed.[22]

And their survey culminated in the following indictment – firmly if cautiously phrased – of the way things were ordered in the industrialised West:

[21] Ibid., pp. 157–68.
[22] Ibid., p. 168.

What men want is not a Utopia, but an objective that is really obtainable, though not without a hazard; a fair chance without too much disfavour; a cause not devoid of idealism. For such they are still prepared to accept discipline. But our present economic life no longer provides a recognisable objective; it denies a fair chance in life to a multitude of our citizens and a fair chance of leadership to those with the will and capacity to lead; and our democracy lacks a cause such as we can follow confidently and with all our heart.[23]

It was in the 1942 Report, however, that the Commission, while discussing 'The Nature and Extent of the Church's Concern in the Civil Order', delivered its most forceful reply to the view that Christians depart from their essential task whenever they turn their attention to questions of social justice.

Christians have often failed [so the message ran] to distinguish adequately between the religious and political spheres, and have thus misled the Church into making pronouncements on questions which it only imperfectly understood. But we hold it as certain that the greater harm has come about through the opposite error – through the indifference of Christians to the maladjustments of that civil ordering of society in which they like others have a part, and the consequent failure of the Church to bring its own light to bear upon the problems so created. If it were merely that Christians were so exclusively absorbed in heavenly things as to be indifferent to the earthly ills of themselves and their neighbours, that alone would spell a serious falsification of the true Christian temper; but it is to be feared that many of us must plead guilty to the even more damaging charge of complacently accepting the amenities, and availing ourselves of the privileges, of a social order which happened to offer these things to ourselves while denying them to others. . . . There can be little doubt that it is to the failure of Christians to realise and act upon these social implications of the Gospel that the present weakness of the spiritual life in our land must in no small part be attributed. We long for a revival of spiritual religion, but there are many who suspect the spirituality to which we call them of making too ready a compliance with a social order that for them means only hunger, slum conditions, unemployment, or sweated labour. . . . Selfishness is of the very essence of the sin from which, in any revival of religion, men need to be redeemed; but what if there be no particular form of this sin from which we more need to be redeemed today than a

[23] Ibid., p. 169.

complacent indifference to the social evils that surround our comfortable lives?[24]

There is some reason to think that the stance adopted by the Commission helped not a little to bring about the almost seismic shift which took place in the social thinking of the country as the War drew to its close – the shift epitomised in the Beveridge Report of 1944 and the inauguration of the National Health Service four years later. Today, politicians and historians alike have their differences about the wisdom or otherwise of the revolution that ushered in the Welfare State, and churchmen and theologians seem to be in similar case. Yet nearly all of them would probably concede that the modern world has not seen very many instances of Christian leaders giving more strenuous – and influential – thought to social and economic problems than was given by the Baillie Commission in the period between 1940 and 1945. For the dominant part he played in its labours, almost as much as for his contribution to 'pure' theology, John Baillie may be said to have earned a secure place in the history of twentieth-century Scottish religion.

c. Loyalties – Reformed, Catholic and Ecumenical

Seekers after a concise yet comprehensive account of the doctrine of the Church which underlay the Baillies' life's work can hardly do better than turn to the pronouncements of the Commission just examined, and in particular to that portion of its 1943 Report which was republished three years later under the heading 'The Church of Christ – Its True Nature and its Universal Mission'. It is a document which may confidently be taken as presenting the views not only of the Commission as a whole but also especially of its masterful convener, whose clarity of thought and incisiveness of judgment are discernible in almost every phrase.

'The Church', it begins, 'is essential to the Gospel. Apart from the fellowship which we are privileged to enjoy within it the Christian salvation and the Christian way of life cease to have real meaning.' Then follows a description, on fairly traditional lines, of the Unity, Catholicity, Apostolicity and Sanctity of this indispensable institution. On its Unity, attention is drawn, in

---

[24] Ibid., pp. 34 and 49.

phrases which echo some of the most favoured affirmations of the Ecumenical Movement, to what St Paul had to say on the subject:

(a) He stresses not only the one Spirit, but also the one body; not merely the spiritual but also the corporate unity of Christ's Church. . . . (b) He does not speak of the unity of the Church as an ideal; he speaks of it always as a reality. . . . (c) He always thinks of this unity as a sacramental unity, signed and sealed by baptism and participation in the sacred meal.

On its Catholicity, the Commission contends that

To say that the Church is one is at the same time to say that it is universal. . . . The later usage of the term to distinguish one section of the Church, claiming to be alone orthodox and legitimate, from heretical and schismatic bodies, marks a shift to both a more intellectualistic and a more hierarchical emphasis. . . . When the Church was first rent asunder by schism, and throughout the greater part of its subsequent history, the various resultant bodies tended each to exclude the others as not belonging to the true Church of Christ, which they conceived themselves alone to represent; but in our own day a more tolerant and charitable view is widely taken, the former mutually exclusive 'sects' being regarded rather as differing 'denominations', all of which are recognised as 'branches' of Christ's Church. Nevertheless the existence of such disunity within the Body of Christ gives rise to grave problems.

On the Church's Apostolicity, the Commission makes the following comment:

This means that it is continuous with the Church of the New Testament, and founded on the witness of the Lord's first disciples. . . . The means by which this apostolic succession has been maintained and transmitted have, as is well-known, been the subject of much controversy, but of the reality and importance of the succession itself there can be no doubt. . . . Like the Ephesians to whom Paul wrote in the first century, we also in Scotland in the twentieth century 'are built upon the foundation of the apostles and prophets, Jesus Christ himself being the chief corner stone'.

On its Sanctity, finally, the judgment made by the Westminster Divines that 'The purest Churches under heaven are subject both to mixture and to error' leads on to a declaration that the Church on earth is a society, not of the just but of the justified, not of the righteous but of the forgiven and the redeemed. And it is itself a redeemed society – no mere collection of redeemed individuals, but a society entrance into whose fellowship constitutes the salvation of the individuals comprising it.[25]

Building on these convictions, the Commission went on to discuss a host of related topics; and a few of its more revealing comments merit attention. Referring to Cyprian's famous *'extra ecclesiam nulla salus'*, the Report observes, felicitously, that 'The truth is not that adherence to the Church (still less to one branch of it) is a formal pre-condition of salvation; the truth is rather that entry into the divine–human fellowship is what salvation means.'[26] The case for infant baptism is strongly argued, with conspicuous dependence on Calvin and the Westminster Confession, and the Commission's views on both baptism and confirmation are summed up as follows:

What is important is the recognition that there is an age to which . . . individual testimony is proper, and also an age before which it would be unnatural and hurtful to demand it, and that, nevertheless, those of earlier age may be just as truly beloved servants of Christ, yielding to Him the only kind of service of which they are capable or which at that age He desires from them, and accepted by Him as cherished members of His mystical body.[27]

There is also an interesting section on 'The Church of Faith and the Church as Visible Institution', in which the course of thought is traced from the New Testament through Augustine to the catholic orthodoxy of the Middle Ages, Wycliffe and Hus, Calvin and the Westminster Divines to the present day, and approval given to the assertion (by J. H. Oldham, in one of the Oxford Conference volumes of the 1930s) that 'Within the Church as an organised society the true Church has to be continually recreated.'[28]

Against this doctrinal background, it is possible to discern the presence of two strands, not necessarily compatible with each other in every respect, in the churchmanship of the Baillie brothers.

[25] Ibid., pp. 64–75.
[26] Ibid., p. 76.
[27] Ibid., p. 81.
[28] Ibid., pp. 82–5.

On the one hand, from childhood upwards their outlook bore the unmistakeable imprint of Reformed Protestantism, and even in their maturer years they never ceased to be deeply involved in the life of their own communion, the Church of Scotland, and passionately concerned for its welfare. On the other hand, with the passage of time their catholic sympathies came increasingly into view, and from the 1930s to the 1960s there can have been few church leaders who surpassed them in enthusiastic advocacy of the Ecumenical Movement and whole-hearted participation in its activities. Each of these strands – the denominational, that is, and the ecumenical – requires to be examined before a fully rounded picture of the Baillies' contribution to mid-twentieth-century ecclesiastical life can be drawn.

First, then, the denominational strand. Throughout their adult years both John and Donald played a full part in the life of the congregations with which they were associated, as well as in the proceedings of the lower and higher courts of the Church – kirk session, presbytery and General Assembly. The clearest instances of their congregational and parochial involvement were provided by Donald's ministries at Inverbervie, Cupar and Kilmacolm, as well as his service on the kirk session of Martyrs church, St Andrews, during his tenure of the Chair of Systematic Theology at St Mary's College. Their participation in the courts of the Church reached its peak when John, who had already made a unique place for himself as convener of the 'God's Will Commission', was called in 1943 to the office of Moderator of the General Assembly of the Church of Scotland.

Nor is it without significance that under John's leadership the Baillie Commission balanced its world-wide vision with a solicitous regard for the state of ecclesiastical affairs in Scotland itself. The 1943 Report, in particular, looked with an affectionate if critical eye on such matters as the recruitment, supervision and training of ministers, the use of personnel generally, worship, evangelism and preaching. While much in Scotland's religious inheritance was gratefully acknowledged (not least the parochial system, the eldership and the centrality of 'the preaching and teaching function of the ministry'), quite radical changes were also suggested. Some of these, such as the composition of a new catechism or the revival of 'superintendents' to oversee the work of parish ministers, did not ultimately commend themselves to the Kirk. But others – closer oversight, from the centre, of every aspect of ministerial life; a probationary year for young ministers and a fixed retiring age for their seniors; greater frequency of Communion; and, above all, admission of women to the eldership and even, conceivably, to the ministry of Word and Sacraments – were to be acted upon by the next generation.

Even the Commission's final Report (submitted to the General Assembly of 1945 and entitled 'The Conclusion of the Whole') sounded a note of unapologetic admiration for the Church of Scotland and its heritage in worship, government and doctrine:

> By the use of the simplest means its mode of worship has, at its best, been marvellously effective in creating a sense of awe and reverence in the presence of God. Its system of government by a series of church courts from General Assembly to kirk session has so successfully provided for united consultation and action on the national scale that it has served as a model for many communions. Its emphasis on sound doctrine, which has given a certain theological quality to the proclamation of its message, has saved it from absorption in the cultivation of subjective emotion and has enabled it to keep the Faith once delivered to the saints.

Nor did it manifest any inclination to submerge regional peculiarities or denominational distinctiveness in a blandly uniform, icily regular super-Church – as the very next sentences made abundantly clear:

> None of these elements in our heritage must in any way be surrendered, but they must rather be thought of as constituting the most valuable contribution we have to make to the spiritual enrichment of the greater Church for which we pray. The way to a reunited Christendom is not through a weakening of the distinctive witness of the separate communions but rather through such a convinced and convincing exposition of each as will prompt those who represent the others to think whether they have not here something to learn as well as to teach. Nor can we hold it desirable that even the completest possible pattern of future reunion should involve the ironing out of all such regional and sectional divergencies of tradition. The disappearance of such diversity of usage and of emphasis could, at least under earthly conditions, only spell impoverishment.[29]

[29] Ibid., p. 180.

Alongside this denominational strand in the Baillies' thinking, and in a kind of contrapuntal relationship with it, there was always present the other – ecumenical – strand. We have seen how eloquent the God's Will Commission could be in its praise of the Presbyterian heritage, but the eulogy just quoted was immediately succeeded by a solemn warning:

> Such ecclesiastical patriotism is not enough. . . . A world situation demands a world church. . . . Because the situation facing us all is so largely a single situation, we can meet it only by presenting to it a united Christianity. . . . We desire therefore to record in the strongest possible terms our sense of the duty now laid upon our own Church to throw itself with single-minded zeal into the convergent efforts now being made towards the development of a true ecumenical consciousness throughout the whole Body of Christ.[30]

'A world situation demands a world church.' The simple phrase expresses a belief by which both John and Donald seem to have been inspired throughout their adult years, and it would hardly be an exaggeration to say that neither of them could have loved the Scottish Kirk so much had he not loved the *Una Sancta* more – or equally, at the very least.

Their strongest early stimulus to concern for the world-wide Church apparently came from 'Edinburgh, 1910', the great World Missionary Conference of which John R. Mott was the chairman and J. H. Oldham the secretary. Indeed, one of the most telling passages in the Baillie Commission's 1943 Report on 'Division and Unity' might almost be taken as the convener's recollection – after more than thirty years – of what he had heard at the meetings of that never-to-be-forgotten assembly:

> When European missionaries and indigenous Christian leaders of all denominations [in the younger Churches overseas] discuss the main problems of their work, two main questions are constantly raised. The one is whether the younger Churches can thrive and grow as a mere loose federation, each part of which continues to parade as the reason for its separate existence beliefs and practices which it does not itself regard as being of really vital importance. The other question challenges the Churches of the West. Can they hope to carry out effectively their preponderant part in the fuller evangelisation of the world, unless they confront men with a unity of witness and a

[30] Ibid., pp. 180–2.

cohesiveness of effort which cannot be attained so long as present divisions prevail?[31]

For well over twenty years after 'Edinburgh, 1910' (at which, of course, they were no more than onlookers), the brothers had little or nothing to do with high-level inter-Church relations. Only when John moved from America back to Scotland and Donald from parish ministry to university teaching did their growing reputation as theologians combine with their enthusiasm for Christian unity to bring them to prominence in the Ecumenical Movement. Then – half way through the 1930s, that is – they both began to be prominently involved in its 'Faith and Order' activities. Donald played a major part in the Edinburgh Conference of 1937. John, who had been a member of the British Council of Churches almost from its inception in 1942, was elected to the Central Committee of the World Council of Churches at the first great Assembly held in Amsterdam in 1948. The second Assembly, at Evanston in 1954, appointed him – a signal honour – one of six World Presidents. Donald's last important contribution to the Movement was made at Lund (Sweden) in 1952; but for a long period before then he had served as chairman of the subcommission on *Intercommunion*, whose Report with that title was published in 1951.

On the home front, Donald was serving as convener of the Church of Scotland's Inter-Church Relations Committee at the time of his death; while John was a member of the panel of Church of Scotland negotiators who, after protracted conversations with their counterparts in the Church of England, the Scottish Episcopal Church and the Presbyterian Church of England, produced the controversial 'Bishops Report' in 1957.

It is not so easy to detect John Baillie's hand in what was officially called 'Relations between Anglican and Presbyterian Churches' as in the reports of the God's Will Commission. For one thing, he was not the permanent chairman of the Church of Scotland panel. (Donald had originally been nominated for that office, but he died in October 1954. Thereafter it was held in rotation by John, Professor William Manson and Dr 'Archie' Craig.) For another, the Church of Scotland representatives were

[31] Ibid., pp. 93–4.

much less free to determine their agenda than the Baillie Commission had been – as well as being understandably circumscribed by their association with the delegates of other communions. Nevertheless, one cannot but think that Scotland's most eminent theologian – Principal of New College, ex-Moderator of the General Assembly and one of the leading figures in the World Council of Churches – must have had a very considerable say in the debates, and been in general agreement with the conclusions as published.

Throughout the conversations, a central question had been whether oversight in the Church should be conciliar (as in Presbyterianism) or individual (as in Anglicanism): by presbyteries, synods and General Assembly, or by bishops. In the end of the day – and there were some at least who regarded this as a notable breakthrough – the negotiators opted for an answer which could be described as embodying the 'both . . . and' rather than the 'either . . . or' approach. In the words of 'Archie' Craig's biographer, Elizabeth Templeton, they recommended that

all the participating churches should recognise this diversity of practice as compatible with the continuity and catholicity of the Church, and should show that recognition by incorporating in their structure the modes of participation which were cherished by both. Thus, the Presbyterian churches would modify their structure in the direction of adopting a form of episcopacy which was acceptable to both, while the Anglicans would develop a form of order in which ordained ministry and laity would be more closely linked in decisions concerning movement and doctrine.[32]

The fateful recommendations, acclaimed by some as displaying statesman-like resourcefulness and denounced by others as either devious or hopelessly unrealistic, were published at the end of April 1957. They were then subjected – in Scotland, at least – to lengthy and intensive scrutiny; and it was not until the General Assembly of 1959 that the Kirk's final verdict was given. By a majority of 34 in a total vote of 566, the commissioners declared their opinion that (in the phraseology of the victorious motion) 'the proposals are unacceptable in that they imply a denial of the Catholicity of the Church of Scotland and of the validity and

---

[32] E. Templeton, *God's February: A Life of Archie Craig, 1888–1985* (1991), p. 91.

regularity of its ministry within the Church Catholic'. The tide of inter-Church *rapprochement*, which had been flowing in Britain ever since the 1930s, looked as if it might be on the turn; and the immediate resignation of Dr Craig, the convener of the Assembly's Inter-Church Relations Committee, seemed to mark the end of an era.

At the time of the crucial debate John was out of the country on a lecture tour in the United States, and one can only guess as to the difference which his presence might have made. In any case, it has to be remembered that his best days were by then in the past: in 1954 he suffered a devastating blow in the death of his brother, and two years later he retired from New College at the age of seventy. On his return to Scotland he soon became seriously ill, and his depleted energies were spent in the preparation of his Gifford Lectures rather than on the defence of a lost cause. We may, however, be sure that he deeply regretted the failure of a uniquely determined effort to end the age-old conflict (one of the most profound and protracted in Christian history) between Episcopacy and Presbytery, and that if anything could have disturbed the remarkable serenity of his last days it would have been a realisation that the high-water mark of ecumenical advance in the twentieth century had already been reached – and, in all probability, passed.

Like his brother, Donald spent a great deal of time and energy in the committee work which was (and is) such an essential part of the Movement. Yet conceivably his most enduring service to the cause was made neither in the Inter-Church Relations Committee of his own denomination nor on the Faith and Order Commission of the World Council of Churches but through the pages of his posthumously published lectures on *The Theology of the Sacraments*. There, more clearly than anywhere else, is made plain his passionate desire to reconcile warring traditions and, if possible, to blur the edges of conflicting orthodoxies – to attain (as he himself says in the opening chapter) 'such a deeper and more Christian understanding as could draw together those of the Catholic and those of the Protestant tendencies'.[33]

The first half of the book considers the nature of the sacraments in general, and their place in the life of faith, before going on to

---

[33] D. M. Baillie, *Theology of the Sacraments*, p. 41.

outline a defence of infant baptism which – while drawing on the insights of recent New Testament scholarship – does not deviate in essentials from traditional orthodoxy, Catholic or Reformed. Throughout these chapters the author's conciliatory temper is constantly in evidence. After discussing whether the principle of a 'sacramental universe' (so dear to theologians from the Catholic wing of the Church) can be reconciled with the Reformed belief that a sacrament depends entirely on the divine word of promise, he concludes: 'It is only when God speaks and awakens human faith that the natural object becomes sacramental. But this can happen to material things only because this is a sacramental universe, because God created all things visible and invisible.'[34] On the relationship between faith and grace in the sacraments, he rejects both the *ex opere operato* doctrine of medieval Catholicism and the popular Protestant view that the efficacy of the sacraments depends on the faith of the receiver; he prefers to say that they operate *through* faith. 'God', he writes,

> works faith in our hearts. He bestows on us the gift of faith, gaining our confidence, not forcing it. His graciousness overcomes our mistrust, His grace creates our faith, so that when we come to Him it is really *our* faith, and we come willingly. In order to bring about this end He uses means – words, smiles, gestures, symbolic gifts, which we call sacraments.[35]

He will have nothing to do with the 'Catholic' view of the sacraments as extensions of the Incarnation, arguing against it that the Incarnation did not go on for ever but came to an end; since then the divine Presence is with us in a new way through the Holy Spirit working in the Church by means of Word and sacraments. At the same time he is concerned to emphasise that Incarnation and sacraments are inseparable. 'It is', as he puts it,

> the essence of the Christian sacraments that they could not have existed but for the historical incarnation. They have continuity with it, they point straight back to it, they can only be celebrated in the redeemed community which it created, and only by those who within that community have been set apart in a succession which connects us through the ages with the origins of our religion.[36]

[34] Ibid., p. 47.
[35] Ibid., p. 54.
[36] Ibid., p. 66.

It is, however, in the second half of the book that Donald Baillie's eirenic spirit is most patently obvious. 'Doubtless', he remarks at the outset to his Presbyterian readers,

> we should all wish to criticise the Anglo-Catholic doctrine of the eucharist.... But if we cannot get beyond a merely negative criticism, we may, when asked for our doctrine of the Lord's supper, be found offering a stone instead of bread.... Surely if we criticise Roman or Anglo-Catholic eucharistic doctrine it will be because we claim that we have some better and richer and higher belief about what God gives us in the sacrament. But I am not mainly concerned to criticise the doctrines of those other traditions, or to make a gulf between them and our own views: I would be much better pleased if it emerged from my discussion that they and we are nearer to each other than we sometimes think.[37]

After an interesting examination of 'the dramatic symbolism of the Lord's supper', in which sympathetic use is made of modern Catholic insights and stress laid on the fact that 'the eucharist consists of a complex of elements, words and actions', he goes on to ask, 'What are the realities that it [the sacrament of the Lord's Supper] ought to symbolise if it is to be true to the Gospel of Christ? . . . What are the things signified?'[38] His answer involves a discussion of two 'elements of meaning' that have traditionally been found in the sacrament: the Real Presence and the eucharistic sacrifice.

On the former, he begins with a reminder that when we speak of God's presence (whether in creation as a whole, to human-kind, to believers, or in the sacrament) we must think not of a local or spacial presence but of a spiritual, personal relationship. In the theology of the sacraments, he contends, all the churches, Lutheran and Reformed as well as Roman and Anglo-Catholic, have periodically offended against this principle; indeed, he draws attention to certain crudities in thought and expression of which one or other has been guilty. Nevertheless he believes that every tradition at its best has clearly desired to avoid such crudities, and that in essentials they are all of one mind and heart. His considered – and reconciling – judgment, therefore, is as follows:

[37] Ibid., p. 93.
[38] Ibid., pp. 93–6.

Surely what the Roman doctrine at its best is struggling (with a very inadequate metaphysic) to conceive is the reality and objectivity of the divine presence as something prevenient and given, if only we will accept it.

And surely it is the same truth that we presbyterians are endeavouring to express in a safer and surer way when we say that in the sacrament Christ is as truly present to the faith of the receiver as the bread and wine are to his outward senses. 'Present to the faith of the receiver' – that is the most real presence conceivable for a divine reality in this present world. The most objective and penetrating kind of presence that God can give us is *through faith* . . .

This does not mean that somehow we conjure up the divine presence by believing in it, or that we produce the faith out of our own resources, and that in response to our faith God gives us His presence. Nay, God is prevenient, and faith depends on His actions; He calls it forth, and that is His way of coming to dwell in a man or a company of men. That is what He does when He uses the symbolism of the bread and the wine, the words and the actions, to give Himself to *us* in the sacrament of the Lord's supper.[39]

On the eucharistic offering (perhaps an even more controversial aspect of sacramental doctrine), Baillie is concerned to suggest that, apart from Rome, the difference between the churches 'may not be so extreme as is often supposed'. Both the Thirty-nine Articles of Anglicanism and the Westminster Confession of the Reformed tradition repudiate the sacrifice of the Mass. Yet their violent reaction against medieval abuses and superstitions should not prevent us from asking whether the sacrament of Holy Communion, properly and fully understood, does not contain something of the element of oblation, sacrifice or offering – and Baillie's answer is a very positive one.

Among the arguments that he advances are these. First, all our worship may be regarded as an offering to God (cf. the Shorter Catechism on prayer as 'an offering up of our desires unto God'). Second, while condemning the 'Popish sacrifice of the mass' the Westminster Confession itself speaks of the Communion Service as including 'a *spiritual oblation* of all possible praise to God'. Third, 'while in the sacrament it is profoundly true that God is the giver and we are the receivers, it is also true that receiving

[39] Ibid., pp. 100–1.

God means giving ourselves to Him; and indeed . . . God's giving of Himself to us and our giving of ourselves to Him are but two ways of describing the same thing'. Fourth, in offering our prayers, our praises and ourselves to God we also recall Christ's self-offering, without which we can do nothing – and of course that sacrifice of His, made once on Calvary, is also an *eternal* sacrifice, having its direct, "vertical" relation to every moment of our sinful human history'.[40]

Gathering together his entire argument so far, Baillie believes that we may say something like this on the whole subject: 'in the sacrament, Christ Himself being truly present, He unites us by faith with His eternal sacrifice, that we may plead and receive its benefits and offer ourselves in prayer and praise to God'. And if we *can* say that, 'then surely we Protestants, we Presbyterians, have our doctrine of eucharistic sacrifice'.[41] Whether or not this interpretation finds favour with theologians from the warring traditions referred to is perhaps doubtful, though it is impressively supported by quotations from Roman and Anglo-Catholic writers, as well as John Calvin, which purport to show that the gulf between 'Catholic' and 'Reformed' may not be so wide as is often imagined. At any rate, we may hope for general sympathy with Baillie's passionate desire, revealed yet again in the closing pages of *The Theology of the Sacraments*, to minimise the differences and maximise the agreements between the various ecclesial traditions. Stressing the corporate nature of the Communion, and alluding – with some pride – to Archbishop Brilioth's opinion that the Reformed Churches' most distinctive contribution is to be found in their emphasis on the note of fellowship at Communion, he ends with a statement and a question:

> Unless our sacramental service maintains at its very heart that note . . . of Christian solidarity, of fellowship in the body of Christ, it will not be the holy communion at all. . . . May it not be that both the doctrine of the Real Presence and the doctrine of the eucharistic offering begin to come right and to take their true shape when they are controlled by the idea of the sacrament as a corporate act of the one body of Christ?[42]

40 Ibid., pp. 112–17.
41 Ibid., p. 118.
42 Ibid., p. 124.

'Christian solidarity' and 'fellowship in the body of Christ': in phrases such as these may be found the most convincing explanation open to us of the ecumenical commitment of both John and Donald Baillie. But no study of their churchmanship should end without a word concerning the personal piety which inspired and sustained it. In John's case, it is necessary only to mention his *Diary of Private Prayer* (which since its first publication has sold more than 125,000 copies in Britain alone, and has been translated into over a dozen languages), and Isobel Forrester's reference in 'A Cousin's Memories' to the 'three clear focal points' in his study at Whitehouse Terrace in Edinburgh: 'the big, uncluttered desk by the window', 'the big leather chair, where he often sat far into the night reading' and 'the prayer desk by the window with its little pile of well-worn versions of the Scriptures and of devotional books' where in solitude he read and thought and worshipped.[43] As for Donald, John Dow's reminiscence of him has a few sentences whose truth many contemporaries have confirmed:

> Nothing but the peremptoriness of an early morning train could persuade this man of God to omit family worship at his own table. Unfailingly by 8.40 each week day down College Street came the familiar figure in the old mackintosh, gown over his arm, often looking pale, ill and fragile, on his way to morning prayers in the University Chapel: others might steal a morning off, he with more excuse would not. When he was a worshipper, there was the promptness of the real participant in every response. When he himself conducted the service, we could not but be drawn closer by the tones of his voice and the sincerity of his words. In addressing a newly-ordained minister his final stress was on the danger of letting carefulness about many things cut out the one thing needful – personal devotion.[44]

The brothers' last substantial contribution to scholarship, John's Gifford Lectures, ended by quoting Kierkegaard's dictum that 'Truth is not an objective statement about certain relations of being, but a form of existence in which such relations are actualised', followed by a prayer from Henry Vaughan.[45] It was

---

[43] I. Forrester, 'John Baillie: A Cousin's Memoirs', in J. Baillie, *Christian Devotion* (1962), pp. xxi–xxii.

[44] J. Dow, Memoir, p. 16.

[45] J. Baillie, *The Sense of the Presence of God: Gifford Lectures 1961–2* (1962), p. 261.

a peculiarly appropriate conclusion; for in their preaching, their application of the Faith to social issues and the very practical service they rendered both to the Church of Scotland and to the ecumenical Christian community, as well as in their theological teaching and writing over some forty years, John and Donald Baillie provided their own generation and posterity with an impressive example of theological truth embodied in life, and piety and learning harmoniously combined.

Chapter 12

Church History in Edinburgh
c. 1840–c. 1990

There have been two chief centres for the study and teaching of Church History (along with the other components of a theological curriculum) in Edinburgh during the last 150 years or so: the University's Faculty of Divinity and the New College of the Free, later the United Free, Church of Scotland. In both institutions, which merged in the 1930s as a result of the union of the Church of Scotland and the United Free Church, the teachers of Church History have almost without exception been not only historians of the Church but also *Church historians* – the Church's servants as well as its chroniclers and analysts.

This was certainly the case at New College. From its origins in the 1840s, the professors were all ministers of the Free (after 1900, the United Free) Church, just as the great majority of its students were candidates for the Free Church ministry. The ecclesiastical orientation of the place was incontrovertible, and may be ascertained from even the briefest scrutiny of the part played by its teachers in contemporary Church life.

After some ten years of parish ministry, *David WELSH* became Professor of Ecclesiastical History at Edinburgh in 1831. A protégé of Thomas Chalmers, he was deeply involved in the Non-Intrusion movement. As Moderator of the Disruption Assembly, he headed the seceders' procession on 18 May 1843, and from then until his death he was a leading figure in the youthful Free Church. He helped to formulate its schemes for school and university education, and did more than anyone else to raise funds for the erection and endowment of the 'New' College on its splendid site in the heart of the city. Becoming – inevitably – its first Professor of Church History, he crowned his services to the infant seminary by supervising the inauguration of its superb theological library.[1]

Welsh's successor, *William CUNNINGHAM*, was also both churchman and scholar. He had been a parish minister before joining the New College professoriate on the morrow of the Disruption – initially as second professor of Divinity, and then as Professor of Divinity and Church History. Among the Non-Intrusionists before 1843, and the Free Church leaders thereafter, none was more of a fighter than Cunningham. The tally of his controversies is almost endless: with the 'apostate and perjured' Voluntaries, with McLeod Campbell's 'Rowites', with Moderates like Dr Inglis and Dr Cook, with Free Church favourers of rival colleges in Aberdeen and Glasgow and, of course, with Arians, Arminians, Socinians and 'Papists' of every age including his own. Whether because of his bellicosity or in spite of it, Cunningham was one of Scotland's most prominent and honoured ecclesiastics from the 1830s to the 1860s. The Free Church General Assembly elected him to its Moderatorship in 1859; and as Professor of Church History, and Principal of New College after Chalmers's death in 1847, he played a unique part in fashioning – and personifying – the distinctive ethos of his communion.[2]

When *Robert RAINY* came to the Chair he was already marked out as a coming Church leader. Deflected from a career in medicine by the euphoria of the Disruption, he had joined the first generation of students at New College. After brief ministries in Huntly and Edinburgh, he was called in 1862 to succeed Cunningham in what was looked on as the intellectual and spiritual powerhouse of Scottish Evangelicalism. From the very outset his exceptional debating and administrative gifts made him master of both the General Assembly (which he attended for more than forty years) and the Free Church as a whole. Principal of New College from 1874 until his death, he pronounced with magisterial authority on nearly all the vital religious issues of the day, Evolution, Biblical Criticism, Confessional Revision and Religious Establishments included, and was the only minister in modern times to be thrice elected Moderator (in 1887, 1900 and 1905). His position in the

[1] A. Dunlop, 'Memoir of Dr. Welsh', *Sermons by the late Revd. David Welsh. D.D.* (1846).

[2] R. Rainy and J. Mackenzie, *Life of William Cunningham, D.D.* (1871).

Free Church could seriously be likened to that of an archbishop in other ecclesiastical bodies.[3]

The commitment of New College's Church historians to the Free Kirk was equalled by that of their opposite numbers in the University's Faculty of Divinity to the 'Auld Kirk'. All were ordained ministers of that Church, and all had served in its parishes for longer or shorter periods.

James ROBERTSON, who ministered at Ellon from 1832 until his presentation in 1844 to the Chair vacated by Welsh at the Disruption, had been one of the ablest representatives of the Moderate party throughout the Ten Years' Conflict. After his appointment, he did much to restore the morale and the fortunes of the battered Establishment, and his election to the Moderatorship in 1856 was more than usually well deserved.[4]

Robertson's successor in 1861, *William STEVENSON*, came late to the Chair (he was in his middle fifties), after strenuous ministries in Arbroath and South Leith. It is perhaps hardly surprising that he is remembered more for his services to the Church than for his scholarship, considerable though that was.[5]

Robert WALLACE was Professor of Ecclesiastical History for only four years, from 1872 to 1876, during which he was also minister of Old Greyfriars (and thus Edinburgh's last clerical pluralist). He had a remarkable subsequent career as – successively – editor of the *Scotsman* newspaper, barrister and Liberal MP; but his earlier years had been spent in parish ministries, and while a professor he was one of the most vocal leaders of the 'Broad Church' school within the Church of Scotland.[6]

The last nineteenth-century occupant of the Ecclesiastical History Chair, *Malcolm Campbell TAYLOR*, made a special place for himself in university administration, serving for some time as secretary of the Court and (from 1884 to 1899) as Dean of Divinity. But he had previously ministered in the prestigious pastoral charges of Dumfries Greyfriars, Montrose, Crathie and Edinburgh Morningside, and seems to have continued to

---

[3] P. C. Simpson, *The Life of Principal Rainy*, 2 vols (1909).

[4] A. H. Charteris, *Life of the Revd. James Robertson, D.D.* (1863).

[5] *Fasti Ecclesiae Scoticanae* (new edn, 1915), vol. I, p. 164; A. Grant, *The Story of the University of Edinburgh* (1884), vol. II, pp. 312–13.

[6] *F.E.S.*, vol. I, pp. 43–4; J. C. Smith and W. Wallace (eds), *Robert Wallace: Life and Last Leaves* (1903).

carry a good deal of weight in ecclesiastical as well as academic circles.[7]

During the present century, the picture has changed much less dramatically than one might expect. Before the great watershed of the Union of the Churches in 1929, certainly, the professors' ecclesiastical affiliations were quite as close, and obvious, as ever.

Alexander Robertson MACEWEN, an ordained minister of the United Presbyterian and then of the United Free Church, served congregations in Moffat and Glasgow before being called to Rainy's Chair in 1901; and his publications were, at least in part, tributes to the religious tradition from which he sprang. Deeply involved in the negotiations which led to the United Presbyterian–Free Church Union of 1900 and in the protracted 'Church case' that followed, he spent a considerable proportion of his last years in committee work. He helped to plan 'Edinburgh 1910', the celebrated World Missionary Conference, and was one of the United Free Church's chief representatives in reunion negotiations with the Church of Scotland. Appropriately enough, he ended his days as Moderator of the General Assembly of the United Free Church.[8]

Hugh WATT (who survived – and more than survived – into the post-Union era) was every bit as much a churchman as his predecessor, holding pastoral charges within the United Free Church before being elected to the Chair in 1919. His notable administrative gifts and his obvious concern for the welfare of New College students and alumni were recognised, and given even further scope, by his elevation in 1946 to the Principalship of New College. The year of his retirement saw him called to the Moderatorship of the General Assembly.[9]

---

[7] *F.E.S.*, vol. I, p. 85; D. T. Rice and P. McIntyre, *The University Portraits* (1957), pp. 200–2.

[8] D. S. Cairns, *Life and Times of Alexander Robertson MacEwen, D.D.* (1925).

[9] A. C. Cheyne, 'Hugh Watt', in J. H. Burnett, D. Howarth and S. D. Fletcher (eds), *The University Portraits, Second Series* (1986), pp. 206–8; R. L. Small, 'An Appreciation', in D. Shaw (ed.), *Reformation and Revolution: Essays Presented to the Very Revd. Principal Emeritus Hugh Watt. D.D., D. Litt. on the 60th Anniversary of His Ordination* (1967), pp. 11–16.

The only conceivable exception to the 'churchly' character of Edinburgh's Church historians in the period before the fusion of New College and the University's Faculty of Divinity was *James MACKINNON*. Though trained in Divinity as well as in Arts, and licensed to preach by the Church of Scotland, he was never ordained; and after brief and temporary appointments in Scotland and South Africa he spent the years between 1890 and 1908 lecturing in History – *not* Ecclesiastical History – in Queen Margaret College, Glasgow, and the University of St Andrews. His early publications reveal no particular interest in or commitment to Church concerns, but after his elevation to the Edinburgh professorship a marked change of direction can be discerned. While he never played a prominent part in Church life, his attention focussed increasingly upon the Patristic and Reformation periods. Until his retirement at the beginning of the 1930s, and indeed for more than a decade thereafter, he poured out a stream of substantial works on well-nigh every subject traditionally included in the Church History curriculum at Edinburgh. Devoid of even a touch of zealotry or clericalism, he expressed with erudition and unflagging diligence the distinctive viewpoint of liberal Christian scholarship. Against a background of conflicting ideologies and Britain's descent once again into total war, he could hardly have performed a more valuable service for the Church of his time.[10]

Mackinnon's pupil, *John Henderson Seaforth BURLEIGH*, came to the Chair in 1931. Soon after, a complete union was effected between the University's Faculty of Divinity and the former United Free Church's New College. The change meant that for a time Church History was taught by *two* professors, one (Burleigh) in the old University Chair, the other (Watt, followed briefly by Torrance), in the so-called 'Church' Chair. From 1952 onwards, however, no further appointment was made to the latter, and a succession of lecturers filled the gap. It might have been expected that the merging of Faculty and seminary – and the ending of New College as an exclusively ecclesiastical institution – would entail a perceptible loosening of the age-old connection between theological teaching and Church life: as a matter of fact, the next

[10] Rice and McIntyre, *Portraits*, pp. 141–2; D. F. Wright, 'James MacKinnon', in *Dictionary of Scottish Church History and Theology* (1993), p. 524.

half-century provided little evidence (at least so far as Ecclesiastical History was concerned) that this had happened.

Like nearly all his predecessors, Burleigh was an ordained minister. He had served in pastoral charges in Fyvie and Dundee before coming to the Chair, and his subsequent services to the Church were many and various. Convener for a time of the onerous Church and Nation Committee, he was also a member of the ecumenical group who produced the famous 'Bishops Report' in 1957; he was elected Principal of New College in 1956 and Moderator of the General Assembly in 1960.[11]

Thomas Forsyth TORRANCE, who held the 'Church' Chair from 1950 to 1952 before being translated to the Chair of Christian Dogmatics, carried on the tradition of ecclesiastical commitment. His career had begun with ministries in two parishes, and as a professor he soon acquired a remarkable reputation in Church circles at home and abroad. He played a prominent part in the Ecumenical Movement, was joint founder and editor of the *Scottish Journal of Theology*, set new standards of scholarly energy and crusading zeal during his convenership of the Kirk's Commission on Baptism, and was called to Moderatorship of the General Assembly in 1976.[12]

At the time of writing (1998), all the teachers of Ecclesiastical History at New College since Burleigh's retirement are still alive. It is therefore neither necessary nor desirable to give more than a very brief account of them here.

After six years as a lecturer in the Department, *Alexander Campbell CHEYNE* (the author of this study) succeeded his old teacher in the Chair in 1964. Like all his predecessors save one (Mackinnon), he was an ordained minister of the Church of Scotland, though he never served full-time in a parish. The Church appointed him Principal of New College in 1984, and he was called to the Moderatorship of Edinburgh Presbytery shortly after his retirement in 1986.[13]

---

[11] A. C. Cheyne, 'In Memoriam: The Very Revd. John Henderson Seaforth Burleigh, M.A., B.D., B.Litt., D.D.', *Records of the Scottish Church History Society*, vol. xxxii, pt. 2 (March, 1985), pp. 101–2.

[12] John McIntyre, 'Thomas Forsyth Torrance', *New College Bulletin* (August, 1979), pp. 1–2.

[13] A. E. Lewis, 'The Authority and Artistry of Alec Cheyne', *New College Bulletin* (Autumn, 1986), p. 3.

The present occupant of the Chair, *Stewart Jay BROWN*, took up his duties in 1988. He is neither an ordained minister nor a licentiate, but his background in the United States – and his work on Thomas Chalmers – have familiarised him with Church attitudes and practices, and no one could accuse him of indifference to, or lack of sympathy with, the traditional concerns of College and Faculty.[14]

From the 1950s onwards, the teaching at New College has been augmented and enriched by a succession of lecturers. *James S. M'EWEN* filled the vacancy created in 1952 by Torrance's move to Christian Dogmatics. A Church of Scotland minister with considerable experience in various parishes, and a fine teacher and preacher, he transferred to the Chair of Church History at Aberdeen in 1958.[15] On the promotion of his successor, Cheyne, to the Edinburgh Chair after Burleigh's retirement, *David F. WRIGHT* was called to the lectureship. The first Englishman to hold an appointment in the Department, Wright apparently had no difficulty in transferring from Evangelical Anglicanism to Scottish Presbyterianism, and was soon playing a full part in the ecclesiastical life of his adopted city and country; his administrative gifts were demonstrated during a term as Dean of the Faculty.

Andrew C. Ross came to the Department in 1966 as the first lecturer with special responsibility for the History of Missions. Ordained by the Church of Scotland, he had spent eight years in Malawi as a minister of the Church of Central Africa (Presbyterian), and the fact that from 1978 to 1984 he was both Principal of New College and Dean of the Faculty indicates the special place he occupied in the esteem of both Church and University. *Peter C. MATHESON*, a licentiate of the Church of Scotland, joined the Department in 1965, and for twenty years it benefited from his exceptional teaching skills. He was called to the Chair of Church History and Christian Doctrine at Knox College, Dunedin, New Zealand, in 1985.

On Matheson's departure, financial considerations – it was a period of unusual stringency – might have made it impossible to fill the vacancy had it not been for the munificent endowment of

---

[14] 'Professor Stewart J. Brown', *New College Bulletin* (Autumn, 1989), p. 2.

[15] *F.E.S.*, vol. x, p. 430.

a Lectureship in the History and Theology of the Reformation by the Kirby Laing Foundation. To this newly created lectureship in memory of Sir John Laing, a prominent Christian industrialist, there came in quick succession two young scholars who both (as it happened) could be said to represent a Methodist contribution to the predominantly Presbyterian scene at New College: *Susan HARDMAN MOORE* from the University of Durham and *Jane DAWSON* from the University of St Andrews. Dr Hardman Moore was not only the Department's first woman teacher but also its first Methodist lay preacher; she did much for both the ecclesiastical and the academic life of Edinburgh before moving to King's College, London, in 1992. Her successor, Dr Dawson, also had a Methodist background, but her special expertise – in the English and Scottish Reformations – placed her in the mainstream of New College's traditional interests.

Although lecturers only made their appearance on the Mound in the 1950s, it is difficult now to think of Church History there without them.

Church History in its entirety covers a vast field, both in time and space, but its Edinburgh practitioners have always paid special attention to the Early Church, the Protestant Reformation and Scottish Christianity.

Welsh's full course of teaching spanned three sessions, the period down to Constantine being studied in the first year, that from Constantine to the end of the thirteenth century in the second, and the fourteenth, fifteenth and sixteenth centuries in the third. Cunningham adopted an approach that was more thematic than chronological; but if his *Historical Theology* (2 vols, 1862) is anything to go by (and we are assured that it represents the substance of his class lectures) the doctrinal controversies of the Early and Reformation periods took up the greater part of his attention.

As for Rainy, the College Calendar of 1874–75 provides the following description of the topics which he hoped to cover:

> In the Junior Class the Lectures begin with a brief survey of the History of the Church during the period covered by Canonical Scripture. Afterwards the topics which are chiefly dwelt on are the age of the Apostolic Fathers, that of the Apologists, the controversies regarding the Trinity and the Person of Christ, the history of Sacerdotal and

Sacramental tendencies and their results, the Pelagian controversy; and following upon this, the features and influences which prevailed in the Middle Ages in so far as the time enables the subject to be overtaken. In the Senior Course, a few lectures on the Reformation are followed by a survey of the Popish controversy, and this by a notice of the characteristics of the Lutheran and Reformed Churches respectively. The Socinian and Arminian controversies succeed; and these are followed by a survey of the rise of Rationalism in Europe, and of the effects it produced in Theology, especially in Switzerland and Germany, which leads to a notice of the modern German Schools. As an appendix to the course, in order to supply a fuller view than the textbook presents, the history of the Scottish Church is traced continuously down to the Disruption, and attention is directed to the principles which it illustrates. Special courses on particular subjects are occasionally introduced.[16]

With minor emendations, Rainy's programme continued basically unchanged down to his retirement at the beginning of the twentieth century.

Once the difficulties created by the 'Church case' (1900–05) had been got out of the way, MacEwen settled down on not dissimilar lines. In 1907–08, for example, the Junior Church History Class (attended by third-year theology students) took as its subject the period 'from New Testament times to the close of the fourth century, including Augustine, and extending to the Christological controversies of the fifth century'; Scottish History was examined during the last month of the session. The syllabus of the Senior Class (attended by students in their fourth and final year) was described as follows: 'During the first month, the transition from ancient to modern Church life will be exhibited in connection with the Scottish Church. Thereafter, the Reformation movement will be set forth and scrutinised, and the most important historical developments of Modern Christianity will be traced.'[17]

No major changes were introduced by Watt. Throughout the 1920s, lectures to the Junior Class dealt with the Early Church, both before and after Constantine, together with 'some aspects of the Medieval Church'; the Senior Class studied the Lutheran

[16] *The College Calendar for the Free Church of Scotland, 1874–75* (n.d.), pp. 26–7.
[17] *The College Calendar for the United Free Church of Scotland, 1907–08* (1907), p. 22.

Reformation (in seminar), together with the Swiss, French and English Reformations, before Christmas, and post-Reformation history, particularly Scottish, after Christmas.[18]

A very similar pattern was followed by Auld Kirk teachers in the University. Indeed, no really substantial changes took place until the 1960s, when – against a background of rapid academic expansion and reappraisal nationwide – the BD curriculum as a whole was reshaped and the Church History component within it radically restructured. For the first time in more than a century, students were not introduced to the subject by a full, year-long course on the Early Church. Instead, 'Ecclesiastical History I' consisted of a general survey from the beginnings to the present, though special attention was still directed to the traditional priority areas. In the new ordering of things, this introductory class might provide some students' only acquaintance with Church History; but those who wished to take their studies further were offered, in 'Ecclesiastical History II', a course entitled 'Major Themes in the History of the Church', in which such topics as Christians and Jews, War and Peace, Forms of Piety, Controversies and Controversialists and 'Grass Roots' Christianity (the local manifestations of movements such as Puritanism and Tractarianism) were examined at a more advanced level. In their third and final BD year, specialists were able to select from a wide range of subjects – Augustine, the Crusades, the Fourth Lateran Council, the Urban Reformation, the Church in the Modern World and so on – and to study these intensively, with much use of original sources.

The result of these changes is that Ecclesiastical History as now taught at New College probably ranges more widely than ever before – though some may wonder whether depth of treatment has (at least for the average student) suffered in the interests of breadth.

Also increasingly evident is a less theological, more distinctively historical, view of the discipline.

The older approach, now abandoned, may be seen at its most consistent and extreme in the 'prelections' of Cunningham. An

---

[18] *The College Calendar for the United Free Church of Scotland, 1927–28* (1927), p. 37.

address delivered by him at the ceremonial opening of New College in 1850 contained the following remarks on the title of the Department and the proper content of its teaching: 'This is usually known by the name of Church History, but as I have hitherto treated it, and mean to continue to treat it, it might, with more propriety, be designated Historical and Polemical Theology, as distinguished from, and supplementary to, Systematic Theology.'[19] Never again was the subsidiary – and frankly theological – role of Ecclesiastical History stated with such assurance and precision.

Rainy's lectures, it is true, were also largely concerned with the history of Christian thought and the great controversies which had engaged so much of his predecessor's attention; but in the younger man we can detect a greater awareness of the whole *context* in which the Church's thinking took place, and a greater readiness to consider not just its theology (central as that must always be) but every aspect of its many-faceted life. As he observed in his 1862 inaugural, 'The true religion, being the religion for man, could not but be historical – that is to say, implicated with history, entering into history and coming out of history. It is a religion indeed of principles, truths, laws; but it is and always was a religion of facts, events, historical transactions. . . . Revealed religion and historical fact are indivisible.'[20]

The down-to-earth standpoint thus articulated is also apparent across the denominational divide in Rainy's late-Victorian contemporaries, Stevenson and Wallace, though Taylor seems to have reverted to the older view of his subject as a branch of historical theology. But it is in the twentieth century that the understanding of Church History as being related at least as much to History in general as to Theology has come to full expression.

Of the two United Free professors appointed before the 1929 Union, both had undergone an education which almost guaranteed a continuance of the new outlook. MacEwen's undergraduate years at Oxford made the admirer of John Cairns the United Presbyterian traditionalist a disciple also of Jowett and Ruskin. Watt was the first occupant of the Church History Chair to possess an honours degree in History. On the Auld Kirk side, Mackinnon

[19] *Inauguration of the New College of the Free Church, Edinburgh, November 1850* (1851), p. 64.

[20] Simpson, *Rainy*, vol. I, p. 204.

held 'secular' teaching appointments, and published volumes on a wide range of historical topics, before coming to the Regius Chair of Ecclesiastical History in Edinburgh.

What might be called the Cunningham tradition was even less in evidence from the 1930s onwards. Burleigh's *A Church History of Scotland* (1960) was actually criticised by one American reviewer for being 'little concerned' with the development of theology.[21] His successor, Cheyne, was, like him, a BD of Edinburgh, but before studying, and then teaching, at New College he had graduated in History at Edinburgh, undertaken historical research at Oxford (again like Burleigh) and held a lectureship in History at Glasgow. He valued his association with the 'secular' historians of Edinburgh University's History Board, of which he was for a time convener, almost as much as his relationship with the theologians in the Divinity Faculty. The present incumbent of the Chair, Stewart Brown, obtained his doctorate in History and Divinity from the University of Chicago; but his first degree (from the University of Illinois) was in History, and he had lectured in History at North-Western University and the University of Georgia before coming to Edinburgh in 1988. Among the lecturers, Ross, Matheson, Hardman Moore and Dawson were all likewise trained historians whose experience and interests precluded an exclusively theological approach to their subject.

The older, predominantly theological, mindset perhaps re-appeared during Torrance's brief tenure of the Church History Chair. After his departure, however, the attitude discernible in Rainy, Stevenson and Wallace, and even more clearly in Mackinnon and his successors, resumed its almost unquestioned sway. It was strikingly expressed, some time in the 1970s, in a short unpublished paper by Matheson for use in the Department's 'General Survey' course.

> Church History [it was argued] is, paradoxically, a secular discipline within a Divinity Faculty! Certainly it deals with the Church, and the very concept of the latter implies a theology. Its concern, too, is focussed on the Church in all its aspects, the history of its organisation and liturgy, its piety and theology, its creeds and catechisms. Yet it does all this *in a secular way*, arming itself with the techniques and criteria of the secular historian.

[21] S. A. Burrell, *Church History*, vol. 30 (1961), pp. 245–6.

And the conclusion was this: 'In a Divinity Faculty the role of Church History is to bring us down to earth. . . . It is a thoroughly secular discipline within an eminently theological perspective.'

'A secular discipline with a theological perspective': that is a description of the work of their Department with which all, or nearly all, of Edinburgh's twentieth-century ecclesiastical historians would have whole-heartedly agreed.

No account of Church History at Edinburgh, however summary, can afford to overlook the publications of those who were its chief practitioners from the early years of the Victorian age to the eve of the twenty-first century. As already noted, their lectures concentrated upon three aspects of their subject: the Early Church, the Protestant Reformation and Christianity in Scotland; and the same concentration is evident – until recent decades, at any rate – in their published work.

On the Early Church, the only considerable publications of the Victorian period – apart from Cunningham's two-volume *Historical Theology* (1862), which, as its title reveals, can scarcely be reckoned a work of history – came at its beginning and its end, and both from New College. Neither Welsh's *Elements of Church History*, vol. 1, *Comprising the External History of the Church during the first Three Centuries* (1844) nor Rainy's *The Ancient Catholic Church* (1902) possesses much more than curiosity value today; but both are works of undeniable learning, and need not fear comparison with similar overviews of a textbookish kind by contemporary scholars in England, Germany or North America. Shortly after his appointment to the Chair, Welsh spent several months of study in Bonn, Heidelberg and elsewhere, and his acquaintance with the German literature on his subject, as well as the classical sources, is impressive. Moreover, as the thoughtful and wide-ranging introduction to his *Elements* makes plain, he had a philosophic cast of mind which armed him against the temptation to utter superficial if 'edifying' judgments and made him a true historian rather than a mere annalist. Rainy for his part possessed a subtle (some would say convoluted) mind which qualified him to deal with the complexities of Patristic thought, while his administrative ability and experience undoubtedly deepened his appreciation of the great ecclesiastics of former days.

In the present century, only Mackinnon has ventured into the area of general surveys of the Early Church. Of his trilogy, *The Historic Jesus* (1931), *The Gospel in the Early Church* (1933) and *From Christ to Constantine* (1936), the two earlier volumes may be said to belong to New Testament studies rather than to Church History. The third, a rewriting of the lectures delivered by him during his twenty-one years' tenure of the Chair, is modestly offered 'in the belief that the experience of an old teacher [he was then in his mid-seventies] might be of some service in guiding . . . a new generation of students'.[22] Like all Mackinnon's work, it is based on careful research meticulously footnoted, and if its theological stance may have seemed a little old-fashioned even in the 1930s, it impresses as the product of an independent, well-stocked and generous mind, and is still a useful work of reference for the non-specialist.

Mackinnon's pupil, Burleigh, was later to become known as one of the leading authorities on the history of the Scottish Church, but he made his early reputation in the Patristic field. His Croall Lectures (1949) on Augustine's *City of God* were a stimulating introduction to some important aspects of the thought of the great North African Father, while his scholarly reputation was further enhanced by his edition (with fresh translations) of *Augustine's Early Writings* in the Library of Christian Classics series (1950). Around the same time, Torrance published his *The Doctrine of Grace in the Apostolic Fathers* (1948), a study which – though hardly history – prompts a comparison with Cunningham in the realm of historical theology.

Rather surprisingly, no substantial work on the Reformation period was published by Edinburgh's Church historians during the nineteenth century – unless we include Cunningham's massive *The Reformers and the Theology of the Reformation* (1862), which is to all intents and purposes a theological handbook.

Things changed after the First World War. Mackinnon's *magnum opus, Luther and the Reformation* (4 vols., 1925–30) mediated the findings of the Continental 'Luther Renaissance' to English-speaking readers. Britain's foremost Luther scholar of the next generation, Gordon Rupp, rightly observed that this was

[22] J. MacKinnon, *From Christ to Constantine: The Rise and Growth of the Early Church (c. A.D. 30 to 337)* (1936), p. ix

'a signal service'. He went on, however, to remark: that 'The chief criticism must be that he (Mackinnon) commits the one unforgivable sin of Luther study, which is to make Luther dull, and provokes the reflection that his brand of theological and historical liberalism singularly unfits him to interpret Luther's theology':[23] an excessively harsh judgment on a work which is still a valuable, because detailed and well-documented, guide to the reformer's career. (Opinions may perhaps differ about the dullness!) Mackinnon's two subsequent volumes, *Calvin and the Reformation* (1936) and *The Origins of the Reformation* (1939), display the distinctive strengths – and weaknesses – of all his work. Lack of sympathy perhaps weakens the one, while more recent studies of late-medieval thought give a dated appearance to the other; yet even today they are not without value as careful and compendious introductions to their subjects.

Since the 1950s, Reformation studies have not ceased to engage the attention of Edinburgh's Church historians. On the borderland between history and theology, Torrance organised a new translation of *Calvin's New Testament Commentaries* (1959–72) and was associated with a reissue, in three volumes, of *Calvin's Tracts and Treatises* (1958); he also published a number of theological studies on Reformation topics, such as *Calvin's Doctrine of Man* (1952), *Kingdom and Church: A Study in the Theology of the Reformation* (1956) and *The Hermeneutics of John Calvin* (1988). Still in the theological field, Wright translated and edited the *Commonplaces of Martin Bucer* (1972) as well as editing essays on *Martin Bucer: Reforming Church and Community* (1992). And that new life could be injected into what the Victorians understood by Reformation history will be seen when some of Matheson's contributions to the subject are presently taken note of.

Throughout the entire period from the 1840s to the 1990s, Scottish history has attracted a good deal of attention from Edinburgh's Church historians. Admittedly, the occupants of the University Chair during the nineteenth century were far from productive. Robertson wrote virtually nothing. Stevenson's scholarly and quite lively *The Legends and Commemorative Celebrations of St Kentigern, his Friends and Disciples* (1874) has been described – a little dismissively – as 'The best thesaurus

[23] G. Rupp, *The Righteousness of God: Luther Studies* (1953), p. 53.

of the legends of St Kentigern.'[24] Wallace's *George Buchanan*, for the Famous Scots series (1899), slight as it is, was left unfinished. Taylor published only a few semi-popular articles. The New College men did much better. Welsh's admiring *Account of the Life and Writings of J. Brown M.D.* (1825), his old moral philosophy teacher, is of little interest today. But Rainy's brilliant *Three Lectures on the Church of Scotland* (1872), though fiercely partisan (it was a reply to a course delivered just a few days previously by Dean Stanley), should still be required reading for anyone who wishes to understand the central concerns – and deepest prejudices – of Scottish Presbyterians over several centuries; while his biographical works, the *Life of William Cunningham* (1871) and *Memorials of Robert Smith Candlish* (1880) – the former written in association with James Mackenzie, the latter with William Wilson – are, despite their strongly Victorian flavour, indispensable accounts of the men and their times.

A. R. MacEwen, the earliest of New College's history teachers in the present century, was equally prolific. His boldest venture, the two-volume *History of the Church in Scotland* (1913, 1918), may strike today's reader as somewhat old-fashioned and in need of extensive emendation. Yet as MacEwen himself remarked about the histories of John Cunningham (1859) and George Grub (1861), 'All students will acknowledge that narratives written at these dates require to be re-written, and that estimates which then seemed adequate must be reconsidered.'[25] Furthermore, the fact remains that nothing on quite the same scale has appeared since MacEwen's time, and that even today's revisionists concede that cautious use may still be made of his account. In any case, it is probably his biographical works which show him at his best. More than thirty years separate his short memoir of his father (1877) from his *Antoinette Bourignon, Quietist* (1909); in between came the *Life and Letters of John Cairns* (1895) and *The Erskines* (Famous Scots, 1900), for which he most deserves to be remembered. If Cairns was the presiding genius of the United Presbyterian Church, it could almost be said that Ebenezer and

[24] J. A. Duke, *The Columban Church* (1932), p. 186.
[25] A. R. MacEwen, *A History of the Church in Scotland*, vol. I: 397–1546 (1913), p. vii.

Ralph Erskine *were* the original Secession; together, MacEwen's volumes bring these giants and their tradition attractively – and in the main convincingly – to life, and *The Erskines* merits description as a religious classic.

Between the end of the First World War and the outbreak of the Second, Edinburgh's Church historians published virtually nothing about their own country apart from Mackinnon's two volumes, *The Social and Industrial History of Scotland from the Earliest Times to the Union* (1920) and *The Social and Industrial History of Scotland from the Union to the Present Time* (1921) – neither of which was principally concerned with ecclesiastical affairs.

Things have been very different since. Watt's *Thomas Chalmers and the Disruption* (1943), though deeply indebted to the standard Victorian biography by W. Hanna, was a concise and readable contribution to the centenary celebrations; *Recalling the Scottish Covenants* (1946) and *John Knox in Controversy* (1950) reworked familiar material in the author's pleasantly unpretentious way. Of more permanent value were *Published Writings of Thomas Chalmers: A Descriptive List* (1943) and *New College, Edinburgh: A Centenary History* (1946), the latter a substantial, indeed indispensable, work based on an intimate acquaintance with the archival material. Watt, it should be remembered, had not only been Secretary of New College Senate for a number of years: he was also an excellent teacher, who through his supervision of postgraduate students – many of them returning to their religious roots from North America – promoted much worthwhile research into post-Reformation Scottish history. Indeed, both Torrance's retranslation, with an introduction, of Robert Bruce's sacramental sermons, *The Mystery of the Lord's Supper* (1958) and J. S. M'Ewen's *The Faith of John Knox* (1961), a perceptive and lucid analysis, can be seen as following the lead of their one-time professor.

The quater-centenary year of the Scottish Reformation saw the publication of Burleigh's *A Church History of Scotland* (1960), the first general survey to appear for over a century. Its comprehensiveness, clarity, balance and broad sympathies won general acclaim, and after nearly forty years it looks like continuing for some time yet as the standard introduction to the subject.

Burleigh's successors, Cheyne and Brown, have both concentrated on relatively modern topics. Much of Cheyne's work is contained in articles on such eminent nineteenth- and twentieth-century ecclesiastics and theologians as Caird, Tulloch, Robertson Smith and the Baillie brothers; but he has also published *The Transforming of the Kirk: Victorian Scotland's Religious Revolution* (1983), together with an edited volume, *The Practical and the Pious: Essays on Thomas Chalmers (1780–1847)* (1985) and – a brief reassessment for the Ter-Jubilee of 1843 – *The Ten Years' Conflict and the Disruption: An Overview* (1993). Brown's *Thomas Chalmers and the Godly Commonwealth in Scotland* (1982) immediately took its place as the authoritative modern biography and one of the finest pieces of ecclesiastical history produced this century. It was followed by a volume of essays co-edited with Michael Fry, *Scotland in the Age of the Disruption* (1993); and students of the period now await the appearance of his Chalmers Lectures on *The Crisis of National Religious Establishments: England, Scotland and Ireland, 1833–45*. Nor would the picture be complete without mentioning that the Ecclesiastical History Department may claim a large share in two volumes edited by Wright in collaboration with others: essays on *The Bible in Scottish Life and Literature* (1988) and the monumental *Dictionary of Scottish Church History and Theology* (1993), many of whose contributors have either taught or studied at New College in recent years.

We have seen how the teaching of Church History in Edinburgh gradually extended beyond the traditional areas – Early Church, Protestant Reformation and Scottish Christianity. A similar broadening of interest and sympathy is also evident in the publications of staff members. Watt may have begun the movement with his little sketch, *Representative Churchmen of Twenty Centuries* (1927). Matheson certainly gave a wider meaning to Reformation studies with *Cardinal Contarini at Regensburg* (1972) and *Argula von Grumbach: A Woman's Voice in the Reformation* (1995), as well as editing *The Collected Works of Thomas Muntzer* (1988). He also illuminated a crucial phase of German history with his documentary compilation and commentary *The Third Reich and the Christian Churches* (1981) and gave a new dimension to an old subject with *The Finger of God in the Disruption: Scottish Principles and New Zealand Realities*

(1993), an account which might have surprised men like Welsh and Cunningham. Perhaps most innovative of all, Ross's fascinating *John Philip (1775-1851): Missions, Race and Politics in South Africa* (1986) is far more than the conventional missionary biography, while his *A Vision Betrayed: The Jesuits in Japan and China, 1542-1742* (1994) breaks fresh ground with its combination of Chinese and Japanese history, missiology and religious studies.

Prediction is not part of the historian's task, but such recent developments as these suggest that Church History in Edinburgh has not only a productive and interesting past to look back upon but also a productive and interesting future ahead of it.

Chapter 13

New College, Edinburgh 1846–1996

It is never easy to ascertain or describe the essential characteristics of a great and long-established institution; and in the case of New College, which has not only survived the changes and chances of over one and a half centuries but displayed throughout that time a vigorous and varied intellectual life, the task is particularly daunting. One obvious way of approaching the subject, however, is to sketch the history of the place from its beginnings down to the present day, in the hope that at least some of its enduring concerns and achievements may thereby be discovered – and that is what will be attempted in the following pages.

The story now to be told seems to fall into two clearly distinguishable epochs, divided from each other by twentieth-century Scotland's most important ecclesiastical event: the Union in 1929 of the United Free Church and the Church of Scotland, which between them included the majority of all the country's Presbyterians. That Union led, among other things, to the merger of New College (then a basically denominational seminary, though of unusually catholic sympathies and remarkably ambitious scholarly pretensions) with the University of Edinburgh's Faculty of Divinity, and so ushered in the era in which we still live.

Each of these broad divisions – before 1929, and after – may be divided into three shorter periods of time, almost as obvious and hardly less significant. Our material therefore organises itself under the following six headings: Phase 1, the 1840s and 1850s (the early Victorian College); Phase 2, from the 1860s to the end of the nineteenth century (the mid- and late-Victorian College); Phase 3, from 1900 to 1929 (the United Free Church College, from the Union with the United Presbyterians to the later and larger Union with the Church of Scotland); Phase 4, from the

1930s into the 1950s (the College as the oldest living collegians first knew it, before, during and after the Second World War); Phase 5, the 1960s and 1970s (when the long-term implications of the coalescence of Church College and University Faculty became increasingly evident); and Phase 6, the tumultuous 1980s and 1990s, better known to others than to the present writer, but in which he discerns a mingling of promise and menace in almost equal proportions.

* * *

During the summer of 1843 – the summer of the Disruption – the leaders of the infant Free Church, with Thomas Chalmers at their head, had much to think about; but the need for a theological college seems never to have been far from their minds. On the opening day of the new body's first General Assembly, a committee was set up 'for providing means for the education of students for the ministry', and only a day or two later the members of that committee expressed the conviction that a Theological Faculty with a curriculum equal to that of Scotland's existing Theological Faculties was absolutely essential for their purposes. At the beginning of July 1843 the first three professors – Chalmers, Welsh and Duncan – were named, to be followed soon after by Cunningham. That same month saw the purchase of 80 George Street, Edinburgh (in the heart of the New Town), 'for the accommodation of a college'.[1]

Such were the soaring aspirations of Chalmers and his associates (they thought of a rival to the existing University's 'Old College' rather than a mere theological seminary) that something more splendid than the George Street building was quickly deemed necessary. Some three years later, therefore, on 3 June 1846, Principal Chalmers laid the foundation-stone of 'the New College' on the Mound, overlooking the city's main thoroughfare, Princes Street, and hard by its most distinctive

[1] The early days of the College are described in S. J. Brown, 'The Disruption and the Dream: The Making of New College, 1843–1861', in D. F. Wright and G. D. Badcock (eds), *Disruption to Diversity: Edinburgh Divinity 1846–1996* (1996), ch. 2; also H. Watt, *New College, Edinburgh: A Centenary History* (1946), esp. ch. 2, 'Mainly about buildings', pp. 10–13.

landmark, the Castle Rock. The end of the beginning came in November 1850, when the opening of the just-completed establishment was celebrated in a three-day jamboree of sermons and addresses: by the current Moderator of the Free Church, by Principal Cunningham (Chalmers's successor as head of the College), and by each of the professors, now seven in number.[2]

There could be no doubt as to the main purpose of the new institution. Of primary concern to all its founders was what today would be called 'ministerial formation' – by which they understood not simply instruction in the practicalities of ministry but an all-round theological education in accordance with the highest possible academic standards. Graduation in Arts, it was assumed, would normally precede entrance upon Theology; and with Scottish Presbyterianism's traditionally intellectual bias the leaders of the Free Church were determined that the pursuit of the classic disciplines (Old and New Testament language and literature, Church History and Systematic Theology) should be carried on at University level, with all the appropriate rigour and range. Indeed, so intense was the desire to avoid all cultural narrowness, and to create what almost amounted to an alternative university, that the original Senate included professors of Moral Philosophy, Logic and Natural Science as well as of the strictly theological disciplines; while the drive for excellence found expression in the despatch of Cunningham to the States in July 1843 to investigate 'the constitution and working of the most eminent of the American theological institutions'.[3]

At the laying of the foundation-stone in June 1846 the College's *Ur-Vater*, Dr Chalmers, expressed thoughts about its future role which were almost certainly shared by all his colleagues. It would, he believed, perform two principal functions. First, by its instruction of ministerial candidates in the right understanding and right handling of Holy Scripture, it would provide both Church and country with 'that richest blessing, the blessing of well-filled pulpits and well-served parishes'. Second, by their participation in what he called 'the warfare of argument', its teachers would 'man the towers and bulwarks of the Church', and repel 'the inroads both

---

[2] The addresses delivered on the occasion are to be found in *Inauguration of the New College of the Free Church, November MDCCCL* (1851); cf. also Watt, ch. 5, 'The Formal Opening of the Completed Building'.

[3] Brown, esp. pp. 35–6; also Watt, p. 10.

of infidelity and of heresy'. Phrased otherwise, he saw the College as a servant of the Church, the educator of its future ministers and at the same time the proclaimer and defender of Christian truth by what he described as 'an academic treatment in the hand of academic men'.[4]

The intimate connection between College and Church which Chalmers hoped for was indubitably realised. Despite all its other commitments, the Free Church from the outset willingly assumed responsibility for the New College and everything connected therewith. The generosity of church folk had made possible the purchase of the Mound site; a small group of well-wishers was persuaded to donate what was then the very large sum of £20,000 to meet the basic building costs; almost half as much again was subscribed to pay off loans and unforeseen expenses; and while students' fees contributed greatly to the College's ordinary revenue, the backbone of its finances – from the 1840s right through to the end of the 1920s – was the annual collection taken in the congregations of the Free, and later the United Free, Church. As Principal Watt put it in his invaluable centenary history, 'there was distinctly evidenced in the average member a determination that no future minister would be hampered through any remediable deficiency in his equipment'.[5] Even in today's vastly altered circumstances it might still be appropriate to remind New College's staff and students of the biblical dictum: 'Other men laboured, and ye are entered into their labours.'

Naturally enough, the Church's concern for its College found expression in general oversight as well as in financial support. While internal discipline was the responsibility of the professors, they themselves were clearly answerable to the Church courts. Nominated and elected on the floor of the Assembly, they were inducted to their charges by the local presbytery. The courses they taught and the views they expressed were subject to Assembly scrutiny and the possibility of Assembly condemnation. Today's scholars may be horrified at such disregard for academic autonomy, but before censuring it too severely they should bear one or two quite substantial considerations in mind. For one thing, in those days there was much greater agreement on

[4] Text in Watt, pp. 2–4.
[5] Watt, p. 88.

essentials, both inside and outside the Church, than would now
be the case. For another, if Robertson Smith at Aberdeen discovered the limits of professorial freedom, A. B. Davidson and
Marcus Dods at Edinburgh were allowed to express opinions
almost as radical as any we know today. And of course the
scholarship produced by a system that has long been abandoned
was not markedly inferior to anything presently in evidence: men
like Cunningham, Rainy, Davidson, Dods, H. R. Mackintosh,
A. R. MacEwen and William Manson were chosen by arrangements more democratic than those now prevailing – and possibly
just as reliable.

Which brings us to that aspect of New College life which the
men of the first generation would have rated more important –
its worship only excepted – than anything else: I mean, the world-
view inculcated there. For that, we turn to the professors. David
Welsh died as early as 1845, and Chalmers followed him two
years later. The character of the place was therefore largely
determined by those who survived them and taught successive
cohorts of students from the 1840s right on into the 1860s: John
('Rabbi') Duncan, who professed Hebrew and Old Testament;
Alexander Black, New Testament; James Buchanan and James
Bannerman, Divinity; and William Cunningham, Ecclesiastical
History. All strike me as more 'hard-line' in their brand of
Calvinist theology than either Welsh or Chalmers.

Duncan almost defies categorisation. Of formidable linguistic
expertise, with eccentricity to match, and self-described as 'a
philosophical sceptic who has taken refuge in theology', he was a
mystic and a poet rather than a dogmatist. Yet even at his most
imaginative and rhapsodical he evinced a veneration for the letter
of Scripture which even his more down-to-earth, scholastically
minded colleagues could not exceed.[6] Black, who figures in the
Fasti of the Free Church as 'a man of vast erudition . . . able
to converse in nineteen languages and correspond in twelve',
published little; but the tenor of all his teaching may be gauged
from the affirmation which he made during the 1850 lecture-
marathon that 'The doctrine of the plenary inspiration of the

[6] W. Ewing (ed.), *Annals of the Free Church of Scotland*, vol. 1 (1914),
p. 54; S. Isbell, 'Duncan, John (1796–1870)', in N. M. de S. Cameron (ed.),
Dictionary of Scottish Church History and Theology (1993), p. 262.

Word of God . . . constitutes the very basis of sound theological study.'[7] Buchanan had been a celebrated preacher in the traditional mould before ever he was called to New College. Thereafter he published a succession of weighty treatises on Christian doctrine which fully justify his description as 'a Reformed theologian of the old school'.[8] Bannerman, who had risen to prominence during the Ten Years' Conflict before the Disruption, later published exhaustive studies in the fields of ecclesiology and pneumatology – the latter being hailed, quite recently, as a 'magisterial presentation of the concept of the plenary inspiration of Scripture'.[9]

But it is Cunningham who more than any of them embodies the fiercely conservative, combatively orthodox, high Calvinism of New College in its earliest phase. An out-and-out admirer of the great Genevan reformer, to whom he paid many tributes, he was a doughty controversialist whose enemies ranged from Arians, Socinians, Arminians – and of course 'Papists' – to a great array of contemporary deviants. He believed that 'The whole Bible is composed, even as to the words of which it consists, through the immediate agency of the Holy Spirit', and argued that no future developments in theology could possibly endanger the work of Protestantism's founding fathers and the great seventeenth-century Puritans.[10] Today, many regard him, with some justification, as little more than a bigot and a din-raiser; yet he was also warm-hearted, truly learned, and an inspiring teacher, and Marcus Dods (no uncritical admirer) aptly named him 'Grand Councillor and Senator of the Free Church of Scotland'.[11]

Led by men like Cunningham and his colleagues, New College in its opening years was marked by a passionate and self-sacrificing loyalty to old-style Protestantism, to the distinctive principles and piety of the Free Church of Scotland, and to an unyieldingly strict

---

[7] *Annals of the Free Church*, vol. I, p. 49; *Inauguration of the New College*, p. 147.

[8] *Annals of the Free Church*, p. 50; N. R. Needham, 'Buchanan, James (1804–1870)', in Cameron (ed.), *D.S.C.H.T.*, p. 107.

[9] Needham, 'Bannerman, James (1807–1868)' in *D.S.C.H.T.*, p. 56.

[10] W. Cunningham, *Theological Lectures* (1879), p. 409; A. C. Fraser, *Biographica Philosophica: A Retrospect* (1905), p. 161; cf. also R. Rainy and J. Mackenzie, *Life of William Cunningham* (1871).

[11] M. Dods (ed.), *Early Letters of Marcus Dods, D.D.* (1910), p. 118.

interpretation of biblical authority; and on that loyalty its very considerable international renown was built.

* * *

Cunningham died in 1861. In 1862 Robert Rainy succeeded him in the Chair of Ecclesiastical History, and in 1863 Andrew Bruce Davidson was appointed to the Old Testament Chair. Between them, Rainy and Davidson dominated the College and largely set its tone from then until the beginning of this century; and under their aegis took place the momentous transition from the theological conservatism of Cunningham and his co-adjutors to the liberal evangelicalism of the second phase of our history.

Of course, countervailing forces were also at work during those mid- and late-Victorian years, as even to mention the names of George Smeaton, Alexander Duff, James Macgregor and Thomas Smith – all of them cast in an older mould – should make plain. Nor was the intellectual revolution the only development of importance in the College's story. Rich financial resources were steadily accumulated, chief among them being the Cunningham Fellowships (awarded to the ablest students in each final year), the generous Craigfoodie bequest of David Meldrum (presently used to provide a valuable augmentation of teaching resources) and the Book Scheme (which helped many an impecunious student to lay the foundations of a theological library). Two new teaching posts were instituted: the Chair of Evangelistic Theology, whose first occupant was the veteran missionary pioneer, 'Duff of India', and the Fulton Lectureship in Elocution, which may have done something to improve the manner if not the content of Scottish preaching. The 1870s saw the birth of Professor W. G. Blaikie's brainchild, the College Dinner, a notable enhancement of community spirit in the place. And no history of the College would be complete without a mention of the increasingly professional Home Mission work carried on by the student body, first in the West Port area of Edinburgh, then in the Cowgate, and finally (with residential accommodation from the nineties onwards) in the slums of the Pleasance.

But it was the theological transformation effected by Davidson and Rainy – assisted, during the last decade of the century, by

Marcus Dods – that won the College widespread acclaim (and opprobrium), and made it a peculiarly exciting place in which to study.

Of all the influences at work in this transformation the most profound and far-reaching was undoubtedly a greatly heightened historical awareness. Rainy's Cunningham Lectures of 1873, entitled *The Delivery and Development of Christian Doctrine*, contain the following judgment: 'In our day . . . what meets us is the question, "How will you face and what will you make of history . . .?"'[12] His Old Testament colleague, Davidson, tacitly posed the same question, and answered it throughout a lifetime of teaching and writing dedicated to the advocacy and exemplification of the critico-historical approach to Holy Scripture. As one of his contemporaries put it: 'For him, the historical delivery of the Old Testament was authoritative as truly as the contents; and the divine meaning was not to be ascertained without a critical knowledge of the original speakers and circumstances. Upon that basis, modest and humble though it was, great doctrinal superstructures might be raised. But the critical . . . basis of fact must first be laid.'[13]

Armed with this conviction, Davidson brought the literature of the Old Testament dramatically, indeed electrifyingly, to life, altering forever his students' attitude to the Bible as a whole. As pointed out in ch. 6, *supra*, they now came to regard it not so much as a quarry of texts easily removable from their original setting, or a compendium of dogmatic propositions, but as the record of a particular people, their life and literature, over many centuries; and the conviction dawned upon them that in respecting Church traditions and confessional deliverances *less* than what the text actually said they were returning to the faith and practice of the sixteenth-century reformers at their best. Of course there were dangers in the new approach. It could foster the view that the Bible was for literary and historical experts only. It could be warped by naturalistic or positivist pre-suppositions – or represented as coming 'in paper parcels from Germany'. It could reduce

[12] R. Rainy, *The Delivery and Development of Christian Doctrine*, Cunningham Lectures (1874), p. 227.
[13] A. T. Innes, Biographical Introduction, in J. A. Paterson (ed.), *The Called of God, by the late A. B. Davidson* (1905), p. 33.

'the impregnable rock of Holy Scripture' to shifting sands. But those who adopted it found themselves the possessors of a new sense of liberation and a belief that the Bible's riches were being opened up in a manner scarcely conceivable under the old ordering of things. That revolutionary novelty, believing criticism, had found a home in New College – a home from which it has never subsequently been evicted.

The fusion of faith and critical scholarship may well have been the College's outstanding achievement during the mid- and late-Victorian period. Many difficulties were created for Christian belief by the advances then being made in the realms of geology, biology and history. But as one thinks not only of Davidson but of the open-mindedness, sensitivity and balance shown in Rainy's London lectures on *The Bible and Criticism* (1878), his inaugural address as Principal on 'Evolution and Theology' (1873), and the sermon he preached on 'Faith and Science' during the University's tercentenary celebrations ten years later (1883), not to mention Dods's great commentaries in the Expositor's Bible series, one is inclined to agree with Principal Oswald Dykes of Westminster College, Cambridge (himself a New College *alumnus*), when he affirmed in 1900 that 'It was . . . the [New College] teachers' awareness of all the current problems in their latest form, combined with their unshakeable loyalty to the Catholic and Evangelical faith, that continued to draw the constant stream of questing students from many Churches.'[14] One also begins to appreciate the distinctive character, and the value, of New College's contribution to nineteenth-century life and thought.

* * *

In many respects the third (or United Free Church) phase of the College's history, which spanned the years from the Church Union of 1900 to the still greater Union of 1929, can be regarded as a continuation of the second.

The scholarly eminence of the teachers was in no way diminished. In the first decade of the new century, the loss of Davidson, Rainy and Dods was compensated for by the advent of A. R. MacEwen, the masterly biographer of the Erskines and John

[14] Watt, p. 90.

Cairns and author of a two-volume history, still useful, of the Kirk down to 1560; H. R. Mackintosh, Edinburgh's most distinguished theologian (with Robert Flint and W. P. Paterson) between Cunningham and John Baillie; and Harry Kennedy, a pioneering scholar who anticipated later work on the Greek of the New Testament, eschatology, the mystery religions and the theology of the Epistles. Along with them should be mentioned the variously gifted J. Y. Simpson, last in the College's line of Professors of Natural Science. They were joined, in the years just before and just after the First World War, by Adam Welch, an *Alttestamentler* who brilliantly combined many of the characteristics of his predecessors, Duncan and Davidson, and Hugh Watt, the archetypal 'college man' and chronicler of its history. It would be hard to point to any other contemporary institution in Great Britain which could boast a more able body of theological scholars and teachers.

Again, there was no dimming of the College's reputation as a centre of believing criticism, now embodied in three very remarkable Principals: Dods, Whyte and Martin. Having survived a full-scale heresy trial at the outset of his professorial career (in 1890), Dods went on to publish an influential summary of the Liberal-Evangelical position in *The Bible: Its Origin and Nature* (1905), and his summons to follow Rainy as head of the College in 1907 may be taken as indicating the Church's implicit approval of his stance. Alexander Whyte was, with R. S. Candlish (his predecessor from 1843 to 1873 as minister of Free St George's Church in Edinburgh), the only pastor of a congregation to be called to the Principalship. As every reader of the biography by G. F. Barbour will know, Whyte was a striking blend of the Evangelical and the Liberal. An admirer of the Puritan divines and a supporter of Moody and Sankey, he had also signed a student petition in favour of A. B. Davidson's appointment as professor and – later in his career – spoken eloquently in Assembly on behalf of Robertson Smith. Succeeding Dods as Principal in 1909, he once declared his belief that 'the true Catholic . . . is the well-read, the hospitable-hearted, the spiritually-exercised Evangelical'.[15] As for Alexander Martin, Professor of Apologetics and Pastoral Theology from 1897 to 1927 and Principal from

---

[15] G. F. Barbour, *The Life of Alexander Whyte* (5th edn, 1905), p. 389.

1918 to 1935, this son of a staunch Free Churchman was more responsible than anyone else on the United Free Church side for the Union with the Church of Scotland in 1929. Like John Baillie after him, he had grown out of traditional Calvinism into a freer theological air; but his essential position is aptly epitomised in the title of his Cunningham Lectures: *The Finality of Jesus for Faith*.

Union with the United Presbyterian Church brought a certain enrichment in the way of financial and other resources. The Jubilee celebrations at the same time (1900) inspired a host of physical improvements, including the construction of the Rainy Hall and the opening of new classrooms in the Ramsay Lane area on the north-west side of the College. The curriculum was extended to include lectures on a number of previously neglected subjects: religious education, sociology, Church praise, and – rather more innovative – 'The Bible in Literature'. From 1902, a 'School for Christian Workers' operated through evening classes. And just after the 1914–18 War the New College professors collaborated with the University's Divinity Faculty and other colleges in the city to establish a Postgraduate School of Theology which would eventually bring a great influx of graduate students to Edinburgh and make it one of the research centres of the theological world.

So far, so good; but two real disasters – one of relatively local concern, the other of global magnitude – darkened the scene between the beginning of the century and the end of its second decade.

The first was a direct result of the long-hoped-for Union of the Free and United Presbyterian Churches which called the United Free Church into existence in 1900. Horrified by what they saw as an abandonment of Disruption principles, a tiny minority of Free Churchmen laid claim, as the rightful heirs of Chalmers and his associates, to the entire property of the pre-Union Free Church – and in August 1904 the supreme court of appeal, the House of Lords, gave judgment in their favour. The ruling proved impossible to carry out, and eventually Parliamentary intervention was required to secure a more equitable settlement. But for the New College community – whose entire complex of buildings had initially to be vacated – the immediate consequences were dire. Between October 1904 and January 1907 they were obliged to find alternative accommodation, partly in the Pleasance Settlement and partly in the University. Moreover, even after the lost premises had been recovered the endowments built up over several decades were seriously depleted by enforced transfers to the continuing Free Church. The expansive mood of 1900 was perhaps never recovered.

Though less instantly devastating, the First World War marked an even more significant divide in the College's history. Classes were decimated as students joined up and replacements dwindled away, and some men never came back. Along with all the other losses of that world-shattering conflict must be reckoned the optimism which had characterised the late-Victorian and Edwardian periods. 'Never glad confident morning again', and a more sober mood pervaded the Churches and their theology. At the same time, the exigencies of war undoubtedly drew the different religious bodies closer together, leading *inter alia* to increased cooperation between New College and the University's Faculty of Divinity. The way was being paved not only for the great Church Union of 1929 but also for that fusion of College and Faculty which would open a new era for them both.

* * *

The fourth phase of New College's history covers almost exactly one-quarter of a century, from the Union of 1929 to the mid-fifties (or from ten years before the Second World War to ten years after it).

Among the teachers, many of the previous generation continued to play an influential part. The torch, however, was passing to younger figures like William Manson (New Testament), Daniel Lamont (Practical Theology) and the Church historians Hugh Watt (from the 'Free Kirk' side) and John Burleigh (from the 'Auld Kirk'). The determinative years were probably the mid-thirties, when – in quick succession – came the appointments of John Baillie (1934), Norman Porteous (1935), G. T. Thomson (1936) and Oliver Rankin (1937). Tom Torrance and Matthew Black did not arrive until 1950 and 1952 respectively, and the period drew to a close with the coming of James Barr in 1955 and John McIntyre in 1956.

It was, of course, the Union of the Churches, with the consequential merger of New College and Edinburgh University's Faculty of Divinity, which gave its character to this fourth phase. The implications for New College were spelled out in the section of the Churches' 'Basis and Plan of Union' entitled 'Relation of Divinity Halls to the University'. Among its provisions were the following:

> statutory confessional tests for theological Chairs in the University to be abolished;
> electoral boards equally representative of Church and University to be set up to make appointments to Chairs – with the requirement of a two-thirds majority decision to ensure that no Chair could be filled by someone unacceptable to the Church;
> existing United Free Church professors to become professors in the University's Faculty of Divinity;
> students preparing for the ministry of the Church to be matriculated students of the University;
> New College to be maintained as a college of the united Church for the use of the enlarged Faculty.[16]

These provisions were gradually put into effect by a series of Parliamentary Acts and binding agreements between Church and University which extended from the Universities (Scotland) Act of Parliament in 1932 and the Agreement between Church and University in 1933 to an important Order in Council in 1952. The result – a combination of the resources of College and Faculty and a concentration of all theological teaching on the Mound – had far-reaching consequences for staffing, physical environment and general ethos.

As far as staffing was concerned, at the outset of the 1930s the refashioned institution could boast of nine professors altogether: in 'Divinity', 'Ecclesiastical History', 'Hebrew and Semitic Languages' and 'Biblical Criticism and Biblical Antiquities' from the pre-Union Faculty; and in 'Dogmatics', 'Church History', 'Old Testament Language, Literature, and Theology', 'New Testament Language, Literature, and Theology' and 'Apologetical Theology, Christian Ethics, and Practical Training' from the pre-Union College. Subsequent rationalisation somewhat reduced

[16] J. T. Cox (ed.), *Practice and Procedure in the Church of Scotland*, ed. by J. B. Longmuir (5th edn, 1964), pp. 374–8.

that number, and future appointments to all Chairs became the business of a Board of Nomination on which Church and University were equally represented. The new symbiosis found striking expression when Professor W. A. Curtis (Dean since 1928) assumed the joint office of Dean and Principal in 1935.

What the post-Union state of affairs would mean for the College's physical aspect was not so immediately evident. The Church still retained ownership and control of the buildings, while making them freely available to the University for the purposes of its Faculty of Divinity. In the long run, a huge financial responsibility was transferred from Church to University, though during the first decade or so the University may well have appeared to be the greater beneficiary. New College's library had always been one of its finest assets, but more adequate accommodation for the ever-expanding store of books became available when the former Free High congregation moved from its home on the east side of the main quadrangle to a new location elsewhere in the city. The consequent rehousing of the library – a massive exercise on any reckoning – was completed in 1936. The old stackrooms were released for use as classrooms and examination rooms; the old library hall became the Martin Hall; and in essentials the College approached the lay-out still recognisable today.

The spirit of the place also underwent changes. For one thing, within the Evangelical consensus of the teachers tensions gradually emerged between John Baillie's eirenic Liberalism and G. T. Thomson's campaigning Barthianism – though from his appointment in 1946 J. S. Stewart (whose fame as one of Scotland's greatest preachers attracted students from all round the world) was perhaps a mediating influence. For another, as the conviction grew that professional training for ministry in the Church must be conducted with all the technical expertise that only a university could supply, so what was coming to be called 'Practical Theology' began to play an increasing role in the curriculum. Most significant of all, while the College's commitment to the service of the Kirk remained unquestionable – between 1930 and 1950 three professors (Mackintosh in 1932, Baillie in 1943 and Watt in 1950) were called to the Moderatorship – it became less identifiably denominational in character than ever before. Indeed, one could even argue that there was a certain turning-away from ecclesiastical to more exclusively academic concerns. As John McIntyre, looking back some years later, pointed out, the union of College and Faculty had involved an amalgamation of two views of theological education, the Church-directed and the University-directed, and the end was not yet: 'it remained to be seen whether the amalgam was to be theologically credible, or whether one . . . of the components would claim superiority'.[17]

* * *

A considerable number of accessions to the staff ushered in the fifth phase of the College's existence. Senior figures from earlier days, Burleigh, Porteous and Stewart, were of course still active and influential well into the sixties. But in addition to Torrance and McIntyre a further band of younger men came to Chairs: George Anderson (Old Testament) in 1962, Cheyne (Ecclesiastical History) in 1964, Blackie (Christian Ethics and Practical Theology) and Hugh Anderson (New Testament) both in 1966. The transformation which took place between the early sixties and the late seventies was no doubt partly due to them. Yet with hindsight one can see that forces greater than any individual or group of individuals were at work. The harvest of the Union of the Churches and the merger of College and Faculty had pretty well been gathered in by this time, and decisions made in the world of politics and academia were as responsible as ecclesiastical events and interests for the way things developed.

Supremely important were the consequences of a Report on Higher Education produced between 1961 and 1964 by a committee under the Chairmanship of Lord Robbins. New universities came into being, older ones were encouraged to expand and diversify; and among the institutions affected, financially and in other ways, was Edinburgh University's Faculty of Divinity. An article that appeared in the very first number of *New College Bulletin* (Easter 1964) conveys the forward-looking temper of the time. After outlining an impressive range of developments, contemplated or already under way, its author ended – optimistically – thus: 'We have every reason to believe that, as a result of the Robbins Report . . . , and the will of the government to put it into effect as soon as possible, our hopes will be fulfilled

---

[17] *New College Newsletter*, no. 4 (Dec. 1975), p. 3.

and our plans implemented sooner than we had once thought possible.'[18]

An early sign of the current expansionism was given in staffing arrangements. In addition to the professors, a number of lecturers had begun to make their appearance: ten full-time, seven part-time by 1964. A little later, student numbers started to rise, from a total of 212 in 1966 to 314 in 1975. The degree structure was also completely refashioned. The BD could now be taken either as an ordinary degree (without previous qualifications in Arts) or with honours; students also began to be enrolled for a new MTh degree and for various diplomas and certificates. Alongside these changes, moreover, innovative teaching methods made their appearance: duplicated course outlines, seminars, project and role-play groups, field work.

The increase in staff and the new educational techniques – together with a sharp rise in the number of women students, particularly after the Church of Scotland admitted women to the ministry in 1968 – were accompanied by equally significant changes in the physical environment. As already noted, the College continued to be Church of Scotland property even after all the activities of the University's Faculty of Divinity had been relocated there. For a number of reasons, this did not prove entirely satisfactory; and the eventual solution – decided on as early as 1961, but not fully implemented until more than a decade later – was the legal conveyance of the College and adjacent properties from the Church to the University, with the crucial proviso that if the Faculty did not provide an acceptable course of training for Church of Scotland candidates the buildings should revert to Church ownership. The full import of the transfer did not become immediately obvious. Its physical consequences were soon evident in completely renovated, much more 'user-friendly' accommodation. The library at the heart of the College found itself immeasurably better supported, with a larger staff and a professionally qualified librarian in charge. But along with these relatively straightforward changes came others that were subtler and more far-reaching.

As portentous as any was the introduction – again, in the early seventies – of new degrees (BA and MA) in Religious Studies.

---

[18] *New College Bulletin*, vol. I, no. 1 (Easter, 1964), p. 15.

Drawing on the resources not only of the Divinity Faculty but also of a number of Departments in Arts and Social Sciences, these degrees provided an opportunity for studying all the major world religions, as well as for employing a variety of approaches to religion, in well-nigh every conceivable permutation and combination. For some years recruitment was slow, but increasing numbers of students were eventually attracted. As a result, the College gradually became more closely linked with the rest of the University, and less exclusively a home for future ministers studying Christian theology, than ever before.

At the same time as the rise of Religious Studies was undermining the old identification of theological with ministerial education, a new approach to the latter also began to be adopted. By the end of the seventies, William Tindal's successor as Professor of Practical Theology, James Blackie, had inspired and overseen a radical metamorphosis of the subject, so that when *his* successor, Duncan Forrester, took over the department in 1979 he could sum up the attitude which he shared with Blackie as follows: 'In the modern world it is not enough to pass on an accepted and recognised pattern of ministerial practice; ministers must be enabled to think critically and theologically about their work, to innovate, and to respond creatively and faithfully to unprecedented situations.' And he added, even more significantly, that 'Practical Theology must interact, not only with other theological disciplines but with sociology, social work, medicine, counselling, psychiatry, and so on.'[19]

Before leaving New College in the sixties and seventies, a word must be said about the growing spirit of ecumenism discernible there. It had always been an outward-looking place, as well as a kind of Mecca for Evangelical Protestants around the world. The first great Missionary Conference ('Edinburgh 1910') met in the Assembly Hall nearby, and its secretary, J . H. Oldham, had studied in the College. With the creation of the Postgraduate School of Theology in 1919 it began to attract researchers from a very wide spread of churches and countries. One of the College's most distinguished Principals, John Baillie, became a President of the World Council of Churches; Baillie, Burleigh, Tindal and Torrance were all signatories of the so-called 'Bishops Report';

[19] *New College Newsletter*, no. 10 (August 1979), pp. 5–6.

and although inter-Church relations suffered something of a set-back thereafter, several members of staff kept the ecumenical flame burning. John McIntyre fraternised with Anselm scholars at Bec, and Tom Torrance dedicated one of his publications 'To the Church of Scotland, the Church of my father, and the Church of England, the Church of my mother and my wife, in the earnest prayer that they may soon be one'.[20]

It was hardly surprising, therefore, that special relationships began to be formed with (among others) the Scottish Episcopal College and the Dominican House, both in Edinburgh, and the Roman Catholic seminary at Drygrange in the Borders. Most striking of all, clergy and laity from non-Presbyterian denominations began to be appointed to teaching posts: John Zizioulas from the Orthodox tradition, Robin Gill from the Church of England and Noel O'Donoghue from Irish Catholicism (to name only a few). What William Cunningham would have had to say to all this must be left to the imagination, but one suspects that the generous-minded Chalmers might just conceivably have given it his approval.

* * *

No period in the College's history has seen a more perplexing blend of encouragement and discouragement, the welcome and the regrettable, than that which began around 1979 with such defining events as the retirement of Tom Torrance and the appointment of James Mackey to succeed him – together with the departure to St Andrews of Bill Shaw (first non-professorial member of staff to hold the joint office of Principal and Dean) and the arrival in Practical Theology of Duncan Forrester.

This latest phase has not been lacking in accessions of teaching strength and academic prestige. The well-established exchange of students with the University of Tübingen was followed by a similar arrangement with Dartmouth College in the USA. Soon afterwards, the Centre for the Study of Theology and Public Issues was set up 'to encourage work on the interface between theology and the Churches and social issues of the day'.[21] Then two

[20] T. F. Torrance, *Royal Priesthood* (1955).
[21] *New College Bulletin* (October 1984), p. 8.

remarkable transfers of personnel and resources were effected. The Centre for the Study of Christianity in the Non-Western World came south from Aberdeen under its Director, Andrew Walls, and quickly built up a strong lecturing team as well as acquiring a new professorial post. About the same time, Glasgow's Principles of Religion specialists moved east – one of them, Alistair Kee, being subsequently promoted to a Personal Chair. Meanwhile the Department of Ecclesiastical History, just weakened by New Zealand's capture of its Reformation expert, Peter Matheson, was fortunate enough to attract the munificent endowment of the Laing Lectureship in Reformation History and Thought. In 1986, New Testament was compensated for the loss of Hugh Anderson by the arrival of that 'benign hurricane', John O'Neill. In 1987, the vacant Chair of Ecclesiastical History was happily filled by Stewart Brown from the USA, author of the standard modern study of Thomas Chalmers. And in the early 1990s the College's standing in the University and beyond was enhanced by the appointment of Principal Sir Stewart Sutherland to a Personal Chair in the Philosophy of Religion and by the launching of the *Edinburgh Review of Theology and Religion.*

These causes for satisfaction have, however, been counter-balanced by several problematic or even positively disturbing developments, some at least connected with the 'market philosophy' of central government in the Thatcher years. Drastic financial cut-backs, and the proliferation of burdensome systems of assessment and control, have damaged staff morale and limited teaching effectiveness. Inadequate funding has kept vacant the Old Testament Chair since George Anderson's retirement in 1984 and the Divinity Chair since John McIntyre's in 1986. Departing lecturers have not been replaced, and courses have had to be withdrawn. The phenomenal rise in student numbers, which has not been met by a proportionate increase in the complement of teachers, has created a host of difficulties. And the heterogeneity of the student body since the recent boom in Religious Studies has raised quite fundamental problems about the College's purpose and identity.

To some observers within the Church of Scotland, an early harbinger of trouble came with the appointment – to the Thomas Chalmers Chair of Theology! – of James Mackey, a laicised Roman Catholic priest. A tumult of protest arose from disgruntled

Presbyterians, and fundamental questions were posed. Had the Board of Nomination gone beyond its powers? Should the terms of association between Church and University be renegotiated? Was it perhaps time, as the College's founders had decided in 1843, for the Church to go its own way, reclaiming unfettered freedom – and onerous responsibility – in the management of ministerial education? In the end, that particular storm blew itself out. The General Assembly of 1980 acknowledged that the Edinburgh Board of Nomination had acted in proper accordance with the procedure laid down by the Universities (Scotland) Act of 1932. It also indicated general satisfaction with the way in which appointments were made to established theological Chairs, and expressed disapproval of 'any suggestions which might impair the good relations which exist between the Church and the Universities'.[22]

So far, so good; but the winds of change continued to buffet those who hankered after a College like that presided over by Alexander Martin or William Curtis, not to mention Rainy or Cunningham. The Kirk no longer seemed able to produce really high-quality candidates for professorial Chairs, so that time and again selection committees had to look beyond it for their choice. Its over-all say in appointments, moreover, was steadily decreasing – partly because of finance-driven University decisions to keep certain established Chairs vacant, partly because of a growth in the number of lectureships and Personal Chairs (neither of which required approval by a Board of Nomination with its statutory quorum of Church representatives). And of course the ever-declining ratio of ordinands to other students made its own contribution to the gradual emergence of a less Church-orientated, almost certainly more 'secular', climate of opinion in the College.

Try as it may, the Church has found no solution for these problems. The most important attempt, which was made by a special Assembly Committee meeting at the end of the eighties under the chairmanship of Principal Johnston of Heriot-Watt University, avoided the wilder suggestions that had been made by excited partisans. The proposal, for example, that the Church itself might undertake the funding of vacant Chairs or lectureships was rejected outright. But for the rest the committee confined

---

[22] *Reports to the General Assembly* (1980), p. 382.

itself to expressing confidence in the basic goodwill of the University authorities, to reminding all parties of the legal settlement that had been negotiated in the aftermath of the 1929 Union, and to emphasising the very considerable advantages of that settlement. Finally, its response to all who, from the Mackey appointment onwards, had longed for the pre-Union state of affairs – an exclusively Church-funded, Church-managed College – was given in these dismissive but eminently realistic words: 'It would be inadvisable to tamper with existing legislation.'[23]

* * *

With that pronouncement and its slightly lukewarm acceptance of things as they are our tale draws near its end. The historian is not a prophet, at least in the predictive sense; and only a very bold or a very foolish person would dare to foretell the future, long-term or short-term, of New College. 'It may be that the gulfs will wash us down: It may be we shall touch the Happy Isles.' Yet the temptation to conclude with one or two brief comments and one or two modest hopes is irresistible.

The story has been of unceasing – sometimes almost over-whelming – change, so that *semper eadem* is not a claim which even the College's most enthusiastic admirers would make for it. Perhaps we should simply console ourselves with Newman's assertion that 'In a higher world it is otherwise, but here below to live is to change, and to be perfect is to have changed often'! Nevertheless I believe that through our very mutation certain overarching continuities are to be discerned.

The four-fold task of the University (Professor Jaroslav Pelikan has recently reminded us) may be described thus: to advance knowledge through research, to transmit knowledge through teaching, to preserve knowledge in scholarly collections and to diffuse knowledge through publishing.[24] New College has proved deficient in none of these. When one thinks of the service rendered to the *preservation* of knowledge by our inconvenient but marvellous library, one is inclined to rate it the College's crowning glory. But then one remembers the remarkable succession of

[23] *Reports to the General Assembly* (1991), pp. 552–4.
[24] J. Pelikan, *The Idea of the University* (1992). p. 76.

outstanding scholars and teachers who have adorned the place throughout its 150 years: the peerless Chalmers, of whom David Masson observed that 'merely to look at him day after day was a liberal education';[25] or Cunningham with his 'luminous and powerful mind' (to quote Marcus Dods yet once more);[26] or Davidson, whose treatment of every subject, according to S. R. Driver, was always masterly and judicial, yet whose teaching was such that, as J. Strahan tells us in the biography, 'on the great lecture days' students 'came down from the top-storey classroom to the Common Hall moved with feelings of pity and awe, thrilled with aspirations of faith and hope';[27] or the omnicompetent Rainy, described by Gladstone as 'unquestionably the greatest of living Scotsmen',[28] dominating the College as he dominated the Church for over thirty years; or H. R. Mackintosh, that 'figure' (according to a particularly able student) 'of incandescent granite',[29] one of the very select band of Scottish divines to be awarded a DD by Oxford University; or Adam Welch, whose lectures could reach such heights of intensity that 'note-taking became a sacrilege' and 'every pen was laid aside and men sat awestruck and in silence';[30] or my own teacher, John Baillie – erudite, judicious, humane, master of a beautifully lucid, almost poetic literary style, and able (as Professor Newlands has remarked) to combine openness to liberal scholarship with unapologetic devotion.[31] There have indeed been giants in the place.

Besides advancing, transmitting and preserving knowledge, New College has also played a notable part in its diffusion through published works. A constant stream of high-quality writings has spread its name across the world: Cunningham's weighty volumes and Davidson's pioneering articles and reviews; the brilliant

[25] D. Masson, *Memories of Two Cities: Edinburgh and Aberdeen* (1911), p. 81.

[26] A. Whyte, *Former Principals of New College, Edinburgh* (1909), p. 22.

[27] J. Strahan, *Andrew Bruce Davidson* (1917), pp. 132–3 and 292.

[28] P. C. Simpson, *The Life of Principal Rainy* (1909), vol. II, p. 163.

[29] E. Templeton, *God's February: A Life of Archie Craig, 1888–1985* (1991), p. 15.

[30] G. S. Gunn, Memoir, in A. C. Welch, *Kings and Prophets of Israel*, ed. by N. W. Porteous (1952), p. 28

[31] G. Newlands, 'Divinity and Dogmatics', in Wright and Badcock (eds), *Disruption to Diversity*, p. 126.

polemic of Rainy's *Three Lectures on the Church of Scotland*; the fresh and authoritative New Testament studies by Marcus Dods, Harry Kennedy and William Manson; A. R. MacEwen's perceptive cameo of eighteenth-century Scottish Dissent, *The Erskines*; H. R. Mackintosh's classics, *The Doctrine of the Person of Christ*, *The Christian Experience of Forgiveness* and *Types of Modern Theology*; Adam Welch's powerful challenges to received opinion in Old Testament scholarship; J. S. Stewart's eloquent Cunningham Lectures on Paul, *A Man in Christ*; John Baillie's *Our Knowledge of God*, *And the Life Everlasting, Invitation to Pilgrimage* and (his Gifford Lectures) *The Sense of the Presence of God*; and John Burleigh's standard survey, *A Church History of Scotland* – together with more recent works from which it would be invidious to select. There is no denying the solid worth of the College's contribution to the literature of scholarship.

That the tradition of sound learning will continue into another century is fairly certain. But alongside the scholarship there has always existed a dedication to the service of Christ and His Church without which New College would never have come into existence or survived over 150 years. In one of the most interesting and persuasive articles contributed to *Development to Diversity*, the volume published to mark the College's sesquicentennial, Dr Gary Badcock contends that 'the milieu of faith, and specifically faith in the Scottish Reformed tradition, is what has made and what makes New College what it is'. He goes on to argue that out of this distinctive religious understanding has come

> not only the College's commitment to learning but also its international outlook, its placing of worship at the heart of community life, its stress on the centrality of Biblical authority, its pastorally-oriented theology, its openness to all the insights derivable from other disciplines, other systems of thought, other values, and its tradition of acting as a 'clearing-house' for theological ideas.[32]

It would be very hard to disagree with his analysis.

Take away the Faith, and allegiance to it, and not much that is characteristic of the New College story would remain – just as service rendered to the Church and support received from it in return are among its constant themes. One small instance of this

---

[32] G. Badcock, 'New College and the Reformed Tradition: The Promise of the Past' in Wright and Badcock, p. 277.

is the fact that every single decade since the 1840s has seen a member of the College staff being called to the Moderatorship of the General Assembly. More important, religious commitment has been a prevailing feature of all the College's most influential leaders from the 1840s onward. Remember how it was 'the Christian good of Scotland' to which Chalmers dedicated his multifarious talents; how Davidson once pleaded for 'a clear-cut Christianity, standing out sharp against the sky, with a chasm between it and the world'; how Rainy, on call to Huntly Free Church at the outset of his career, declared, 'I can honestly say that to be a minister of the Free Church is an honour I would not exchange for anything earthly'; how Robertson Smith, the most brilliant student ever to sit on the college benches, once assured the Assembly that 'in the Bible alone I find God drawing near to men in Christ Jesus and declaring to us in Him His will for our salvation'; how Adam Welch, whose life was by no means free of tragedy, nevertheless remarked. 'I am not conscious of any time when I did not know that I was surrounded by stately dependabilities'; and how John Baillie, after scrutinising his own early experiences, concluded, 'I stand now, as I stood then, under the sovereign constraint of One who has never ceased to make it known to me that He claimed me for His own and required me for His service. . . . I have no choice but to set my feet upon the pilgrim's way.'[33] At New College, godliness and good learning, devotion and intellectual acuity, have never been far apart.

To the advantages of this conjunction numerous witnesses have testified over the years, from the Hungarians and Irish of the mid-nineteenth century to the Koreans and Americans of the late-twentieth.

> Used to the more or less anonymous atmosphere in a crowd of nearly one thousand divinity students [a young visitor from Heidelberg wrote recently] I found a lively community of people not only studying together but trying to build up a Christian community as well – by daily prayers, various commitments outside the Faculty, a common meal. I would not have been able to experience this at home.[34]

[33] T. Chalmers, 'Churches and Schools for the Working Classes' (1844), p. 21, and elsewhere; Strahan, *Davidson*, p. 296; Simpson, *Rainy*, vol. I, p. 111; W. R. Smith, 'Answer to the Form of Libel', p. 21. cf. *supra* p. 136; G. S. Gunn, Memoir, p. 43; J. Baillie, *Invitation to Pilgrimage* (1942), p. 47.
[34] *New College Bulletin*, no. 12 (Sept. 1981), p. 8.

And – echoing her tribute – a member of the teaching staff at Dartmouth College, in Edinburgh as part of the exchange arrangement with that institution, has told how his charges found in New College 'what they had been told to expect, but did not really expect: namely, the attitude of faith and commitment which is not only proper but essential to a first-rate theological Faculty'.[35] Will the tradition continue into a new century? One cannot be certain. As early as 1850, Professor Campbell Fraser (soon to move from New College to the Chair of Logic in the University) issued a warning.

> This [he said], like other institutions, may stand while there is a work in society for it to do, and while it is honestly doing the work, by truly creating and guiding opinion and wielding a moral force. But when the work is done or left undone, neither old endowments and associations, nor ecclesiastical or civil patronage and power, can make head against the great law of the universe, which either gradually or suddenly sweeps it away![36]

Fifty years later, at the Jubilee celebrations of 1900, Oswald Dykes, a distinguished former student, cut even closer to the bone.

> Let the divinity school [he counselled] once be severed from the practical uses it had to serve, let theology be cultivated as a purely intellectual or scientific interest, let their divines cease to be themselves men of God, or let those studies which are vital to the Church fall into the hands of scholars who were aliens from the faith which they investigated, and they stood in danger of a theology barren because undevout, unprofitable to the souls of men. No greater calamity could befall the Church.[37]

Whether Dykes and Fraser were scaremongers or not, and whether the ideals which they shared with innumerable servants and friends of New College, then and now, were deserving of survival, must be left to the present generation of staff and students, and those who come after them, to decide. But it would be ungracious to end on a hesitating or minatory note. As we celebrate this ter-Jubilee, our strongest feelings must be of discriminating gratitude for the past and modest confidence for

---

[35] Ibid., no. 13 (1982), p. 5.
[36] Watt, p. 47.
[37] Ibid., p. 85.

the future. As one of the College's ablest and best-loved *alumni*, the late Professor Alan Lewis, wrote in 1987 on the eve of his departure for a Chair in Austin Seminary, Texas:

> To the benefit of its associates far beyond our personal deserts the college enjoys an admiration and affection that sometimes seem to verge on awe. And rightly so: for while no one who knows us from the inside would romanticise our present reality, or even our past, we do know how much of our history is a little awesome, and how much there is today to be excited by, as of tomorrow to be hopeful for.[38]

[38] *New College News*, no. 3 (Autumn 1987), p. 3.

Index of Names
and Authors Cited

Index of Subjects